FEMININITY AND THE PHYSICALLY ACTIVE WOMAN
Precilla Y. L. Choi

GENDER, LANGUAGE AND DISCOURSE
Anne Weatherall

THE SCIENCE/FICTION OF SEX
Annie Potts

THE PSYCHOLOGICAL DEVELOPMENT OF GIRLS
AND WOMEN
Sheila Greene

JUST SEX?
Nicola Gavey

WOMAN'S RELATIONSHIP WITH HERSELF
Helen O'Grady

GENDER TALK
Susan A. Speer

BEAUTY AND MISOGYNY
Sheila Jeffreys

BODY WORK
Sylvia K. Blood

MANAGING THE MONSTROUS FEMININE
Jane M. Ussher

THE CAPACITY TO CARE
Wendy Hollway

SANCTIONING PREGNANCY
Harriet Gross and Helen Pattison

ACCOUNTING FOR RAPE
Irina Anderson and Kathy Doherty

THE SINGLE WOMAN
Jill Reynolds

'ADOLESCENCE', PREGNANCY AND ABORTION

Constructing a Threat of Degeneration

Catriona Macleod

Routledge
Taylor & Francis Group

LONDON AND NEW YORK

First published 2011
by Routledge
27 Church Road, Hove, East Sussex BN3 2FA

Simultaneously published in the USA and Canada
by Routledge
270 Madison Avenue, New York NY 10016

Routledge is an imprint of the Taylor & Francis Group, an Informa business

Typeset in Times by Garfield Morgan, Swansea, West Glamorgan
Printed and bound in Great Britain by TJ International Ltd, Padstow, Cornwall
Cover design by Terry Foley, Anú Design

This publication has been produced with paper manufactured to strict environmental
standards and with pulp derived from sustainable forests.

British Library Cataloguing in Publication Data
A catalogue record for this book is available from the British Library

Library of Congress Cataloging-in-Publication Data
Macleod, Catriona.
Adolescence, pregnancy, and abortion : constructing a threat of degeneration / Catriona
Macleod.
p. cm.
Includes bibliographical references and index.
ISBN 978-0-415-55339-1 (hb : alk. paper) – ISBN 978-0-415-55338-4 (pb : alk. paper)
1. Sex instruction for teenagers. 2. Teenage pregnancy. 3. Abortion. I. Title.
HQ35.M33 2010
306.874'3–dc22
2010007376

ISBN: 978-0-415-55339-1 (hbk)
ISBN: 978-0-415-55338-4 (pbk)

TO THE TWO BOYS WHO TAUGHT ME ABOUT
THE EMBODIMENT OF PREGNANCY AND
MOTHERING: LIAM AND AIDAN

CONTENTS

ACKNOWLEDGEMENTS

The ideas reflected in this book are the result of many years of work in the area of 'teenage pregnancy' and abortion. During this time, my research has been funded by the Johan Jacobs Foundation, the National Research Foundation, and Rhodes University's Joint Research Committee, all three of which I gratefully acknowledge. My thinking has been honed by many debates and discussions with numerous colleagues. Here I mention only two, whose intellectual and personal support has been of enormous value to me: Kevin Durrheim and Andy Gilbert. I have had the good fortune of working with a number of excellent research assistants. They are: Tracy Morison, Natalie Donaldson, Phindi Mnyaka, Jateen Hansjee, Jessika Rama and Pumeza Luwaca. My husband, John Reynolds, and my two children, Liam Macleod Reynolds and Aidan Macleod Reynolds, to whom this book is dedicated, constantly remind me of what is important in life.

ABBREVIATIONS

ACDP   African Christian Democratic Party (South Africa)
APA   American Psychological Association
CLA   Christian Lawyers Association (South Africa)
CSG   Child Support Grant (South Africa)
CTOP Act Choice on Termination of Pregnancy Act (Act 92 of 1996) (South Africa)
PAS   post-abortion syndrome
SABC3   South African Broadcasting Corporation's television Channel 3

1

SETTING THE SCENE

On 14 November 2006, *Special Assignment*, a weekly programme aired on the South African Broadcasting Corporation's television Channel 3 (SABC3), was entitled *Silent Cries*. The programme is about teen-aged women who conceive and decide to terminate their pregnancy (which, under legislation introduced in 1996, is legal up to twelve weeks on request and thereafter under specific conditions). The following description of the programme appeared on the *Special Assignment* website (Special Assignment 2006):

> Girls as young as 12 years are having multiple abortions – without their parents' consent. This week a Special Assignment investigation reveals that many teenagers regard termination of pregnancy as another form of contraception and disregard the consequent dangers of HIV infection. We follow four girls as they enter clinics and prepare for their procedures. They tell us why they have opted for abortions and how they feel going through with them. While two of the girls are still in high school, the other two are university students. Out of the four girls, two are repeat cases. Since the Choice on Termination of Pregnancy Act was passed in 1996, the demand for abortions has increased. Last year about half a million pregnancies were terminated in South Africa. According to the Act, a pregnant woman who asks for an abortion cannot be turned down. 72 000 teenagers missed school last year because they were pregnant. From our investigation it would seem that many underage girls are successfully exploiting two loopholes in the Act. Firstly, they don't need permission from their parents to get abortions, and secondly, the Act doesn't stipulate how many abortions a woman can have in her lifetime.
>
> (*Special Assignment* 2006)

The actual programme starts with the following question:

Do you know where your teenage girl is? She could be in a clinic waiting to get through her most difficult test yet, terminating her pregnancy alone and without your consent. Girls as young as 12 years are having abortions. We ask, 'Are teenage girls confusing abortion with contraception?'

(*Special Assignment* and SABC)

The tone and content of the programme clearly had an effect on some viewers as evidenced in the blogs that appeared shortly after it aired. This is an example of one.

I have just finished watching *Special Assignment*. . . . I have never really formed an opinion on abortion. The main reason behind that is that as soon as I do form an opinion on it, it is my moral duty to act on it, and well, I'm lazy. What did strike me as the nurse carried out the biological waste to the dumping area, is what a waste of potential that was. And I'm not talking about the child that almost was, but more about the people that would have surrounded it.

(Time 2006)

The issues raised in this *Special Assignment* programme and the blog are what this book is about – young women conceiving, young women being pregnant, some young women giving birth and some young women requesting a termination of pregnancy. The manner in which these issues are spoken about, and the implications of these representations, are the central focus of the book. Readers will notice, as they proceed through the material that follows, that I have not used young women who are sexually active, or who are pregnant, or who are undergoing a termination of pregnancy as the object of study. Instead of focusing attention on the pregnant teenager herself, the concern here revolves around public representations of 'teenage pregnancy' and abortion and around what enables us to make the kinds of statements that are evidenced above.

For example, in the extracts above, young women are represented as 'girls', people who sneak away from adult supervision in order to terminate a pregnancy, who confuse contraception with abortion, who are irresponsible regarding the possibility of HIV infection, and who irresponsibly 'exploit' current legislation. Throughout the *Special Assignment* programme these young women are referred to as 'schoolgirls', 'girls', 'youngsters', 'underage girls' and 'underage kids'. They are represented as ignorant, immature, neglectful and risk-taking. Whatever else they may be, in the eyes of the presenters of this programme, they are not adults, not capable of independent decision and not mature enough to be involved in sexual activity, to carry a pregnancy or to decide independently on a termination of pregnancy.

In addition to positioning young women in this way, the programme intimates that 'teenage pregnancy' and abortion are causes for social concern. The demand for abortion is increasing, it is stated, with the implication of a strain being placed on the public health system. Many young women are missing school as a result of pregnancy, which implicitly defines them as becoming educationally and possibly economically challenged. Thus, not only are these 'girls' responsible for their individual suffering through their immature acts, but also they are contributing to social problems. Many of these themes will emerge in the discussions that follow.

In addition to examining how young sexual and reproductive women are represented, this book is about the research and social practices that allow for particular discursive constructions. For example, in the *Special Assignment* programme there is the social practice of addressing an audience. The implicit audience of the programme is exactly the person who wrote the blog featured above – an adult who will form an opinion on the matter. It is addressed to adults who are concerned about the well-being of their own children and of children in general, people who would want to have a say in what teen-aged women do. The people that the programme is about – young women who are pregnant and considering an abortion – are not addressed. They are not, for one moment, considered as a possible or reasonable audience.

The approach taken in this book

The usual types of questions asked by social science researchers in the field of early reproduction are: What causes 'teenage pregnancy'? What are the consequences of early motherhood? What are the consequences when a teenager has a termination of pregnancy? Are young women able to make decisions on their own when it comes to a termination of pregnancy? What are the best interventions to prevent pregnancy and to ameliorate the consequences of early reproduction or termination of pregnancy? All these questions focus attention on the individual teenager – examining her individual emotional, cognitive and social characteristics to explain why she gets pregnant, why she mothers in a certain way, how she makes a decision about her pregnancy, how she responds to abortion, and how best to help her.

This will not be the focus of attention in this book. Instead, I analyse how we, as academics writing in journals and books, as health professionals talking about young women who are pregnant, as journalists and TV programme directors producing written and visual text, and as lay-people writing to newspapers or on blogs, represent young women with regard to reproductive issues. In other words, this book examines public representations – the public discursive context – of early reproduction. The main questions that direct the discussions that follow are: What kinds of understandings concerning young women and reproduction do these representations promote? What kinds of practices enable particular representations? And what are the implications of these kinds of representation?

The reason for this shift (from the standard approach of focusing on young women themselves to focusing on representations about them) has to do with an understanding of the implications of these representations. In analysing the manner in which these young women are defined, measured, categorized, described and spoken about, we start to understand two things. First, we obtain insight into the context (at least the public discursive context) within which these young women experience their lives. In other words, we can begin to explore some of the social constraints and possibilities that may shape their decisions, their interactions and their reactions to a pregnancy. Second, in exploring representations of young women, sexuality, pregnancy and termination of pregnancy, we can begin to understand the ideologies that influence interventions with young people. No intervention is neutral – all are based on particular premises regarding the basic good and the basic nature of the individual. It is these kinds of issues that will be discussed in this book.

In making my argument, I draw on a number of sources of data, including journal articles, newspapers, websites and television programmes. Although these media of communication have different functions, and appeal to different (albeit overlapping) audiences, they have a number of things in common. The first is that they represent the ideas and arguments of people with a certain level of material and educational resource base, with access to, and the ability to use, current information and communication technologies. As such, they potentially produce and reproduce particular representations of reality. The second is that, as public documents, they have 'reach'. Potentially, they may be read by a wide range of people. Third, although supposedly different in function and audience, they espouse remarkable similarity ideologies, albeit in different narrative structures.

In analysing the public discursive context of 'teenage pregnancy' and abortion, I am not claiming to represent, in totality, the social environment within which young people will experience their lives. The public discursive contexts represented in journal articles, websites, television and newspapers (some of which will be accessible globally and some of which will be accessible at national or local level) will interweave in complex ways with local knowledge and practices, at times being re-enforced, at times being appropriated, at times being dismissed or ignored, and at times being actively resisted by practices and interactions at the micro-social level. This kind of context is more suitably studied using ethnographic methods (for an in-depth ethnographic study in South Africa, see, for example, Mkhwanazi 2004).

4

The basic argument

The basic argument advanced in this book is this. Public discussions of 'teenage pregnancy' and abortion, for the most part, construct a threat of degeneration, in which young women are positioned as contributing, through their sexual and reproductive status, to social decline.

Underlying this assessment of young women who conceive and either bear a child or terminate the pregnancy is a discourse of 'adolescence' as a transitional stage, an understanding of 'adolescence' as a shift from childhood to adulthood. Within this discourse, vestiges of childhood remain while the characteristics of adulthood are being developed. It is this assumption of 'adolescence' as transition that allows for the reporters in the *Special Assignment* programme to call young women who have conceived 'girls' or 'children'. Although these women have displayed the biological characteristics of adulthood through being able to conceive, they are assumed to be emotionally and socially immature, and therefore children.

That this discourse is not necessary (i.e. that young people need not be understood in this way) is borne out by historical and cultural variability in the ways in which young people have been constructed. 'Adolescence' as a category of development was invented in the West in the early part of the twentieth century, and has filtered into African understandings of young people through such means as education.

Not only is the discourse of 'adolescence as transition' a historical and cultural construction, but also it contains within it the seeds of its own destruction. 'Adolescence' is inhabited from the inside by paradoxes (child/not child; adult/not adult) that require constant work in order to arrive at merely temporary resolution.

There are various ideologies attached to the discourse of 'adolescence as transition', ideologies that have important effects in terms of research and interventions with young women who are pregnant. The first ideology concerns the linkage, made by early proponents of the notion of 'adolescence', between the transition of the person from childhood to adulthood and the transition of humankind from primitiveness to civilization. Although these early conceptions of 'adolescence' are no longer taken seriously, the threat of degeneration that primitive people posed to civilization continues to haunt our understandings of 'adolescence'. The less developed, in the form of young people, are depicted as posing a threat of degeneration to the more developed, in the form of adults, through their careless and risk-taking behaviour – through engaging in sex, through not taking contraceptive precautions, through requiring additional health and psychological care during pregnancy or during and after a termination of pregnancy, through engaging in inadequate mothering practices and producing the next generation of problematic youth, and through relying on welfare and not being economically active.

In the same way as colonialists created a firm distinction between primitive people and civilized people, current theorists understand adolescence as clearly distinct from adulthood. The second ideology attached to the 'adolescence as transition' discourse, thus, is the construction of an 'imaginary wall' between teen-aged people and adults. This imaginary wall means that young people are treated as a category separate from adults. The similarities in trends among adults and among teen-aged people in a particular social milieu are de-emphasized, and 'teenagers' are investigated and treated as a separable class of people.

The third ideology revolves around the meaning of the transition to adulthood. This transition is no longer one that is socially defined through a range of rituals or rites of passage, but rather an individually based achievement as the 'teenager' progresses through developing the requisite cognitive, emotional and behavioural characteristics of adulthood. There are two implications to this ideology. This first is that the transition, rather than being of short duration as would be the case in social rituals marking the transition to adulthood, is depicted as a drawn out one of anything up to eight years. The second is that, because the transition is an individual achievement, the chances of the process being derailed, for problems to emerge, are high.

The 'adolescence as transition' discourse and the associated ideologies underpin our ways of talking about, our social practices regarding, and interventions with young people who are sexually active and/or pregnant. They form the bedrock of investigative practices with regard to the consequences of 'teenage pregnancy' and of abortion among young women. They are the mainstay of interventions with young people regarding sex and reproduction. And they feed into an othering process that marks black and minority group 'teenagers' as particularly problematic in the social problem of 'teenage pregnancy' and abortion.

Theoretical foundations

The kind of approach I take in this book is broadly referred to as social constructionism. Social constructionism is quite a diverse and debated field. However, there are some commonalities that I shall briefly summarize here (a useful introduction to the field for those wishing to read further is provided by Burr 2003). In the first place, social constructionism is about questioning the inevitability or necessity of understanding things in particular ways. It points out that human characteristics and interactions are historically and socially variable, that ways of being differ considerably according to time and place. In other words, our knowledge of the world, the way we behave and the manner in which we talk about things are socially and historically constructed. In this book I shall discuss how, first, 'adolescence', and second, 'teenage pregnancy' were 'invented' at particular

historical times. I shall also discuss the social variability of the understanding of 'teen-age'.

Second, from this perspective, knowledge is constructed in social interactions between people. In other words, social action and knowledge are
intricately interwoven. Social interaction and action is, of course, not
restricted to face-to-face interaction. It may take a variety of forms, including
communication through journal articles, textbooks, television, the internet
and newspapers, these being the main sources of data included in this book.

Third, social constructionism is critical of what is referred to as 'taken-
for-granted' knowledge. It does not accept common wisdom as truth, but
questions the assumptions that are made in statements of truth. In
particular, it asks how these assumptions may serve the interests of specific
dominant groups. In other words, it is interested in the power relations that
exist between people and how talk is used to produce and entrench these
power relations. In this book, we shall see how an understanding of 'adolescence' as a transitional stage of human development (in other words as
the bridge between childhood and adulthood) allows for the adult
intervention in these young people's lives, interventions that are frequently
infused with moral invectives and ideological injunctions.

Central to social constructionism is an understanding of discourse.
'Discourse' has been defined in a number of ways. For example, Ian Parker
conceptualizes it as 'a system of statements which constructs an object'
(Parker 1990: 191), while Erica Burman states that discourses are 'socially
organised frameworks of meaning that define categories and specify
domains of what can be said and done' (Burman 2008: 2). While there has
been some debate concerning the exact meaning of discourse, what most
versions have in common is that discourse has an underlying regularity and
has constructive effects.

In terms of the first of these, namely its regularity, a discourse presents a
coherent system of meanings. In other words, the statements in a discourse
cluster around culturally available understandings as to what constitutes a
topic (for example the culturally available ways of talking about and
understanding 'adolescence'). This regularity, however, is found amid variability. This means that although there is some regularity and consistency to
discourse, discourses do also change over time. They develop within particular socio-cultural contexts and are historically variable (Macleod 2002).

In terms of the second aspect of discourse, it is argued that discourses do
not simply describe the social world. Instead, they are the mode through
which the world of 'reality' emerges. They construct people and objects
as well as knowledge and truth in particular ways. Norman Fairclough
(1992) distinguishes three aspects of the constructive effects of discourse,
namely the construction of, first, 'social identities', 'subject positions' or
types of 'self', second, social relationships between people, and third,
systems of knowledge and belief. Fairclough calls these the 'identity',

'relational' and 'ideational' functions of language. In this book I shall explore how the 'adolescence as transition' discourse constructs, first, the identity of the young woman as deficient and in need of assistance, second, the relationship between the educator or expert and young woman as one of guidance or facilitation, and third, our knowledge and beliefs about, for example, the consequences of abortion among young women.

Discourse is constructive, but it is also restrictive. It has a dual character, simultaneously constructing and restricting what can be known, said or experienced at any particular socio-historical moment. It is this duality, 'through which action and understanding are simultaneously enabled and constrained, that links knowledge to power' (Young 1987: 114). For example, the discourse of 'adolescence as transition' simultaneously allows certain ways of understanding teen-aged pregnancy and abortion and restricts other ways of understanding them. It enables a particular set of power relations between educator and young women, and restricts other ways of relating. This discourse emerged in a particular socio-historical moment and thus discourses prior to this would have constructed and restricted understandings of young people in different ways to the present times.

Fairclough (1992) describes a discursive 'event' as simultaneously a piece of text, an instance of discursive practice, and an instance of social practice. He explains the latter two dimensions as follows: the 'discursive practice' dimension concerns the nature of the processes of text production and interpretation (e.g. which discourses are drawn upon and how they are combined); the 'social practice' dimension refers to the institutional and organizational circumstances of the discursive event and how that shapes the discursive practice. In this book, I trace discursive events that define 'teenage pregnancy' (and the associated possibility of abortion) as a social problem. The texts which form part of this event are the range of public statements – either written or spoken – about young sexually active or pregnant women. The discursive practices infused in these texts include drawing on an 'adolescence as transition' discourse, which is frequently combined with gendered and racialized discourses. Finally, I analyse certain social practices that shape the discursive practices referred to. Of particular pertinence is how particular research practices, specifically the tendency to design comparative research that fails to take factors other than age into account, provide fertile grounds for the construction of what I term a threat of degeneration.

As indicated above, social constructionism is a diverse field. Within the overarching principles of social constructionism outlined above, I utilize postcolonialist and feminist lenses to inspect the issue at hand. Again both these fields (feminism and postcolonialism) are contested fields of inquiry. Briefly, however, the postcolonial lens highlights how current power rela-tions are embedded in colonial history, with past and present intermingling in dynamic ways to re-enforce or to trouble particular understandings and interactions. In a sense colonialist forms function as a palimpsest: something that is reused or altered while retaining traces of its earlier form (for further discussion, see Macleod and Bhatia 2008). In this book I discuss how the colonialist construction of 'primitiveness', and consequently of a threat of degeneration, continues to haunt our understandings of 'adolescence', which have consequences for how young women and reproduction are viewed. The feminist lens that I utilize is one that attempts to understand gender in terms of the power relations that operate both at a micro-level and at structural levels. In this, women and men are not seen as groups pitted against one another, with one possessing power over the other. Rather power relations are multiple and shifting, as dominant discourses, social practices and social arrangements compete for hegemony (for further discussion, see Macleod and Durrheim 2002).

Location

In our modern, electronic and globalized world, the public discursive context of 'teenage pregnancy' and abortion cuts, in many respects, across axes of location. Ideas, facts, conclusions and taken-for-granted assumptions are widely circulated through the easy access to information allowed by global media and communication technologies, such as the internet and television. Of course, there is contestation and debate, but these are frequently remarkably similar across a range of geographical locations.

In this book, I have drawn on research conducted within the United Kingdom, North America, Europe, New Zealand, Australia and South Africa in order to construct my central argument. Much of the data is sourced from South Africa. There are good reasons for this, other than the obvious fact that I live and work in South Africa.

First, owing to the legalization of abortion in 1996 (in which there is no restriction in terms of age), the HIV/AIDS epidemic which affects young people disproportionately, and the implementation of a strong public sexuality education programme, South Africa represents somewhat of a recent case study in terms of debate about practices regarding young women, sex, reproduction and termination of pregnancy. Second, these data throw into sharp relief the central issues of the book, specifically the colonial foundation of the notion of 'adolescence', and racialized processes of othering that occur in discussions of young women and pregnancy. This is owing to South Africa's colonial and Apartheid past, and its current status as a country with a mixed so-called 'First World/Third World' economy. South Africa was colonized by both the Netherlands and Britain, although British rule lasted substantially longer than Dutch rule. Apartheid practice, which centred on race as a criterion for differentiation, evolved out of the structures of segregation established during the course of colonial settlement and conquest, and became a form of internal colonialism.

9

Although there are debates around race in the literature on 'teenage pregnancy' in many countries, it is virtually forgotten that colonialism forms a palimpsest of the notion of 'adolescence' in the many contexts in which it is deployed on a daily basis. The latter is also true in South Africa. However, South Africa represents a country battling with the legacy of colonialism and racism, as well as gender inequalities that formed part of these systems, and as such provides a rich source of data that speaks to these issues.

Readers should note that I am not suggesting that colonialism was the same everywhere. There were clear differences, for example, between the rationale for rule and the administration of Francophone and Anglophone colonies. Even within colonies, such as South Africa, there were contradictions and contestations (Comaroff 1989). Nevertheless, there were commonalities in colonialist discourse, such as the distinction between primitiveness and civilization, and it is to these commonalities that this book speaks.

An outline of the book

In Chapter 2, I discuss what has been termed the 'invention of adolescence'. The basic argument here is that 'adolescence' has only recently (in the past 150 years, more or less) been seen as separable stage of human development. I explore the sociological and academic trends that allowed for this invention within the Western world, as well as its infiltration into understandings of young people in Africa. I discuss how the invention of 'adolescence' has allowed for the construction of an imaginary wall between teen-aged people and adults, in which teen-aged people are seen as a group apart, as a subcategory with its own unique features and trends, and how this distinction (between teenagers and adults) together with the colonialist roots of the notion of 'adolescence' allow for the construction of a threat of degeneration.

In Chapter 3, I argue that the inevitability of the 'adolescence as transition' discourse breaks down not only when we view it in historical terms, but also when we start unravelling the various paradoxes that it presents. Internal contradictions haunt the basic premises of the 'adolescence as transition' discourse. These internal contradictions are evident in a number of events, such as sex education, the pregnancy of a teenager, and decision-making in the context of abortion. In each of these, the adult/not adult, child/not child nature of the transition are exposed and placed in contradistinction to each other. The purpose of this chapter is to deconstruct the 'adolescence as transition' discourse, an action that allows for a questioning of this discourse that underpins the construction of a threat of degeneration.

In Chapters 4 and 5, I turn to the nitty-gritty of the topic at hand. In Chapter 4 I explore how 'teenage pregnancy' was invented as a social problem in the United States in the late 1960s and early 1970s. At this stage the signifiers 'unwed mother' and 'illegitimate child' collapsed into the supposedly neutral scientific signifier of 'teenage pregnancy', allowing health and social scientists to investigate the negative consequences of early reproduction. These negative consequences have been listed as the disruption of schooling, socio-economic disadvantage, poor child outcomes, health risks, welfare dependency and demographic concerns. In this chapter I trace some of the social practices that allow for this construction of degeneration, in particular the research practices in which comparative work that foregrounds age to the exclusion of socio-economic status and other social issues is conducted.

In Chapter 5, I explore how, despite the fact that abortion seemingly solves the problem of teen-age mothering, it has become the new social problem. This is made possible through research practices that allow for a construction of abortion as medically and psychologically damaging. After providing the legislative framework of legal abortion in two countries (United States and South Africa), I discuss debates on the psychological consequences of (legal) abortion for women in general, and for young women specifically. I show how the notion of post-abortion syndrome has been taken up by the anti-abortion lobby in ways that turns the personal degeneration, implied in the attribution of health and psychological consequences to abortion, into social degeneration.

In Chapter 6, I turn to the thorny issue of 'race' and teen-aged pregnancy and abortion. I trace the connection made between 'race' and social degeneration in relation to young people conceiving and either terminating a pregnancy or bearing a child. I discuss how 'culture' is used in contradictory ways to explain the occurrence of the social problems of 'teenage pregnancy' and abortion among 'black' and/or minority group people.

There are a number of implications inherent in the discourse of 'adolescence as transition' and the accompanying imaginary wall and threat of degeneration. In Chapter 7, I turn specifically to the implication that intervention on the part of the expert is justified. The expert is invested with managing the risks associated with young people and sex, pregnancy, abortion and childbearing. I analyse the talk of some health service providers with regard to the risky behaviours of young women, as well as the recommendations of a number of South African researchers concerning the educational interventions that should occur in young people's lives in order to prevent the occurrence of abortion. Two distinct philosophies emerge: one in which the educator is seen as guide for the young person on the way to adulthood, and one in which the educator is viewed as a facilitator of the development of naturally emerging patterns. I argue that each of these set up power relations based on the 'adolescence as transition' discourse and that other, more liberatory ways of viewing the educational interface between teen-aged women and educator are possible.

Finally, in Chapter 8 I turn to the question of how young women who do indeed have unwanted pregnancies should be viewed. I argue for a shift from the signifier 'teenage pregnancy' to 'unwanted pregnancy'. Although the term 'unwanted pregnancy' is not without its problems, concentrating on 'unwanted pregnancies' achieves three things. These are, first, a shift away from slicing off a segment of women (young women) from other women of similar social and economic circumstances; second, the potential to understand the circumstances under which pregnancy may be deleterious to women, and third; a shift in focus from the individual young woman to the gendered space within which conception takes place. Preventing unwanted pregnancies is clearly an important aim. In this final chapter I start to explore some of implications of a shift to unwanted pregnancy in terms of research practices and service provision.

2

ADOLESCENCE AS
TRANSITION?

On the day following the *Special Assignment* programme (SABC) mentioned in Chapter 1, the following message was posted on 'The Asylum Forum – Electrochat therapy' web-page by Dizzy (The Asylum Forum 2006):

> Who watched this last night – made me question my views on abortion and the law allowing it!!

The following discussion ensued:

Dark Angel: You're joking right? It was sickening to see a 'qualified' nurse telling a 17 year old CHILD that the government does provide child grants so she doesn't have to worry 'bout money if she gets the baby. Please! Are you saying that you'd rather this girl have the baby and raise it herself. Children having children! The reason these girls use abortion as birth control is because they're uneducated. Educate them about condoms and the pill and other methods and they won't use abortion as birth control. (Although as the one lady said, girls using abortion as birth control is a myth). One girl said she won't use the pill because she'll gain weight . . . again, educate her and give her the facts. Some people gain weight on SOME forms of contraceptive but there's not only one kind of pill or contraceptive for that matter! I really can't believe *Special Assignment* and this melodramatic bull got to you!

Darth-sidious: It's a shame that it made you do that, as that was its obvious intention. Poor piece of propaganda crap. Give me a camera crew and I'll quickly also manage to produce a melodramatic documentary, but this one focusing on the harsh realities of children who are abused, are born to

	mothers who do not want them and who cannot afford to look after them.
Dizzy:	No, I'm not kidding!! Having had 2 terminations myself, I know what it's about (and yes, it definitely makes a woman hard!) and while I see where the kids are coming from, they know full well about birth control, but don't want to use it for whatever (pathetic) reason. Yes, they're uneducated and government must stand up and fix it. What really got me is the age that these girls are starting to shag and fall pregnant AND the fact that virginity testing is illegal, but abortions are free and ok for any girl who wants one.
Darth-sidious:	Please explain the logic of your argument to me. What does the fact that the girls are young have to do with the appropriateness of its legality?

We see here a debate in which there is disagreement concerning whether young women should be allowed free access to abortion. However, despite the disagreement, there is one thing that these individuals appear to agree on: the young women in question are in a transitional phase of development. They are simultaneously knowledgeable (know full well about birth control) and ignorant (uneducated), able to make choices (abortion should be their choice) and neglectful (don't use contraceptives, are unable to look after children). They are 'girls' and, paradoxically, 'children having children'.

This kind of understanding is pervasive not only in lay discussions about teen-aged pregnancy and abortion, but also in the scientific literature, as evidenced in the quotes below.

> No more a child but not yet a woman, and now faced with a woman's role and responsibilities!
>
> (Gillis 1990: 121)

> The adolescent's affective development is unstable and variable in nature because they find themselves between the child and adult world.
>
> (Geldenhuys and de Lange 2001: 92)

> In many ways, today's adolescents are privileged, wielding unprecedented economic power. At the same time, they move through a seemingly endless preparation for life. They try one face after another, seeking to find a face of their own. In their most pimply and awkward moments, they become acquainted with sex. They play furiously at 'adult games' but are confined to the society of their own peers. They want their parents to understand them.
>
> (Santrock 2002: 344)

The first quote above appears in a letter concerning 'teenage pregnancy' in the *South African Medical Journal* in 1990. The second is from an article, appearing in a 2001 edition of the *South African Journal of Education*, on the experiences of black 'adolescent' women with respect to termination of pregnancy. Written eleven years apart within the same country, these submissions express the same sentiment. The teenager is not child and not adult, but at the same time both. She is the between, the transition, the paradox. The third quote comes from one of the most popular textbooks in developmental psychology, *Life-span Development*. This book was written in the United States but is labelled 'International edition'. It is by John Santrock and is currently in its ninth edition (2008). In the description quoted above 'adolescents' simultaneously possess adult characteristics (economic power, sexuality) and the markings of a child (they are preparing for or playing at real life, they lack a firm identity and need the care and understanding of adults). The section in which this extract appears is itself replete with references to adolescents' experiences of the transition from childhood to adulthood and to 'adolescence' as a bridge between two states of being (e.g. between 'the asexual child and the sexual adult': Santrock 2002: 345).

Santrock is not alone in his portrayal of 'adolescence'. The dominant understanding of 'adolescence' in developmental psychology is that it represents a time of transition which is natural, inevitable and universal. In this stage, the person moves, following a developmental blueprint, from a simple to a complex organization of physiological, cognitive, emotional and psychological attributes (Burman 2008). 'Adolescence' is seen as a separable period of development in which developmental tasks such as the formation of self concept, the development of an own identity, the gradual assumption of responsibility and shift away from parents, the preparation for a career, adjustments to physiological changes, and the development of abstract thinking and mature moral reasoning are undertaken. As such, vestiges of childhood remain while the characteristics of adulthood are being developed. The 'adolescent' is, in a sense, neither child nor adult, but also, simultaneously, both.

Many, if not most, researchers in the health and social sciences accept the 'adolescence as transition' discourse, proceeding with their research with this understanding as the firm foundation for their further investigations. Take, for example, the following quotes from the introduction sections of research articles.

> Very often, however, the person that decides to terminate a pregnancy is an adolescent, who is still *'en route'* to, or on the threshold of, adulthood. Adolescence is seen as the period of life when major developmental changes take place which challenge the child to make a transition from childhood to full adulthood.
>
> (Olivier et al. 2000: 213)

> The period between childhood and adulthood is a time of profound biological, social, and psychological changes accompanied by increased interest in sex.
>
> (DiCenso et al. 2002: 1426)

The first set of authors is from South Africa. They studied young women's views on termination of pregnancy. The second set is from Canada. They conducted a systematic review of studies that evaluated the effects of interventions with regard to unintended pregnancies among 'adolescents'. In both statements there is a clear demarcation between adulthood and childhood. The 'adolescent' moves across from one state to the other and crosses a threshold. While not an adult, the person is still a child. And in order to make it from one side to the other, the 'adolescent' has to face 'major developmental challenges' or 'profound biological, social and psychological changes'.

But what if this is not necessarily the case? What if the 'transitional stage of adolescence' is not universal, not self-evident or necessarily part of human nature? What if there *is* no developmental blueprint? What if ways of being teen-aged have more to do with social, cultural and temporal understandings than with the physiological, psychological or cognitive processes that occur within individuals?

It is to these questions that I turn in this chapter. In the following sections I trace the historical invention of 'adolescence' within 'Western' society in the early 1900s. By the end of the 1920s, 'Americans . . . considered adolescence a special developmental stage between childhood and adulthood, and perceived young people in ways that would have seemed astonishing only fifty years earlier' (Luker 1997: 35). Following this, I trace how this way of understanding young people filtered into Africa through the mechanisms of colonialism, especially schooling. I discuss some of the implications of the invention of 'adolescence', specifically that it locates the transition to adulthood within individual rather than within social processes, and that it stands, in many respects, in opposition to the construction of femininity.

Particular ideologies regarding 'adolescence' underpin the power relations implicit in an 'adolescence as transition' discourse. As we shall see throughout this book, these ideologies permeate much of our understanding of young people and reproduction. They filter into our public discussions concerning, and interventions with, young people. These ideologies, as outlined later in this chapter, are, first, the connection between the development in time undergone by individual young people and the development in time undergone by humankind from 'primitiveness' to 'civilization'; second, the construction of an imaginary wall between teen-aged people and adults (which mimics the separation constructed by colonialists between 'primitive' people and 'civilized' people); and third, the wresting of the transition to adulthood from social processes and its location within developmental processes that occur within the individual. In the first of these, the fear of a threat of degeneration that accompanied colonial interactions with so-called primitive people continues to haunt our talk about teenagers. In the second, there is an assumption that people in their teens are somehow a category apart, a subsection of the population under the sway of forces that do not affect the rest of people in that particular cultural and social milieu. In the third, the assumption of adulthood responsibilities and the development of adult capabilities are viewed as an individual achievement, with the transition to adulthood taking place over a long period of adolescence rather than through social rituals and rites of passage that take place over a much shorter period.

The invention of adolescence within the West

Historical analysis illustrates that 'adolescence' emerged as a separable category of human development only in recent history. The construction or invention of 'adolescence' as a developmental stage of transition occurred in the West in the beginning stages of the twentieth century, with various academic and sociological trends in a range of Euro-American countries making the emergence of the idea that such a stage exists possible.

Stanley Hall's (1904) treatise on 'adolescence' (*Adolescence: Its psychology and its relations to physiology, anthropology, sociology, sex, crime, religion and education*) was a landmark text in this emergence. Gabriel Compayré notes, with some humour, in 1906, 'A few lines by Aristotle [about adolescence], then nothing for 2000 years until Mr Stanley Hall's 1300 pages' (cited in Koops and Zuckerman 2003: 345).

Stanley Hall's work is credited with initiating the psychology of 'adolescence'. Its description of young people was vastly different to that which had gone before. For example, prior to this, the advice that was given to young people in North America was to assume adult responsibilities as soon as possible. Young men, whether 14 or 25, who left their parents' home to start their own life were enjoined to take up their responsibilities soon and to avoid dangers such as prostitutes. Little attention was paid to issues such as sexual maturation or development. Young women were assumed to be awaiting marriage under the protection of their parents' home. These young women were enjoined to prepare for marriage through cultivating good habits (such as religion, avoiding romantic novels and fashion). Sexual references were avoided although it may be assumed that what the authors of the advice books (usually Protestant clergymen) meant by the end of childhood was the onset of menstruation (Kett 2003).

Stanley Hall saw 'adolescence' distinctly as a time of transition. He is famous in particular for his theory that ontogeny (the history of the individual) recapitulates phylogeny (the history of human kind). Put simply, he believed that the transitional stage that humankind went through to move from primitiveness to civilization plays itself out in a similar form in the developmental transition of humans from childhood to adulthood.

There were three specific changes in thinking that this theory heralded. First, stress began to be placed on the physical changes of puberty. In this way 'adolescence' was popularized as a teen-age specific phase, in contra-distinction with the earlier broad category of 'youth'. Second, 'adolescence' was seen as comprising of a universal change in emotional and social functioning of the individual coinciding with the physical changes of puberty. Third, there would be conflict involved in the transition – 'storm and stress' – as the primitive urges characteristic of childhood competed with the requirements of civilized behaviour characteristic of adulthood (Kett 2003).

The last of these conclusions, stemming from the underlying 'ontogeny recapitulates phylogeny' theory, led to a call for a moratorium on the assumption of adult responsibility. Stanley Hall recommended that the pressure of adult activities should be relaxed for young people. Instead, they should be allowed time in which to test themselves, to experiment, to establish the limits of their capabilities and to develop respect for the orderliness required in adult life. Kett (2003: 358) calls Hall's recom-mendations 'a plea for liberating the romantic idealism of youth'. In other words, Hall saw his project as one that allowed young people to develop according to their true natures, as a call for allowing them the space to be themselves.

It is this theory, the attendant conclusions and call for a moratorium on adult responsibilities that current researchers call the 'invention of ado-lescence'. They state that it was only at this stage that 'adolescence' started to be seen in the Euro-American context as a separable stage of develop-ment (Kett 2003). Whether this is wholly due to the influence of Stanley Hall's work or because of the sociological conditions of the time is up for debate. There were a number of trends within society that corresponded roughly with the Stanley Hall's work. The first was an increased con-sciousness of and segregation according to age. The second was the rise of mass schooling and the third, the outlawing of child labour. Each of these will be discussed below.

In the early to mid-1800s, there was little age consciousness in the Euro-American context. People of a range of ages mixed within families, the workplace and schools. Chronological age played little part in the timing of a person's exposure to various activities. It was rather social status and gender that determined this. For example, students entering Harvard Uni-versity in the United States could be anywhere between the ages of 12 and early twenties. Students were ranked in terms of precedence in gaining acceptance to Harvard, and dining halls and processions were ranked according to the social position of students' fathers. This meant that younger students (e.g. 14 year olds) frequently enjoyed precedence over older ones (e.g. 20 year olds) (Kett 2003).

Age segregation began in the last two quarters of the nineteenth century. Educators who sought to reform schools argued that pupils should be classified according to age and ability. This, they said, was a better way to impart knowledge to the pupils and to ensure fair competition between the pupils. This led initially to the removal of very young children (3 to 5 year olds) to separate infant schools and of older ones (16 to 17 year olds) who were seen as a disruptive influence in the ungraded schools. Gradually over time graded schooling was introduced with pupils entering the first grade at age 6 and leaving the eighth grade at age 14 (Kett 2003).

The second sociological factor contributing to the invention of 'adolescence' was the rise of mass schooling. State-sponsored mass schooling originated in Western Europe 'in the "long" nineteenth century, from Prussia (1763) to Belgium (1914), despite great variation in societal characteristics and histories [of these countries]' (Ramirez and Boli 1987: 3). Ramirez and Boli (1987: 3) understand the rise of mass schooling in Western Europe within 'the broader civilizational network within which these nation-states operated . . . [and] as an outcome of European competitive processes'. Thus European states funded and managed mass schooling to enhance national polity.

Some more localized explanations for the rise of mass schooling have also been provided. For example, in the first half of the twentieth century the rate juvenile labour reduced dramatically in America owing to a decline in agriculture, the sector within which many young people – mostly males – were employed. There was an increase in the number of adults immigrating to America thus providing a supply of 'reliable' labour, and changes in technology meant that the kinds of labour in which young people engaged in became obsolescent (Kett 2003).

The third factor contributing to the invention of 'adolescence' was legislation outlawing child labour. Although working children were not a new thing, the kinds of labour that children (and adults) engaged in after the industrial revolution were quite different from the standard labour engaged in agricultural or home manufacturing activities. Children were now expected to work long hours in factories under unhealthy and taxing conditions. In the late 1800s and early 1900s there was a strong lobby to outlaw child labour. For example, in Britain the rate of child labour in the textile industry, one of most infamous in terms of its employment of children, halved between 1835 and 1890 with the passing of the Factory Acts and the inspection of the factories (Nardinelli 1980). In the United States, by 1900 twelve states had 14 as the minimum age for employment in the manufacturing sector. By 1910, this number had increased to thirty-two states (Basu 1998).

While these trends occurred throughout the Euro-American world, leading to what has been termed a universalization of adolescence, local variation in social conditions meant that there was variability in how 'adolescence' was represented and responded to, and how quickly the concept took root. For example, in his comparison of two cities, Pomfret (2001) argues that the concept of 'adolescence' found more fertile ground in Nottingham, Britain, than in Saint-Etienne, France, in the late nineteenth and early twentieth centuries. He ascribes this to local norms of working life, demographic conditions, and the influence of the family.

The construction of adolescence in Africa

Adolescence is often said not to exist in [pre-colonial Africa], and this idea is true in the sense that the unmarried young became, upon marriage, much like the older generation that preceded them.
(Caldwell et al. 1998: 137)

In the article in which this statement is made, Caldwell et al. (1998) trace changes in understandings of young people in Africa and Asia. The statement intimates that the transition to adulthood heralded by the social event of marriage in pre-colonial Africa was replaced, through the process of colonialism, by the concept of 'adolescence' as a form of transition.

Of course, knowing what pre-colonial Africa was 'really' like is basically impossible as our understandings are always already tainted by the interpretations of the early explorers in their writings, or by written interpretations of oral history. What we do know is that the social structures and interactions of pre-colonial Africans were fundamentally different from those of the colonial powers they encountered. Also, the process of the meeting of colonial understandings and structures with indigenous ones was not a simple one characterized by the replacement of indigenous understandings and structures with colonial ones. Instead these two social systems met, conflicted, challenged, annihilated in some instances, hybridized, and interweaved. Part of this process was the construction of 'adolescence', at least as an ideology, in Africa.

One of the main mechanisms for the construction of 'adolescence' in Africa was the introduction of schooling, initially via the missionaries and later through colonial government intervention. This is not to say that education did not exist in pre-colonial Africa. While education was adapted to the particular social circumstances of a particular region, what education had in common in pre-colonial Africa was the use of games and story-telling as educational tools, apprenticeship in a particular activity, and initiation practices. Learning took place within a community setting and involved many people as teachers (White 1996). What colonialism brought with it was the notion that education should take place in separate classrooms, that children should be grouped according to chronological age, that instruction should occur on a daily basis with a particular designated teacher, and that performance in a particular skill should be assessed via the examination. Although there were differences between Anglophone and Francophone colonies in how the educational system was implemented and what purpose it was to play within the colonies, the basic structure of schooling was similar.

The major contribution of schooling was to introduce 'the anticipation of a period of adolescence in which young people were still dependent and unmarried' (Caldwell et al. 1998: 140). Furthermore, it removed young people from the general community activities of production and reproduction and brought age peers together in a group. It transferred deference for authority from the system of the family and clan to a non-relative appointed by missionaries or the government. It cancelled out the apprenticeship style of learning and implied preparation for an entirely new set of activities (Caldwell et al. 1998).

Colonialist powers' intervention in education had a particular rationale. Education began to be seen as the key to bringing Africans to a higher level of civilization and understanding. For example, Albert Charton, Inspector-General of French West Africa, in a book entitled *African learn to be French* published in 1930, writes: 'Africa is not capable of evolving a fully formed intellectual culture of her own'. He concludes that France may assist by 'holding out a helping hand to the indigenous culture, which though more simple, is yet closer to life' and that 'school is a focus for all the influences at work for the uplift of native life' (Charton 1930, cited in White 1996: 15).

Thus, for young Africans, the idea that 'primitive' societies evolve into 'civilized' ones operated on two levels as age and race intersected. Through the school, young people in Africa became the bridge not only between child and adult life but also literally between an entire society's so-called primitive character and so-called civilization. In the West theorists comfortably stated that ontogeny recapitulated phylogeny (namely that teenagers' move from childhood to adulthood resembles the move of humankind from primitiveness to civilization), with the implication of semblance rather than actuality. In Africa, the burden of ontogeny (moving across the bridge between childhood and adulthood created by formal schooling), plus of phylogeny (shifting Africans from so-called primitiveness to so-called civilization) rested with young people.

This is not to say that there was no resistance to the imposition of schooling in Africa. In the Eastern Cape of South Africa, for example, what were called the 'Red' people, named for their custom of painting their bodies with red-coloured clay, resisted the introduction of schooling by the missionaries. Some researchers have suggested that there was a clear distinction between 'Red' communities and 'School' communities. 'Red' communities sought to protect practices under threat from colonization, practices such as chiefly rule, communal tenure and initiation. 'School' communities, educated in missionary schools, embraced Christian values such as monogamy and emphasized the importance of formal Western-style education. These researchers have been criticized for overstating the distinction between the two groups (Delius and Glaser 2002). Nevertheless, what their work illustrates is early resistance (whether in distinct groups or in a piecemeal fashion) to the introduction of schooling in South Africa. Later on, when government intervention in education increased (chiefly after the First World War), there was resistance by many Africans across the continent to the educational system. One of the arguments was that it perpetuated cultural and political domination, particularly as most of the schools constructed for Africans offered agricultural and artisanal training, thereby promoting a view of Africans as wholly pastoral or, alternatively, suited for low level work (White 1996).

Other than schooling, a number of colonial influences contributed to the construction of 'adolescence' in Africa. Christianity brought with it a disapproval of polygamy, initiation rituals and early marriage. Instead, families were expected to rear children through teen-aged years, send them to school, permit marriage at a respectably mature age and ensure a companionate monogamous marriage (Caldwell et al. 1998). The move to an economy based on the exchange of money created the rationale for schooling as young people needed skills in occupations other than those of their parents'. It also brought with it the growth of towns and the accompanying urbanization. An increasing number of young people, who were either born in urban settings or else moved there, were removed from the traditional patriarchal polygamous family structure. They were exposed to Western youth culture and in turn 'had a good deal to contribute to a global youth culture' (Caldwell et al. 1998: 141).

In summary, thus, 'adolescence has come into being in the developing world because of massive economic, institutional, and social changes brought about by Western colonial and economic expansion and by the move toward a global economy and society' (Caldwell et al. 1998: 149). This does not mean, however, that there is homogeneity in the ways that teen-aged people conduct their lives. In fact, currently, there is great social and cultural variability in what is considered 'adolescence' in Africa. Young people in Africa are, in the words of the editors of a book on research concerning young Africans, a 'plural and heterogeneous categor[y]' (De Boeck and Honwana 2005: 1).

It also does not mean that 'adolescence' and its development is (or was) the same in Africa as it is (or was) in the West. For example, in 1950, rates of child labour (defined as people under the age of 16 participating in paid work) in Africa was higher than it was in the middle of the nineteenth century in Britain when the issue of child labour began to filter into the public arena as a social problem (Basu 1998). What is clear, however, is that the *discourse* of 'adolescence as transition', together with its underlying ideologies, has taken firm root in Africa. It is to these underlying ideologies that we now turn.

The ideologies of adolescence

Although Hall's theory of recapitulation was fairly soon discarded by psychologists, the concept of 'adolescence' took root and soon became part of common sense. It became, as Moran (2000: 19) puts it, 'part of the [American] culture's mental furniture'. The invention of 'adolescence' in the West, its importation into Africa and its establishment as a developmental stage within human life (readily accessible for study by developmental psychologists) have rested on, and simultaneously have propagated, a range of ideologies. In this section I review three of these ideologies. First, I explore how 'adolescence' as a *time* of transition that mimics the transition from primitiveness to civilization rests on an evolutionary understanding of development in time and how the separation of primitiveness and civilization in terms of time perpetuates colonialist understandings. This linkage of individual and collective development allows for the threat of degeneration to occupy our talk of 'adolescent' development. Second, 'adolescence' as a separable stage of human development assumes that the changes that young people undergo and the social phenomena observed among them are somehow different to those observed or occurring among the adults of that particular population. I refer to this here as the imaginary wall. Finally, the concept of 'adolescence' implies that the transition to adulthood is not a social process, but rather something that unfolds within the individual. This implies that there is always the potential for this process to be derailed and for the transition to full adulthood to be incomplete.

'Adolescence as transition' and the threat of degeneration

Nancy Lesko (2001), in a chapter entitled 'Time matters in adolescence', traces a change in scientific thinking. In the seventeenth and eighteenth centuries scientific endeavour centred around investigating static laws and regularities (think, for example, of Newton's theory of universal gravitation and his three laws of motion, both of which explain physical phenomenon according to universal and static laws of nature). In the nineteenth century, however, this was supplemented by an approach in which change and growth over time became the central feature. This movement (from studying static laws and regularities to studying change and growth over time) was closely linked to the development of the theory of evolution, which emphasized development through time. Evolutionary theory, through tracing present-day complex organisms back to earlier simpler forms of life

23

(e.g. humans back to apes), introduced a developmental time consciousness to scientific thinking.

This understanding of development and change in time facilitated two, interlinked theories. The first theory concerned the development of civilization. So-called 'primitive' societies started to be seen as being in less advanced positions on the cultural evolutionary scale. Primitive societies were regarded as occupying (in space) an earlier time in the development of Western civilization. The second theory was that 'adolescence' represents a developmental transition from one state to another. In other words, individual humans could now be seen as developing, changing through time – in a sense, evolving. Stanley Hall (1904), as we saw earlier, linked the developmental stage of transition of 'adolescence' with that of the development of civilization.

Indeed Hall saw himself as a Darwin of the mind (Moran 2000), and engaged in theorizing that is termed social Darwinism (in which the insights gained concerning biological evolution are taken up and conflated with cultural or social evolution). He believed that the prolonged chastity evident among young people in the United States at the turn of the century was a factor in the evolution of the 'civilized' race (see later discussion on the invention of the sexual adolescent). It meant that young people were channelling their energies into developing morality, reason and religious, athletic or artistic competence, qualities that marked the 'civilized' race as more advanced than other races. This belief was reinforced by the work of early Victorian ethnographers who argued that polygamy, promiscuity and incest were part of the sexual morality of the 'lower' or 'savage' races. They noted that this too was how the Anglo-Saxon race had behaved in early periods, but that with the progress of civilization, sexual self-control elevated them above the sensuality of primitive people.

As Lesko (2001: 37) puts it, the concepts of development 'are primarily narratives of fulfillment'. Of importance is what the person or persons doing the developing result in – the end product. The 'adolescent' is developing towards the rational adult and primitive people are developing towards civilization. The overlapping of the tale of individual development and of cultural evolution means the privileging of the white, middle-class heterosexual adult male – the rational person towards whom the 'adolescent' is developing – is implicitly the civilized person. This person is the quintessential end-product, the valorized best result, of development, both for the individual and for the collective. He is the rational person, the essence of moral rectitude and social upstanding, the bread-winner who engages in rational economic decision-making that maximizes economic well-being for himself and his family. This is borne out by the fact that the vast majority of research conducted on 'adolescents' has been with white middle-class teenagers (Dubas et al. 2003): those who are most likely to develop into this quintessential best end-result.

The juxtaposition that the 'development in time' concept brought with it – primitive versus civilized, childhood versus adulthood – and the labour that was implied in the movement from one to the other meant that there was always a danger of degeneration. The less developed, the more primitive, are always in danger of disrupting or undermining the stability of those who are developed or civilized. As Lesko (2001) indicates, in colonial times

> The incitement to worry over teenagers [was] largely sexual anxiety – sexuality that invokes animality, self-abuse, loss of male energy, and antisocial attitudes. Sexual precocity, especially masturbation, was the gateway to degeneration because of its serious consequences for the development of individuals, the nation, and the race.
>
> (Lesko 2001: 39)

Thus understandings of 'adolescence' as a developmental stage, and the possible ways in which this transition may be derailed (i.e. through precocious sexuality) was intricately linked to colonial concerns about degeneration of the civilized into the primitive and contamination of the civilized by the primitive. Hall believed that parents who had successfully sublimated their sexual desires during 'adolescence' would have healthier children who would hopefully repeat the cycle, until 'the race itself was composed of more intelligent, more moral, more advanced persons' (Moran 2000: 18). On the flip side, premature sexuality would lead to racial deterioration. The consequences of this vice would be passed on to the children.

These kinds of concerns continue to be expressed concerning young people who disrupt the 'transitionality' of 'adolescence', those who continue to display the characteristics of childhood, or alternatively, precociously display the characteristics of adulthood. As Lesko (2000: 51) states, 'Teenagers cannot go backward to childhood nor forward to adulthood "before their time" without incurring derogatory labels – for example, "immature", "loose", or "precocious"'. People identified as 'adolescents' are expected to cling to a moratorium on responsibility and decision-making, to remain in a continual time of transition, a time of expectation of adult responsibility. If they engage in activities such as sex and reproduction, they are charged with causing a number of social consequences.

The invention of adolescence and its interweaving with colonialist concerns is not gender blind. DeLuzio (2007) outlines how Stanley Hall conflated his theory of 'adolescence' with the development of the civilized boy. Indeed, his work was dubbed by one of his followers as 'boyology' because of the basic assumption that the quintessential end goal of individual development through adolescence was the white, middle-class, civilized male.

Hall believed that 'savage' behaviour would form part of the civilized boy's behaviour. This he ascribed to the fact that a long period was required for the individual's recapitulation of the development from primitiveness to civilization within civilized society (the period of recapitulation within so-called less advanced societies was viewed as being much shorter). Despite his sanctioning of a moratorium on responsibility in which these primitive urges could be displayed, the final outcome of civilized male development was self-control, adjustment and self-direction. Males were thus invested with the capability of preserving and extending the gains made by the civilized races.

The white middle-class female emerged in all of this as 'the first adolescent' – the budding girl who is 'the quintessential and perpetual adolescent' (DeLuzio 2007: 104). Stanley Hall's rendition of the movement from savage boyhood to civilized manhood required that boys go through a stage of life characterized by the attributes of the civilized female, whom he viewed as being one rung below the civilized boy on the evolutionary ladder. He 'ascribed to all adolescents such self-described "feminine" traits as physical and mental volatility, emotionality, altruism, and religiosity' (DeLuzio 2007: 105). He held up the middle-class girl as the example of a particular adolescent attribute, while at the same time insisting on the necessity of sexual differentiation in development and the primacy of the civilized male in racial advancement.

Ninety years after the publication of Stanley Hall's work, Fine and Macpherson (1994) note:

> When we scoured the literature on adolescent females and their bodies, we concluded that the very construction of the topic is positioned largely from white, middle-class, non-disabled, heterosexual women. The concerns of white **elite** women are represented as *the* concerns of this age cohort.
>
> (Fine and Macpherson 1994: 220, emphases in original)

Thus, contrary to the claims by some (e.g. Hudson 1984) that the tenets of adolescence and of femininity are at loggerheads with each other, the conceptualization of 'adolescence' encapsulates a very specific form of femininity.

The result is that young women occupy the category of 'adolescence' in complex and contradictory ways. Because the discourse of 'adolescence as transition' is presented as universally applicable, teen-aged women are incorporated into its mandate. At the same time, differentiation between women on axes of race, sexual orientation, location, class and ability are subtly infused in representations and practices regarding young women. These axes of inclusion and exclusion in the premises of 'adolescence' create multiple double-binds for young women. For example, commenting on

Carol Gilligan's work with young women, DeLuzio (2007) states: 'Faced with the challenge of both conforming to the standard of adult femininity for "selflessness" *and* achieving the standard of maturity for "separation and independence", adolescent girls found themselves in a lose-lose situation' (DeLuzio 2007: 248). Even those most visible in the tenets of 'adolescence', the white, middle-class, able-bodied, heterosexual women referred to above, have to deal with the contradiction of being the embodiment of adolescence and simultaneously excluded from the implicit masculinist ideal end-goal of development.

These double-binds or lose-lose situations have implications not only in terms of how young women experience their lives, but also in terms of public representations of them. The threat of degeneration implicit in the discourse of 'adolescence as transition' is rendered more real by its complex association with femininity.

In Chapters 4 and 5, I outline research detailing the consequences of early reproduction. While some of these are seen as consequences that affect the individual young women only (e.g. psychological stress as a result of an abortion), most are viewed as a social consequences (e.g. perpetuating the cycle of disadvantage through early childbearing: young women condemning their children, and their children's children, to perpetual poverty). Even those that are viewed as personal consequences are depicted as carrying a social cost (e.g. the provision of psychological services required to assist young women traumatized by abortion). Although the overt colonialist language of degeneration is lost, the implication that young pregnant or childbearing women are contributing to social decline is clear. In a sense, the ghost of a discourse of degeneration haunts our understandings of young women and reproduction. This ghost of a threat of degeneration draws off the colonialist underpinnings of a discourse of 'adolescence as transition' and the association of 'adolescence' with femininity. It also relies on the separation of 'adolescence' from adulthood – the creation of an imaginary wall – in which the trends noted among young people are seldom compared to those of adults living in a similar social and cultural milieu.

Constructing an imaginary wall

The invention of 'adolescence' and its creation as a developmental stage between childhood and adulthood has created a firm distinction between 'adolescence' and adulthood. This separation of 'adolescence' into a distinct stage of development means that trends within this group of people are seen as specific to this group. There is what Moran (2000) calls an 'imaginary wall' created between teen-aged people and adults. This means that the relationship between changes in how people in their teens relate to the world and behave and how adults relate to the world and behave is ignored.

For example, researchers interested in 'teen culture' note changes in teen-aged people's consumption of goods, of their tastes in music and movies, their penchant for particular activities. They use this information to draw conclusions about 'teenagers', ignoring how adults in a similar social milieu consume goods, or what music or movies they prefer, or what activities they engage in (Kett 2003). In concentrating on teenagers alone, these researchers create the impression that somehow there is a 'teen culture' separate from 'adult culture'. But, as Kett (2003: 370) points out, 'young people change all the time, but so do we all'.

If one concentrates exclusively on young people, the impression may be created that somehow it is only the teen-aged people who are changing, who are prone to particular trends. Indeed, researchers seldom compare people in their teens with the adults of a population. For example, Quinton et al. (2001: 492) bemoan the lack of a 'comprehensive, longitudinal, methodologically sound study that compares minor and adult women's psychological adjustment to abortion'.

Where comparative research is provided, the similarities between the teen-aged people and adults make for interesting reading. Take, for example, the generally accepted notion that 'adolescence' as a transitional period implies a period of 'storm and stress', of 'normal' emotional and social turmoil. A group of researchers (Offer et al. 1988, cited in Koops and Zuckerman 2003) who studied teenagers and adults in ten countries found that indeed 24 per cent of the teenagers researched regularly experienced feelings of depression. However, so did 29 per cent of the adults, indicating that the psycho-social experiences of these two artificially separated groups of people in these countries were more similar than initially supposed.

Moran (2000) provides an example specific to the central theme of this book, 'teenage pregnancy'. Much of the concern with regard to young people becoming pregnant has been bolstered by arguments relating to the rate of 'teenage pregnancy'. However, this is seldom, if ever, seen in the context of general reproductive trends. Moran (2000) argues that the rate of 'teenage pregnancy', certainly in the United States, is strongly correlated with the rates of pregnancy among adults of similar race, ethnicity and socio-economic background, and that changes in the rates of 'teenage pregnancy' over time reflect changes in reproduction rates in general. Indeed, as will be seen throughout this book, there are more similarities than differences between younger and older women in relation to pregnancy and abortion.

Wresting the transition to adulthood from social processes

Societies throughout history and all over the world have marked the transition of members of the particular society to adulthood (Anglin et al. 1998). This has taken many forms such as a range of rituals, initiation processes, and various rites of passage. A South African example of this is the Xhosa rites of passage for males (*ukwaluka*) and for females (*intonjane*), from which males emerge stating '*Ndiyindoda*' ('I am a man') and females '*Ndingumfaz*' ('I am a woman' – although female initiation rites have waned recently, male initiation continues with controversy raging concerning 'traditional' practices of circumcision versus 'modern' medical methods).

These rituals and rites of passage mark the entry of a young person into the responsibilities and activities of adulthood. They are social in nature, creating a context in which the social contract between the individual and the collective may be fulfilled. At the conclusion of these social processes, certain ways of acting are enabled and others restrained. The individual is expected to take on particular responsibilities and to contribute in particular ways to the collective. These processes are generally time-limited, spanning at the outmost a number of months.

Thus, transition to adulthood is a process that has, for the most part, been an important social event (Graham 2004). What the 'adolescence as transition' discourse does is to wrest the 'transition' from its social grounding and to locate the process within the individual. The fundamental premise of the theory of 'adolescence' is that the transition to adulthood is an individual matter rather than a social occasion. It is something that unfolds 'naturally' through *individually* based physical, psychological, cognitive and emotional processes. It spans a number of years (mostly seen as between six and eight years) rather than a matter of months. And, as seen in the rest of this book, because it is located within the individual, rather than being a social event, it is in immanent danger of being derailed through a number of risk factors.

This is not to say that young people who live in societies where the 'adolescence as transition' is dominant do not engage in a range of practices and social rituals aimed at marking a transition to adulthood. Activities such as smoking or sexual debut, driving a car or hanging out at a certain place may informally, to a greater or lesser extent, at least partially mark a transition to adulthood. For example, Klein (1994: 675) suggests that drug usage among young men in some rural areas of Nigeria acts as 'something akin to a rite of passage'. Through such usage, young men become distinguished from the traditional world of farming and fishing and instead are associated with the sophistication and adulthood of the metropolis. At other times initiation into adulthood takes a more informal quality. Indeed, Mkhwanazi (2004), in her thesis on 'teenage pregnancy' in a South African township, argues that, with the waning of formal female initiation rites, the management of 'teenage pregnancy' acts as a transition rite in townships, with many of the activities emulating those previously used in female Xhosa initiation.

These kinds of informal or subcultural activities are, however, not incorporated into the very definition of 'adolescence'. Within a discourse of

29

'adolescence as transition', these kinds of interactions form part of the emotional and social development of the individual. It is the *individual's* negotiation of the various social and emotional challenges of development that remains centre stage.

Conclusion

Enright et al. (1987) question whether economic and social conditions influence how social scientists view 'adolescents'. Their answer is yes. To substantiate their argument, they present results from their analysis of eighty-nine articles published in two journals (*Pedagogical Seminary* and *Journal of Genetic Psychology*) during the two depressions and the two world wars. They found that during the depressions, scientific writing on 'adolescence' represented 'adolescents' (in the United Kingdom and United States) as immature, psychologically unstable and in need of prolonged education. Given the scarcity of work during a depression, this rendition of young people assists in taking them out of the marketplace, thereby freeing up work opportunities for adults. However, during the wars, the authors noticed that scientific writing portrayed teenagers as psychologically competent and in need of a truncated form of education. The implications here are clearly that these people ('adolescents') are capable of participating in the activities required during a war, including joining the armed forces or providing technical support. Thus, how 'adolescence' is viewed is intricately linked with the socio-economic conditions prevailing at a particular historical period.

Despite the attempts of developmental psychologists to theorize and explain universal theories of development in 'adolescence', there is nothing inherent to 'adolescence' that makes it a universal stage of transition from childhood to adulthood. Indeed, we have seen in this chapter how 'adolescence' emerged as a separable stage of development in the West only in the early part of the twentieth century. Although Stanley Hall's treatise on 'adolescence' was instrumental in this, there were also a number of sociological conditions that assisted in its invention. These included the increased segregation according to age, the rise of mass schooling and the outlawing of child labour. 'Adolescence' was introduced as a construct in Africa through colonial mechanisms such as schooling, Christianity, an economy based on the exchange of money and the development of towns.

Although there is no uniformity in how teen-age years are experienced by young people in various parts of the world, nor is there complete synchrony between, say, 'adolescence' in Africa and 'adolescence' in the West, and 'adolescence' as experienced by females and by males, there are common underlying ideologies that structure our ways of understanding, talking about and intervening with people viewed as 'adolescents'. In the first instance, the connection of individual development from childhood to adulthood (ontogeny) and collective development from so-called primitive-ness to so-called civilization (phylogeny), proposed initially by Stanley Hall, has perpetuated colonialist understandings of 'adolescence'. In particular the threat of degeneration that colonialists feared from primitive people continues to haunt our understandings of 'adolescence'. In other words, the less developed (young people, primitive people) are depicted as having the potential to destabilize and undermine developed, civilized society. This threat of degeneration takes on a particularly gendered hue with the par-ticular characteristics of 'adolescence' being associated with certain versions of femininity. While young people in general are positioned as threatening social stability, it is particularly young women, and more so poor and/or black young women, who embody this threat.

In the second instance, an imaginary wall is constructed between 'ado-lescence' and adulthood. It is not recognized that the trends noted among young people are often broad sociological trends that affect all people in a particular socio-cultural milieu. 'Teen-aged' people are viewed as a separ-able category, with their own unique patterns and characteristics. In the third instance, with the invention of 'adolescence', the transition to adult-hood becomes something inherent within the person. It is a process occur-ring within an individual who happens to be a certain age. It is an extended phase of about eight years, in which the physiological, emotional and cognitive development of the person marks the transition, rather than any social set of events such as rituals, ceremonies and rites of passage, all of which have a limited time span (at the outmost a few months).

The 'adolescence as transition' discourse not only creates an imaginary wall between teen-aged and older people, but also simultaneously per-petuates and disguises an internal contradiction. Teen-aged people are not adult (imaginary wall), but are preparing for adulthood. They are also not children, but because they are not adult, they are, by definition partially children. It is to this conundrum, this internal paradox that I turn to in the following chapter, showing how these internal inconsistencies are thrown into relief by sex education, 'teenage pregnancy' and decision-making regarding abortion.

3

CONUNDRUMS

Sex education, 'teenage pregnancy', and decision-making in the context of abortion

The words 'adolescence' and 'adolescents' have become so commonplace that they suggest an uncontested reality. However, as we saw in Chapter 2, 'adolescence' is in fact rather a recent invention in human history, a fact that allows us to question the inevitability of the 'adolescence as transition' discourse. In this chapter, I discuss how the 'adolescence as transition' discourse starts to unravel not only when the historical, social and cultural invention of 'adolescence', together with the variability of teen-age, is taken into consideration, but also at various points of paradox. At these points of paradox, the internal inconsistency of the discourse is highlighted. Because in the 'adolescence as transition' discourse, teen-aged people are simultaneously children and adults, but also neither, tensions arise in the very conceptualization of this developmental stage. The inconsistencies inherent in the very definition of 'adolescence' mean that there are points at which the internal oppositions become exposed. These points undermine the fundamental premises of the concept, becoming conundrums which are unsolvable. They resist clear definition into one or the other side of the paradox. Instead they sit uncomfortably with our understandings of living, creating a sense of confusion and lack of resolution.

The three conundrums that threaten the 'adolescence as transition' discourse pertinent to this book are teen-aged (hetero)sexuality, the pregnant teenager, and decision-making in the context of abortion. (The term 'hetero' is put in parentheses before the word 'sexuality' in recognition of the heteronormative assumption that sexuality is heterosexuality to the exclusion of other forms of sexuality.) Teenagers, in the 'adolescence as transition' discourse, may practise at being adult, but may not actually perform adult activities such as having sex, reproducing or deciding on matters as personal and important as abortion. They must prepare for adulthood, but may not actually be adults. Theirs is a perpetual state of disequilibrium, in which activities that foretell of adulthood (such as sex education) must be balanced by a state of innocence that forecloses adulthood. The imaginary wall between 'adolescence' and adulthood must be maintained.

The balance, however, is precarious, requiring constant professional debate, intervention and surveillance as the requirements of foretelling or practising adulthood in preparation for actual adulthood opens the window for the intrusion of adulthood into 'adolescence'. Therefore, when teenagers do engage in sex, when they do conceive and when they do decide of their own volition to terminate their pregnancy, strategies must be put into place to ameliorate the difficulties posed by these activities to our fundamental understanding of 'adolescence'. These include sex education programmes that highlight the dangers of sex, research concerning the negative outcomes of early childbearing, counselling that advises young women to consult their parents or guardians before undergoing a termination of pregnancy. In all of these, teen-aged women are treated as a separable category requiring specialized intervention. The similarities between their circumstances and those of women of similar socio-economic status are glossed over.

In the following I discuss how the internal inconsistency of the 'adolescence as transition' discourse plays itself out in, first, sex education, second, the very notion of 'teenage pregnancy', and third, decision-making in the context of abortion. In the first instance I discuss how the instrumentalist goal of sex education (i.e. when the aim of sex education is to be instrumental in bringing about societal changes) rests on the imaginary wall created between young people and adults. I trace, initially in general and then through two examples of sex education programmes, the tension that is created between maintaining childhood innocence and introducing adult sexual information and images. In the second instance I discuss how 'teenage pregnancy' is constructed as 'children having children' a contradiction that cannot be, but is. Because the discourse of 'adolescence as transition' means that the 'adolescent' is a child (and yet not a child), pregnancy among young women creates a crisis to our understanding of 'adolescents' that must be resolved. I trace how this crisis is dealt with with respect to one particular 'adult' function, namely mothering. Finally, I discuss the debate that rages regarding parental consent or involvement in a young woman's decision to terminate a pregnancy. An internal contradiction haunts the assumptions made by proponents of compulsory parental consent or involvement: women who display 'adult' reproductive characteristics are believed to be children when it comes to deciding whether to terminate or continue a pregnancy.

Teen-aged (hetero)sexuality and sex education

Jeffrey Moran (2000) starts his book entitled *Teaching sex: The shaping of adolescence in the 20th century* with a chapter on the invention of the sexual adolescent. In it, he traces the American social context and the influence of Stanley Hall's treatise on the construction of the 'adolescent' as a sexual being. Stanley Hall's work emerged in a time when sexuality was seen as something to be strictly controlled through self-will. Advice manuals, chiefly aimed at men (although Victorian sensibilities condemned female sexual activity and desire as well), exhorted men to exercise mastery over their unruly sexual bodies. In these books, 'there was no reason a thirty-year-old man could not be as chaste as an infant, if only he would learn to educate his will and exercise that chief bourgeois virtue, self-control' (Moran 2000: 5). Masturbation was the greatest foe, with writers explicating at length the dangers of what was called self-abuse. Sexual respectability was central to the standing of middle-class families, and formed a 'stern guide to personal comportment' (Moran 2000: 13).

Hall similarly placed chastity and self-denial at the centre of his interpretation of 'adolescence'. To him, 'adolescence' represented the period between puberty, which implied a sexual awakening. Marriage was the correct context for the expression of this sexual desire. As Moran (2000: 15) puts it, 'Without the demand for sexual repression and sublimation, the modern concept of adolescence made no sense at all'. As discussed earlier, this imposition of self-control represented the mark of the civilized race. Thus, 'adolescence' represented a period of self-restraint together with the development of higher, evolutionary traits, such as morality, reason and other civilized competencies. Once again, these applied only to males. In contrast, Hall argued that the female 'adolescent's' chief developmental task was to avoid exertions of any type that could interfere with her capacity to reproduce.

Moran (2000) concludes his chapter on the invention of the sexual adolescent with the following statements:

> Meeting the needs of the modern adolescent required a modern method. Medicine, eugenics, psychology, education – all of these modern fields promised to help the adolescent meet the inevitable struggle with sexuality. . . . Having created adolescence, they were bound to manage it.
>
> (Moran 2000: 22)

And so began sex education in the United States. This was born initially out of a confluence of interests between the Child Study Movement (a movement established and led by Stanley Hall with the aim of scientifically studying children and 'adolescents') and the Social Hygiene Movement. One of the aims of the Child Study Movement was the development of the responsible sexual 'adolescent'. The Social Hygiene Movement had as its key focus the prevention of venereal disease and prostitution. These two movements lobbied for the introduction of sex education, finding in each other willing allies (Moran 2000).

Sex education has taken on various forms and has been supported or opposed by various rationales in the United States and elsewhere over the years. What have remained constant are the instrumentalist goal of sex education as well as an implicit contradiction that is difficult to resolve. In the following, I discuss the instrumentalist goal of sex education which is linked to a fundamental separation of 'adolescence' and adulthood. I show how the internal paradox of 'adolescence as transition' haunts sex education in general. This is followed by illustrative examples of sex education programmes from the South African context. Although these two programmes have quite disparate approaches, the internal contradiction of adult/not adult, child/not child inhabits both.

The instrumentalist goal of sex education

The initial aim of sex education in the United States was to resolve the problems of venereal disease, prostitution and sexual degeneracy through interventions with young people. Thus, the first sex education programmes had 'instrumentalist' goals. In other words, they wished to be instrumental in promoting social changes (a decrease of venereal disease and prostitution, an increase in sexual rectitude among the general population) through changing individual 'adolescent's' sexual attitudes and behaviour.

These instrumentalist goals continue to provide the bedrock for the motivation to provide sex education programmes. For example, the British Broadcasting Corporation (2002) reported, 'After warnings about increased rates of sexually transmitted infections, the government says it wants to "raise the status and quality" of sex education'. Sexology SA, an organization that offers, among other things, training to South African teachers in sex education, states that in offering sex education to young people, 'the . . . educator will make a global contribution to the struggle against: HIV/AIDS, STIs [sexually transmitted infections], rape, violence against women and children, unplanned teenage pregnancies, date rape and sex abuse in South Africa' (Sexology SA n.d.). Thus social problems such sexually transmitted diseases, HIV, rape, violence against women and children, sexual abuse, unplanned teenage pregnancy are seen as being solved through sex education aimed at changing the behaviour of individual young people. As Moran (2000) puts it:

> Even as they have reckoned with the novel crises of 'teenage pregnancy' and AIDS in the aftermath of the sexual revolution, sex educators have navigated by familiar stars. The dominance of danger and disease in thinking about adolescent sexuality, a deep faith in the instrumentalist model of sex education, and a conviction that adolescence is somehow a thing apart from adult society

– these are the unchanging boundaries of the universe within which sex education continues to be conceived.

(Moran 2000: 217)

The appeal of the instrumentalist goal of sex education is clear. A range of social problems, as outlined by Sexology SA above, are solved by intervening early in the lives of individual young people. Unfortunately, however, there is scant evidence that sex education programmes have much effect on people's actual behaviour (as opposed to their knowledge about sex). Research using randomized controlled trials indicates that sex education does little to delay the initiation of sex, improve the usage of contraception, prevent unwanted pregnancy or reduce exposure to sexually transmitted diseases (DiCenso et al. 2009; Wight et al. 2002). Despite this evidence, the instrumentalist goal continues to hold sway in both popular and government talk about sex education (Moran 2000).

The implicit contradiction of sex education

The instrumentalist goal of sex education rests on a fundamental separation between 'adolescence' and adulthood (the imaginary wall). In other words, sex education makes a basic distinction between what should be prevented (the possibility sexual disease and danger in adulthood) and the present state of the people to whom it is presented. Sex education implicitly defines teen-aged people as adults in the making, with the end-product, the sexually safe and reasonable adult citizen, towards which teenagers should be moving, defined as different to teenagers' current state.

However, there is an internal contradiction that stalks sex education. Sex education is designed to prevent teen-aged people from engaging in inappropriate or destructive sexual activities. The rationale for aiming this education at young people is to instruct them in correct behaviour before they become sexually tainted. Early attempts by the Social Hygiene Movement in the United States to eliminate venereal disease and prostitution included pamphlets and talks aimed at adults. However, the movement soon realized that these strategies had little effect, as adults 'had already been corrupted by at least a decade of licentious images and experiences' (Moran 2000: 36). The answer that was touted was to reach the youth – those who had not as yet been corrupted.

This rationale continues to be used in arguing for sex education, albeit in a modified form. The language of rights and empowerment underpins such talk. For example, AVERT, an international AIDS charity, states that

Sex education is . . . about developing young people's skills so that they make informed choices about their behaviour, and feel confident and competent about acting on these choices. It is widely accepted that young people have a right to sex education, partly because it is a means by which they are helped to protect themselves against abuse, exploitation, unintended pregnancies, sexually transmitted diseases and HIV/AIDS.

(AVERT n.d.)

Sexology SA, quoted above, refers to educators who provide sex education to teenagers (after undergoing their training) as 'being empowered to inform, educate and develop the learner's sexual knowledge, positive attitudes, healthy sexual lifestyles and responsible sexual behavior' (Sexology SA n.d.). A South African book entitled *Sexuality Education: From babyhood to adolescence* is lauded as a well-timed publication that 'deals with the delicate content of human sexuality and the sexual becoming of the child in a sensitive yet sober way' (Van Rooyen and Ngwenya 2003: back cover).

These quotes point to the contradictory understanding of the 'adolescent' that underpins sex education. On the one hand, for sex education to work, a certain level of maturity is required: sufficient rationality to be able to 'make informed choices', enough emotional maturity to 'feel confident and competent', and an ability to develop knowledge and 'positive attitudes'. On the other hand, a certain level of innocence, of child-likeness is required. Teenagers must be 'helped to protect themselves'; they need 'empowerment' and to be dealt with in a 'sensitive yet sober way'. Thus, the educator requires the raw, innocent but potentially rational and mature material of youth in order to assist in the development of correct knowledge, attitudes and responsibility.

But sex education itself introduces the exact opposite of what is seen as desirable in the young person to whom it is directed. In other words, images, graphics, facts, stories and examples of sex need to be presented in some form or another. The innocent (albeit potentially rational and mature) child is exposed to the sexual facts, activities and, possibly, desires of adulthood. In order to prevent 'adolescents' turning into adults who will engage in wrongful, inappropriate, risky or promiscuous sexual behaviour, information about these adult activities has to be presented to the innocent, to those who are child-like. Moran (2000) summarizes this dilemma concerning early sex education programmes in the United States as follows:

Sex education's defining dilemma therefore consisted of the tension between teaching young people proper information about sex before their minds were thoroughly debauched and avoiding the possibility that this education would itself arouse precocious interest in sexual matters. Between the need for timelessness [i.e. a prolonged period of chastity] and the dangers of suggestiveness lay an exceedingly narrow path.

(Moran 2000: 39)

This conundrum, paradox or dilemma continues to beset sex education programmes today, as evidenced in the following quote from the website Health24: 'Parents are also concerned that sexual information might heighten children's interest in experimentation but many studies have shown that information and education do not encourage sexual activity' (Health24 n.d.).

In the following sections, South African case studies outlining two quite disparate approaches to sex education are discussed. The aim of this is, first, to ground the discussion in actual examples of sex education manuals, and second, to indicate how, despite the fact that these programmes treat their subject matter in different ways and provide different injunctions around sex and sexuality, the internal conundrum concerning the transitional nature of 'adolescence' haunts both approaches.

Case studies on sex education in South Africa

Formal sex education in the schools (in the sense of it being policy and there being a set curriculum) is a relatively new phenomenon in South Africa. Of course, sex socialization has always taken place, with a range of rituals being effected to socialize young men and women into socially acceptable norms of behaviour around sex (see Delius and Glaser's (2002) exploration of some of the processes of sexual socialization in pre-colonial South Africa and the ways in which these were transformed under the influence of Christianity, colonial conquest, migrant labour and urbanization). However, no formal sex education was offered in schools, either white or black, under the Apartheid regime. What was introduced into schools (in 1967 for White schools and in 1981 for Black schools) was a non-examinable subject called Guidance, in which pupils were 'guided' into their roles as future citizens. Dovey and Mason (1984) show how in white schools the emphasis was on cultural interests while in black schools, the economic interests of Apartheid South Africa were emphasized.

Despite representations to the Minister of Education during the Apartheid era to introduce sex education, the Calvinist outlook of the then policy of education, Christian National Education, meant that any open discussion of sex in the schools was frowned upon (Nicholas et al. 1997). After the democratic elections of 1994, numerous educational reforms were instituted, among which was the formalization of a compulsory learning programme called Life Orientation. Life Orientation is defined by the Department of Education as 'the study of the self in relation to others and to society' (Department of Education 2007a: 7). It is an examinable subject. One of the components of this learning area is sexuality education.

Given this, a number of sexuality manuals have begun appearing on the shelves. For the most part, these take a child-centred, humanist approach. However, there are some that are more conservative. I have broadly called the first case study discussed below a liberal humanist approach and the second one, a conservative approach. Both are based on texts written by South African experts.

The liberal humanist approach is epitomized by a volume entitled *Responsible teenage sexuality: A manual for teachers, youth leaders and health professionals* (Greathead et al. 1998). The book is published by the Planned Parenthood Association of South Africa. This association is a national body that provides sexual and reproductive health education, training and services, mostly to underserved communities. The manual is in its second edition and has been used extensively in sexuality education programmes.

In a humanist understanding of sexuality, the individual is engaged in a process of self-development and self-actualization with respect to her (hetero)sexuality. Thorogood (2000) describes sex education programmes (in England and Wales) that take a liberal humanist approach as 'regard[ing] education about sex as a right and as a means of achieving a more personally fulfilling experience of life, albeit implicitly within a stable heterosexual relationship' (Thorogood 2000: 430). In the manual under discussion the following is set as an aim:

> The educator can . . . use this basic material, flavour it with the particular community's moral and cultural viewpoints, and so provide adolescents with a secure basis from which to develop their own responsible, fulfilling and personalised lifestyle.
>
> (Greathead et al. 1998: xv)

Sexuality, thus, is something to be explored, to be worked on, with the ultimate aim of being not only 'fulfilled', but also 'responsible'.

In this process, the person has choices. The individual is viewed essentially as free to consider alternatives and to choose among them. For example, in the above-mentioned manual, educators are enjoined to be aware of their own values and beliefs about teenage sexual relationships. The reason for this is that:

> He or she must try not to project those beliefs and values onto others. This is extremely difficult, but in doing so a young person must be given the opportunity to make an informed and responsible decision. More trusting relationships will develop and these will improve decision-making skills and allow a more informed choice regarding sexual activity; they will need you, the educator, to be open to discussion, without imposing your values and beliefs on them.
>
> (Greathead et al. 1998: 96)

In this rendition, thus, the individual should be provided with an environment in which he or she is free. The individual is accorded decision-making abilities and rationality in terms of sexual activity.

Apart from putting aside their own values and beliefs, educators are enjoined to present alternatives: 'Presenting sexual information in a more balanced manner highlighting the positive and negative effects is not only more honest, but has a greater chance of having an effect' (Greathead et al. 1998: 95).

The conundrum here is that the liberal humanist understanding of the individual (as an essentially free person, able to make choices and to self-actualize given the correct environment) clashes with the understanding of the 'adolescent' as not adult. In the manual referred to here the deficiencies of 'adolescents' are outlined in a number of places:

> This process [of sexual decision-making] is more difficult during adolescence, however, owing to factors like the imbalance of hormones, lack of decision-making skills, traditional risk-taking behaviour, bombardment by sexual images by the media and a belief that adulthood only starts once sexual activity is experienced.
> . . .
> The choice of what to do when the pregnancy is confirmed is too serious a matter for the level of maturity of most teenagers.
> (Greathead et al. 1998: 95 and 154)

Thus the 'adolescent' is simultaneously a decision-making individual, free to choose from alternatives, and deficient in exactly these qualities. The 'adolescent' is both the liberal, self-actualizing individual, and a person lacking in maturity and decision-making capacity, and prone to risky behaviour. He or she is adult and not adult, a conundrum.

This paradox allows for objectivity (the supposed putting aside of values and beliefs) and the neutral presentation of alternatives to be accompanied with an implicit assumption of what the correct choices are. As seen in the quotes above, 'responsible' decisions and 'more informed' choices are expected, with a 'balanced' treatment of the issue having a greater 'effect'. The explicit message of the manual is that teenagers have a choice, but the only correct choices are, in the first instance, abstinence ('Adults generally agree that teen sex is not advisable because of the devastating consequences it can have'; 'There can be no advantages to teenage pregnancy': Greathead et al. 1998: 95 and 154) and masturbation ('It is felt that masturbation is the only means to help young people to cope with their sexual feelings, while at the same time not being burdened with a decision involving sexual intercourse and its consequences': Greathead et al. 1998: 128). In the second instance, where sex does occur, the only option is 'safe sex' ('Reducing the risks and consequences can be seen in the same light as teaching safer

driving techniques to prevent and reduce the incidence of car accidents':
Greathead et al. 1998: 208).

Where the correct 'informed choice' fails, for example in the case of
pregnancy, the options become more blurred. 'Teenage pregnancy' itself is
depicted in this manual as a disaster, with medical, emotional and educational risks being associated with it. Options presented to the teenager
in this instance (termination of pregnancy, adoption, single parenthood,
marriage and fostering) are all depicted as having negative consequences,
with the effect of feeding into promoting the first, preferred options
(abstinence and masturbation).

The distinction between the neutral adult, who is able to put his/her
values and beliefs aside, present alternatives to teenagers and guide them in
the correct direction, and the immature, unstable 'adolescent' is further
entrenched by the depiction of the peer group as providing unreliable
information and being a negative influence in the sexual decision-making
process:

> The result of this [not providing sex education] is that they [teen-
> agers] seek answers from friends ill-equipped to provide correct,
> factual answers. . .
>
> The group may put pressure on the non-conforming individual.
> Adolescents fear the consequences of non-conformity, e.g. ridicule,
> rejection.
>
> (Greathead et al. 1998: xv and 58)

Peers are presented here as providing inaccurate information and as pres-
surizing each other into inappropriate behaviour. This implicitly creates a
divide between the untrustworthy peer/'adolescent' and the trustworthy
adult sex educator.

I turn now to the second case study that epitomizes a conservative
approach to sex education. In this I discuss a book entitled *Sexuality
education: From babyhood to adolescence*. Written by a university lecturer
and a teacher, the book is marketed as being 'suitable for teachers, parents,
social workers, religious leaders – in short, for everybody involved in any
way with children and their sexual maturation' (Van Rooyen and Ngwenya
2003: back cover).

In the conservative approach, moral and religious values and principles
rather than choice are central. Rightful living in accordance with particular,
predefined norms and standards is required, and sex education is about
inculcating these norms and standards. Thorogood (2000), writing about
England and Wales, describes such as approach in the following way:

> There are others who see sex education as essential for promoting
> the 'right' values and behavior. This takes a pragmatic line which

41

recognizes that 'if they are going to do it anyway' an education strategy could influence this behavior to remain within socially acceptable bounds.

(Thorogood 2000: 430)

In the above-mentioned book educators are reminded that 'mere information will not teach children the requirements for decency, nor enable them to meet moral and religious demands. Information should always be in line with the norm' (Van Rooyen and Ngwenya 2003: 60).

The role of the educator or parent in this approach is not to present alternatives or assist the teenager with informed choice, but rather to guide them on the path to rightful living. This rightful living is presented, quite unashamedly as:

The following applicable universal values [which include]:
- abstinence
- total commitment to marriage
- respect for one's own and others' bodies
- obedience to the created order: fundamental masculinity and femininity
- physical purity and chastity
- sanctity of life.

(Van Rooyen and Ngwenya 2003: 58)

Despite the somewhat authoritarian approach that this implies, educators are reminded that they must guide the teenager in a caring and sensitive manner:

it is often her [the educators'] understanding and support that give many girls the security they need so badly during these sensitive years. . . . Educators should assure children that they are not alone, that there is someone who cares.

(Van Rooyen and Ngwenya 2003: 60)

The consequences of educators not guiding teenagers in the path of rightful living are presented as disastrous:

Educators should keep in mind that if they fail to do their duty, outsiders will do it on their behalf – possibly with far-reaching consequences.

To complicate the situation, the child is bombarded from many directions with sex information – information which comes to him or her without the proper norms and accompanying values.

(Van Rooyen and Ngwenya 2003: 60 and 59)

In other words, there is the threat of moral decay should educators not take up what is termed their duty. External forces and bad information sources (pornography and blue movies are specifically mentioned) may corrupt the innately curious teenager, with disastrous consequences.

This approach clearly separates the adult educator, who has internalized the correct norms, developed the correct sexual attitudes, and presumably practises the values stated above, from the teenager who is still in the process of developing these norms and values. And yet the conundrum of the 'adolescent' as 'adult/not adult' lurks just beneath the surface. In the chapter on puberty and 'adolescence', the following is stated about teenagers who are sexually active:

> Guiding the sexually active teenager is in essence *education, sexuality education*, which is the prime right and privilege and responsibility of the parent. The sexually active child is a *child in need*.
> (Van Rooyen and Ngwenya 2003: 62, emphases in the original)

A contradiction is created between the association of the teenager with a child and the fact that this child is engaging in activities clearly demarcated in this book as an adult activity (being sexually active). This is dealt with by depicting the teenager as a person desperately in need of assistance. Thus the resolution of the paradox is not to view the teenager as an adult or to accept the adult activity in which she is involved, but rather to re-emphasize her child-likeness, her need for guidance. The guidance recommended in this case is, 'Inform the child of the correct norm [listed above as abstinence and 'total commitment to marriage'] and point out the dangers involved' (Van Rooyen and Ngwenya 2003: 61).

Thorogood (2000) argues that the various models of sex education, despite being different in approach, achieve essentially the same aim: the production of 'normal' (hetero)masculinity and (hetero)femininity, core categories in the regulation of the social world. In this brief section I have argued that despite having very different approaches to sex education, the two manuals featured cannot escape the internal conundrum of the discourse of 'adolescence as transition'. The teenager is inevitably a child, but not a child, needing to be inducted into adult activities, but simultaneously not ready. In the next section the manner in which this internal contradiction plays itself out in the very notion of 'teenage pregnancy' is discussed.

'Teenage pregnancy'

We saw above how one of the sex education manuals discussed referred to 'teenage pregnancy' as having no advantages. The authors of this text state quite categorically that 'Teenage pregnancy is considered a disaster by most people' (Greathead et al. 1998: 154). They are not alone in expressing this kind of sentiment. 'Teenage pregnancy' is generally seen as a social problem, both within the research literature and within the media. There are exceptions to this, however, with some researchers arguing that 'teenage pregnancy' represents a rational choice for a certain sector of the population. This is called a revisionist perspective and will be discussed in more detail in Chapter 4.

Because of the dominant understanding of 'teenage pregnancy' as a social problem, much of the motivation for sex education aimed at young people is to prevent early pregnancy. As seen above, sex education itself contains within it an internal inconsistency: the aim of maintaining innocence and preventing early pregnancy by introducing information and images of the very thing that you wish to prevent. In this section I discuss how pregnancy in a young woman is the physical manifestation of the paradox of 'adolescence as transition'. When a teenager becomes pregnant, she breaches the socially constructed chronology of age, the transitional nature of 'adolescence'. She is a conundrum, a contradiction, someone who, in the words of Lawson (1993: 102, emphases in the original) 'pollutes the category of *child* and becomes a deviant *adult*'. The following excerpts from a variety of sources illustrate this point:

'Teenagers should play with dolls and leave grown-up things until they are older', says the pregnant blonde 14-year-old girl, struggling to stem the flow of tears from her eyes as she clutches her rounded belly.

(Cassim 1998: 3)

The number of children having children has increased dramatically in the last decade.

(Letsholo 2006: 15)

Ms Naicker brought the attention back to the issue of children having children in rural areas, and how this was to be dealt with. (Welfare and Population Development Portfolio Committee 2000)

But more often a child with her own child is exactly what she seems; a child cradling a living, breathing obstacle to school, qualifications and a stable future.

(Timesonline 2009)

More than 200,000 females in the United States have children before their eighteenth birthday. As one 17-year-old Los Angeles mother of a 1-year-old son said, 'We are children having children'
(Santrock 2002: 358)

The first three extracts are from South African sources. The first is from a South African newspaper article that cleverly uses the rhetorical device of 'from the horse's mouth', together with language that invokes sympathy in the reader thereby making the statement less likely to be judged. The second is from a master's thesis. The third is from the minutes of meeting held by the South African Welfare and Population Development Portfolio Committee meeting in 2000. Thus, we find the metaphor of 'children having children' recurring in a range of forums: newspaper articles, academic treatises and government meetings. The final two statements indicate the global reach of this metaphor. The first of them is from Timesonline, the internet version of a widely read international magazine, and the second from an international developmental psychology textbook.

The wide range of contexts within which the idea of 'children bearing children' appears speaks to the status of teen-aged pregnancy and parenting as an irresolvable paradox. Logically, within the adult/child binary set up by an 'adolescence as transition' discourse, a child cannot bear a child because conceiving, deciding whether to carry to term, and bearing and raising a child are adult practices. With teen-aged pregnancy, adult practices and functions (sexual interaction, reproduction, mothering) are displayed by a person who, owing to her age and developmental status, is not-yet-adult. If this person is not-yet-adult, she must be a child. But this she can also not be owing to her reproductive status. The pregnant teenager is thus adult, but not adult, child, but not child. She is a child having a child, something that cannot be but is.

The tagging together of the words 'teenage' and 'pregnancy' has important effects, implying that these young women are engaging in age-inappropriate behaviour (e.g. having sex, mothering), while reducing their chances of age-appropriate activities (e.g. continuing with education). In the following paragraphs I follow how one of these supposed age-inappropriate activities, mothering, is dealt with.

Mothering, what it is and how it should be performed, is a contested cultural arena. This contestation occurs in numerous spaces, one of which is textual: academic treatises, parenting and childcare manuals, women's magazines. The depiction of mothering in these textual spaces is highly variable. For example, Johnston and Swanson (2003), in their content analysis of the representation of mothers in a number of women's magazines, found a number of double-bind messages. One of these is the natural/unnatural maternal double bind, which the authors describe as 'messages [that] maintain that women are natural mothers and men are incapable of mothering, yet simultaneously tell mothers they need a cadre of (typically male) experts . . . to mother successfully' (Johnston and Swanson 2003: 245).

In my analysis of the South African social science literature on 'teenage pregnancy', I found that rather than the naturalness of motherhood being emphasized, the 'skill' involved in the practice was placed in the foreground

(Macleod 2001). Johnston and Swanson (2003) suggest that in the magazines they analysed this skill is depicted as being developed through the intervention of the expert. In the 'teenage pregnancy' literature that I analysed, however, it is represented as a skill that comes only with maturity.

There is, of course, good reason for mothering to be portrayed as a skill rather than as natural when talking about teen-aged mothers. If mothering were seen as natural in this context, then, given the biological capacity to conceive and bear a child, mothering would follow automatically for teenaged mothers. Thus, the 'adolescence as transition' discourse would be threatened. 'Teenage pregnancy' would become unproblematic, at least in this sense. On the other hand, 'skill' implies that a deficient state may exist, as evidenced in the following extracts:

> The girl is usually unable to comprehend that motherhood is a 24 hour per day, 7 day per week, role and that her responsibility for the child will last for a minimum of 18 years – longer than she has lived. This, plus the teenager's total inability to cope, results in a high incidence of child abuse, neglect and possible abandonment by teenage mothers.
>
> (Greathead 1988: 23)

> The majority who perceived mothering to be very difficult, had a problem in performing every mothering related task. They felt this task is not really for teenagers.
>
> (Mkhize 1995: 86)

> Many authors have indicated that teenage mothers do not have the necessary parenting skills and are therefore not capable of giving their off-spring the care that they need. . . . Although the participants all indicated that they loved their children, they were unaware of any other needs other than the physical needs of their off-spring.
>
> (Dlamini 2002: 115)

> Young parents lack parenting skills. They are impatient, insensitive, irritable and inclined to administer corporal punishment.
>
> (Moses-Europa 2005: 13)

These extracts, spanning nearly twenty years, are written by South African health and social scientists. They all implicitly depict mothering as a skilful activity, something lacking in the case of teen-aged mothers. Thus teenage mothers are portrayed as lacking comprehension of the task, as finding mothering tasks difficult, as being unaware of anything other than the physical needs of the infant, and as being impatient, insensitive and irritable. This creates a space for a linkage between mothering by young women and future negative outcomes for the child. In the first extract, for example, the young mother's 'inability to cope' is linked to abuse, neglect and abandonment.

The representation of motherhood as a skill in the context of 'teenage pregnancy' means that there are two potential ways in which the young woman's motherhood (or potential motherhood if pregnant) status may be understood. In the first, her motherhood is viewed as assisting in the maturing process. For example, SmithBattle (2005), in reporting on her longitudinal study of young mothers in the United States, states that 'Mothering often provides a pathway to adulthood for teenage girls and can promote a new sense of purpose, meaning and responsibility' (SmithBattle 2005: 847). Black and Ford-Gilboe (2004) found that the capacities of 'adolescent' parents, particularly in the area of health and well-being promotion, increased. Thus, by participating in an adult function like mothering, the 'adolescent' may become responsible, and achieve the status of adulthood.

In representing motherhood as a pathway to adulthood, however, researchers continue to draw on an 'adolescence as transition' discourse. Only in this case, the transition has been somewhat concertinaed as there is no intimation that women in their twenties only become adults after bearing children. Note, for example, how SmithBattle (2005) is able to utilize the words 'adulthood' and 'girls' quite comfortably in the same sentence in the above quote.

In the second way in which the young woman's motherhood is understood, the contradiction created by the intersection of 'motherhood = adulthood' and 'adolescent ≠ adulthood' is highlighted, thereby depicting the young mother as inadequate. In their review of parenting programmes aimed at teenagers, Coren et al. (2003) summarize the key features of this understanding:

> Younger parents may lack both knowledge of child development, and effective parenting skills . . . due partly to their inexperience of life more generally. . . . There is evidence to suggest that maternal age can also have an impact on aspects of parenting such as . . . mother–infant interaction . . . attitudes to child discipline . . . and on the development of realistic expectations of infant behaviour and development. . . . There is also a higher risk of child maltreatment among younger parents.
>
> (Coren et al. 2003: 80)

Thus, teen-aged mothers' ability to mother is called into question because of their lack of skill or maturity.

There are two issues that arise in relation to this. The first is the research practices engaged in when reaching the conclusion that young mothers display inadequate mothering skills. Research practices are social practices that have major implications for how people are represented and what sorts of narratives are allowed or disallowed as a result.

In terms of the current question of the mothering skills of young women, it should be noted that 'skill' is a relative term. The question, 'Compared to whom do these young women lack mothering skills?' may be asked. The usual answer, of course, is compared to older (adult) mothers. But, this answer, in and of itself, is insufficient. Mothering occurs within a context and comparing younger with older mothers means that you need to ensure that the two groups are indeed comparable. For example, studies that make comparisons between teen-aged and older mothers without identifying the sample's socio-economic status, or considering factors such as social support, stability of partner relationship, number of children being cared for and educational status, are setting up false comparisons. Because a range of contextual factors, such as financial resources, social networks, government policies and emotional support, influence the mothering relationship, when younger and older women are compared, the two groups need to be equivalent in terms of these various factors (Buccholz and Korn-Bursztyn 1993). Thus, when researchers fail to provide matched comparative samples, they are engaging in social (research) practices that construct the 'imaginary wall' that we spoke of earlier, in which the trends and patterns found among teen-aged people are seen as somehow distinct from the trends and patterns found among people of *similar* background.

Research where contextual factors are taken into account in the comparison of younger and older women has reached some interesting conclusions. For example, Ross (2000) studied the mother–child interactions of teen-aged versus adult mothers in the United States. She found that the young mothers were less responsive to their children than the adult ones. However, once she had taken the various factors mentioned above into account, she found that, in fact, mother–child interaction was not associated with maternal age per se. The difference could rather be put down to differences in such factors as child temperament, total number of children at home, total family income, and family structure, with total family income being the most significant. Similarly, in Kenya, Taffa (2003) found no difference between 'adolescent' and adult mothers of similar socio-economic circumstances in terms of care related to child health.

The second issue relating to research concerning the mothering abilities of teen-aged women concerns the manner in which 'good' mothering is defined. Mothering is an interactional event, one that is steeped in understandings of what parenting should achieve, and the kinds of person parents should mould. In other words, it is a deeply cultural and historical event, feeding off highly variable understandings of the nature of being human. This is frequently not acknowledged by researchers, who accept particular measures of adequate mothering as standards that can be applied to a range of people. Feminist research, however, shows that there is great variability across and within historical periods and societies in terms of child-rearing practices and the relationship between mother and child as well as between both of them and significant others (Glenn et al. 1994).

Decision-making in the context of abortion

In this section, I turn to the third instance in which the paradox inherent in the 'adolescence as transition' discourse becomes apparent: decision-making in the context of abortion. Let us return to the *Special Assignment* programme discussed in Chapter 1. In the programme, the nurse, using the manipulative strategy of fear, advised the young woman she was counselling to consult her parents:

> Nurse: There could be perforations of the uterus whilst we do the procedure, *ne*. Maybe, we could pierce through your uterus and then that would warrant you to be hospitalized, *ne*. And I'm afraid that if you are a minor and you did not involve your parents, what are they going to say? Do you think now it is the time when you have to involve them?
>
> (*Special Assignment* and SABC)

Clearly, in this nurse's mind, young women should not be allowed to continue with an abortion without consulting their parents. However, this is not what the Choice on Termination of Pregnancy (CTOP) Act requires. In the Act, it is stated quite clearly that the only person required to give permission for an abortion is the woman herself. The Act allows women under the age of 18 (legally minors) to undergo a termination of pregnancy without the consent of, or even consulting, her parents. Health service providers may counsel young women to consult their parents, but cannot deny the abortion should they refuse.

This subsection of the Act, however, has caused a fair amount of controversy. This controversy is inextricably linked to the understanding of the 'adolescent', as seen in the quotes from newspapers below:

> If she is old enough to fall pregnant then she is old enough to decide whether to terminate or not, hopefully with the support of caring counselors and doctors if she does not want to involve her parents.
>
> (Steiner 1997)

> How can the law protect a girl barely in her teens when she finds herself expecting a baby? It's far, far too early for a mere child to have to take such decisions.
>
> (No minor matter 1998)

In the first quote, from a letter published in the South African newspaper *The Star*, the author states that as reproduction is a sign of adulthood or maturity, it follows that there should be sufficient cognitive maturity for the person to decide on the abortion. In other words, this person places the pregnant 'adolescent' on the adult side of the child/adult binary that haunts 'adolescence'. The caveat of the requirement of support somewhat undoes this statement, but perhaps this author would state the same for all women considering abortion. In the second quote, from a letter published in the South African newspaper the *Eastern Cape Herald*, the conundrum of 'adolescence' is drawn on in its full force. The person under consideration is a 'mere child', 'barely in her teens', basically a child having a child. Thus, although she is reproductively mature, she is in need of adult protection and support.

The subclause of the South African CTOP Act in which parental consent or involvement is not required for a young woman to undergo a termination of pregnancy caused sufficient controversy for the Christian Lawyers Association (CLA) to challenge it in the High Court. The CLA argued that women below the age of 18 are incapable of making a decision concerning a termination of pregnancy in their own best interests without parental consent or control. They used the following as evidence to back their claim: a termination of pregnancy has a negative effect on a young woman; young women are vulnerable when making such decisions; a young woman is incapable, owing to her developmental status, of providing informed consent; young women are unable to fully appreciate the need for parental guidance (Christian Lawyers Association v Minister of Health and Others 2005). In all of these lack is emphasized. The young person is the opposite of the mature, competent, balanced, informed, decision-making adult.

The CLA failed in its application. The rationale provided by the judge in his ruling is interesting. He held that:

> [T]he plaintiff's approach was a rigid approach to immaturity which was blind to the fact that there were women below that age who were actually mature, much as there were those above that age who were immature. This approach failed to recognise and accommodate individual differences. . . . Any distinction between women on the ground of age would accordingly invade [the young woman's constitutional] rights. . . . [T]he Act served the best interest of the pregnant girl because it was flexible in recognising and accommodating her individual position based on her intellectual, psychological and emotional make-up. . . . [T]he Choice Act makes informed consent, and not age, the cornerstone of its regulation of access to termination of pregnancy. . . . The Act allows all women who have the intellectual and emotional capacity for informed consent, to choose whether to terminate their pregnancies or not. . . .

As to whether a particular individual, irrespective of age, is capable of giving such consent, the Legislature has left the determination of the 'factual' position to the medical professional or registered midwife who performs the act.

(Christian Lawyers Association v Minister of Health and Others 2005: 509)

This approach potentially undoes the 'adolescence as transition' discourse. Young women are put on a par with older women, with the possibility of maturity or immaturity occurring in both categories. The criterion of competence or capacity thus shifts away from age to other criteria (intellectual and emotional capacity).

The difficulty with this interpretation is that it is based on an individualized model of understanding. Although this approach is clearly sufficient to keep the current legislation in place, it fails to fully undermine the possibility of young people as a group being seen as fundamentally lacking. Just because particular individuals under the age of 18 may be seen as mature does not mean the majority are. And indeed, in the implementation of the CTOP Act, health service providers frequently make a distinction between young women and older ones in terms of how they treat them. In a number of research interviews that my students and I have conducted with service providers, we found age rather than individual capacity to be a major factor in their assessment of the situation. For example, one service provider stated:

You *cannot* under any *normal* circumstances allow a thirteen year old to have child. I mean they haven't even started [inaudible] / hmm/. So I find that one tends to be a lot more lenient with teenage pregnancies and we do do them right up to twenty weeks.

The CLA, the judge and people writing in newspapers (as quoted above) are not alone in debating the ability of young women in making these sorts of decisions. This issue has been the subject of international scientific debate in situations where termination of pregnancy is available legally. There are two main facets to the debate. The first revolves around the risk that abortion carries for young women in particular, and the second around the ability of young women to make these kinds of decisions.

Proponents of parental consent when young women make decisions about abortion state that abortion carries substantially more risks for young women than it does for adults. Therefore, the advice and counselling of an older and wiser person is required. Opponents point out that, in fact, owing to research practices with regard to this question, in particular the fact that there is a lack of methodologically sound research that compares young and older women's psychological adjustment to abortion, the answer of whether there are greater risks involved in teenage or adult termination of pregnancy is far from clear-cut.

Opponents of parental consent argue, furthermore, that requiring young people to gain parental permission for an abortion may itself have extremely adverse effects (Rodman 1991). The first potential adverse effect is the possibility of sparking family conflict, and rejection and punishment of the young woman. Making parental involvement voluntary, it is suggested, allows young women to decide whether to inform their parents based on years of knowledge and experience with them. Indeed, data from the United States suggests that most young pregnant women consult an older person before deciding on an abortion and most of these consult their parents (Shields 2006). The second potential adverse effect is that in extending the bureaucratic procedures required in the granting of abortions, whether by parental consent or by judicial bypass (a procedure which operates in some US states in which minors may obtain an abortion with court, as opposed to parental, consent) means delays in the abortion procedure and hence greater health risks for the young woman. Finally, of course, requiring parental consent will lead to a substantial number of young women preferring to seek illegal or 'backstreet' abortions in order to avoid having to involve their parents (Rodman 1991).

The second facet of the debate relates to the ability of teen-aged people to make decisions of this nature. Proponents of parental consent argue that young women are not sufficiently competent to make a decision with respect to abortion. In this view, it is argued that the cognitive abilities of teen-aged people are not fully developed. This, together with the understanding of 'adolescence' as a time of maturational change, rebellion and experimentation, means that young people are 'at risk of acting impulsively' (Trad 1993: 398). In this context the decision-making competencies of teenagers are compromised because of their inability to predict long-term consequences or to consider the perspective of significant others in their decision (Trad 1993).

Opponents counter this argument from a number of perspectives. First, they point to difficulties with the research practices that find differences in young people's and adults' decision-making capacity. The social contexts within which the decisions are being made need to be considered (Adler et al. 2003). For example, in the case of young women, the fear of familial consequences and of stigma, lack of access to a range of resources including professional services, and concerns over confidentiality are contextual factors forming the background for a young person's experience of the decision-making process (at least to a far greater extent than for older women).

Second, they argue that the picture concerning the competence of young people to give informed consent to abortion is a lot more complex than initially supposed. Very often it is assumed that because teen-aged people have been found to be less competent than adults in a range of cognitive abilities, this will extend to decision-making with regard to abortion. Opponents of compulsory parental consent or involvement point out, however, that competence is specific to the area under consideration. Generalizing results from studies conducted with teenagers concerning their cognitive abilities in other areas to their decision-making competencies with respect to abortion is false (Adler et al. 2003). Ambuel and Rappaport (1992), in an American study, researched the question of young women's decision-making as related *specifically* to abortion. They compared three groups of women (legal adults – 18 to 21 year olds; older minors – 16 to 17 year olds; and younger minors – 14 to 15 year olds) who were presenting for a pregnancy test. Some of these women were considering abortion, others not. They found that, with respect to those considering abortion, neither of the younger groups of women differed from the older one in terms of any of the measures of competency that they used in their research.

Third, opponents of compulsory parental consent point out that the concern over decision-making should pertain equally to the decision to continue a pregnancy. Preventing a young person from having a termination of pregnancy simply means that this person, assumed to be too immature to make a decision around abortion, now becomes the mother of a newborn infant with the concomitant responsibility for a number of decisions, including the health-care of this baby. It is argued on the basis of this observation that the underlying reason for advocating parental consent in teen-aged abortion is not really to protect the young woman, but rather to make a termination of pregnancy more difficult to obtain (Stotland 2001).

These controversies, which probably will not be resolved at any time in the near future, point to the conundrum that stalks our understanding of 'adolescents'. Here are young people, pregnant and therefore carrying the weight of responsibility in terms of reproduction. This responsibility, presumed to be competently carried out by adults (or at least those adults who conform to particular norms), now lands in the hands of the 'not adult' adolescent. Should this adult/not adult be allowed to make independent decisions concerning whether to carry the pregnancy to term or to terminate it? And what does this mean for how we understand 'adolescence'? In the light of the abortion politics, then, the status of this adult/not adult becomes the central problem. For pro-choice activists (and researchers) to be consistent in their advocacy of access and choice, they need to engage with the central paradox of the construction of 'adolescence' as a period of transition. They need, essentially, to undermine the assumption that young women are less competent than older ones in order to advocate for the same rights for all women. As we see above, however, a fair amount of labour is required in order to undermine such a central premise of 'adolescence'. The basic assumption that young women are unable to make such decisions in a rational, independent and carefully considered manner is part of the basic fabric of the 'adolescence as transition' discourse. Although opposing it is not impossible, as seen in the decision of the court in the application brought by the CLA, it will not be dislodged easily.

Conclusion

In the 'transitional' understanding of 'adolescence', the 'adolescent' is presented as progressing naturally through a phase of development that separates childhood from adulthood. In this the 'adolescent' is neither child nor adult, but at the same time both. It (the 'transitional' discourse) has been utilized by researchers in the field of 'teenage pregnancy' in a variety of ways. The young woman's transitional developmental status has been employed in explaining her propensity to become pregnant, and her inadequacy in terms of mothering. She has the marks of adulthood (being pregnant, becoming a mother) but she is actually a child in that she became pregnant through lack of knowledge, assertiveness and so forth (Macleod 1999c), and she cannot really mother as she lacks maturity and ability.

The simultaneous exclusion of the 'adolescent' from childhood and adulthood is necessary for, first, the recognition of, and second, the problematization of 'adolescent' (hetero)sexuality. 'Adolescent' (hetero)sexuality can be recognized as teenagers are, at least partially, excluded from the definition of childhood innocence. At the same time, it can be problematized as (hetero)sexuality belongs to the adult domain and teenagers are, at least partially, actually children. Young people are hence depicted as simultaneously saturated with and devoid of sexuality. Sex education, with its instrumentalist goal of producing a better society through educating young people in being good sexual citizens, highlights this conundrum. Young people must be inducted into the world of sex, because they will become sexual beings. At the same time, they are children and should be protected from explicit sexual meanings and, in particular, sexual desire (cf. Fine 1988).

Young women who become pregnant have not only failed to fulfil the tenets of the good sexual citizen, but also have breached our fundamental understanding of 'adolescence' as a time of transition. Here are women who are meant to be preparing for adulthood actually engaging in adult activities such as reproduction. Because the 'adolescence as transition' discourse contains within it the suggestion that the teenager is at least partially child, these women become labelled as 'children having children' – something that cannot be but is. They are the embodiment of a paradox. To resolve this, the 'adult' side of the 'adult/not adult' conundrum is rendered invisible, with childishness being emphasized instead.

When one of the adult activities that these 'children having children' embark upon, namely mothering, is considered, a conundrum needs to be solved. Mothering is frequently portrayed as a natural activity. However, in the case of teen-aged mothers, this portrayal is problematic. Given that these young women have the biological capacity to bear children, seeing mothering as natural would render early reproduction unproblematic in this aspect at least. For this reason, mothering skill, which allows room for a state of deficiency, is emphasized.

Whether young women, once pregnant, should be allowed to make independent decisions concerning whether to terminate the pregnancy has been the subject of debate in policy-making forums, courts of law, academic circles and the media. Proponents of compulsory parental consent argue that young people are substantially more at risk of negative consequences following abortion and that they are less able than older people to make informed decisions. Opponents point out that there is no evidence that abortion is more risky for young people than for older ones and that, in fact, making parental consent compulsory is what would make the abortion more traumatic. Furthermore, they state, decision-making should be looked at in context. The circumstances under which women make decisions should be considered as well the type of decision that is being made. Comparing older with younger women or the cognitive abilities of young people in general with their decision-making concerning abortion is problematic.

Underlying these debates, of course, is the inevitable conundrum of the 'adolescent' as a transitional being. Is she really still a child, unable to make these decisions without adult guidance? Is she basically an adult who can choose between abortion and childbearing with the same degree of competence as adults in similar circumstances? In the end, the 'adolescence as transition' discourse leaves us with a 'neither/nor', 'either/or' and 'both/and' answer – a paradox that cannot be solved.

4

CONSTRUCTING A THREAT OF DEGENERATION

The invention of and research practices
concerning the 'social problem' of
'teenage pregnancy'

In Chapter 3 we saw how 'teenage pregnancy' threatens the basic understanding of 'adolescence' as a period of transition. A person who is not a
child but also a child, who is not an adult but also an adult, displays the
reproductive characteristics of adulthood, thereby threatening the not adult
or child aspect of 'adolescence'.

While 'adolescence' appeared, at least in Western history, about a
century ago, 'teenage pregnancy', as a concept and as a perceived social
problem, emerged much more recently. Depending on which country one
talks about, the notion 'teenage pregnancy' has been around since between
the late 1960s and the early 1980s. In this chapter I shall trace the origins of
the term 'teenage pregnancy', showing how its invention as a social problem
depended on particular understandings of how women should be treated.

Since its invention, the notion of 'teenage pregnancy' has become an
extremely popular signifier. At the time of writing there were 28,900 articles
or books listed on Google Scholar using the key word 'teenage pregnancy',
and 1,170,000 general and 17,900 South African websites on 'teenage
pregnancy'. This is despite the fact that it is an imprecise term. Are we
referring to young women with planned or unplanned pregnancies, to young
women with wanted or unwanted pregnancies, to young women who conceive once married or marry after conception, to young women who
conceive and never marry, or to young women who decide to terminate their
pregnancy?

The term 'teenage pregnancy' almost always has negative connotations.
A few examples will illustrate the point:

- On a World Health Organization website, a podcast of an interview
  with a young mother is posted. The title for the podcast is 'Teenage
  pregnancies cause many health, social problems' (World Health
  Organization 2009).
- Speaking more specifically about a particular country, Santrock (2002:
  358), in a developmental psychology textbook widely used in

undergraduate psychology courses, states, 'Each year more than 500,000 American teenagers become pregnant and more than 70 percent of them are unmarried. They represent a flaw in America's social fabric. . . . The consequences of America's high adolescent rate are cause for great concern'.

• A news article featured on the (South African) Health Systems Trust website is entitled, 'Teenage pregnancy figures cause alarm' (Irin news 2007).

The 'problematic' nature of 'teenage pregnancy' and the fact that it should be cause for concern is a dominant position, virtually globally.

The consequences of 'teenage pregnancy', as listed in the research literature, are the disruption of schooling, the perpetuation of a cycle of disadvantage or poor socio-economic circumstances, poor child outcomes, health risks associated with early pregnancy, welfare dependency and contribution to unacceptable demographic patterns. A more recent concern is the association of HIV and 'teenage pregnancy'.

These conclusions are reached through particular research practices that allow for the emergence of particular discursive constructions, and disallow others. The most pertinent of these is the practice of foregrounding age as an explanatory variable, thereby isolating women from their socio-economic and socio-cultural environments.

Various researchers have started to interrogate these research practices and the associated conclusions. Questions are raised such as whether the evidenced disruption of schooling is owing to the pregnancy or other factors, whether there really is a one-to-one relationship between early reproduction and future disadvantage, and what comparison group is being used in studying the relative health risks and child outcomes of teen-aged mothers.

I argue two things in this chapter. First, the persistence of a 'teenage pregnancy = social problem' position is the sanitized version of the threat of degeneration referred to in Chapter 2. The less developed, in engaging in inappropriate activities such as sex and reproduction (as defined by the 'adolescence as transition' discourse), threaten developed or civilized society. Second, without an 'adolescence as transition' discourse, or with the removal of the imaginary wall, the fundamental premise on which the research is based (that 'adolescence' represents a separable stage of development distinct in virtually every area from adults) falls away.

Not all researchers agree with the 'teenage pregnancy = social problem' equation. These researchers have been called revisionists. These scholars argue that 'teenage pregnancy' and childbearing is not as problematic as supposed. Indeed, they postulate that early childbearing represents a rational and conscious choice for disadvantaged teen-aged women for whom there is little advantage in delaying pregnancy. In fact, it may be functional in a number of ways. For example, young mothers tend have a better access to the familial caretaking nexus than older women, and people living in poverty have a foreshortened healthy life expectancy, which means that early childbearing is functional in the sense of providing longer healthy parenting time (Geronimus 1991, 2004; Preston-Whyte and Zondi 1991, 1992).

The invention of 'teenage pregnancy'

'Teenage pregnancy' has not always been considered a social problem. Indeed, the very notion of 'teenage pregnancy' is, historically speaking, a rather recent one. The media and social policy debates in the United States only started referring to 'teenage pregnancy' as a social problem in the early 1970s (Vinovskis 1988, 1992), when phrases such as an 'epidemic' of adolescent childbearing, and 'children having children' became common parlance. Various negative consequences were associated with 'teenage pregnancy', and programmes to prevent or ameliorate these were introduced. Since the 1970s, there has been a plethora of words written on the pregnant teenager both in academic circles and in popular literature, although interest in the topic in South Africa really only began in the early 1980s.

If 'teenage pregnancy' was not viewed as a major social problem prior to the 1970s, why the sudden rise in interest and concern? Researchers, commenting on developed countries, have suggested a number of potential answers. One is that as women's nutrition increases, so the age of menarche decreases. Thus young women are able to conceive at a younger age and are therefore more at risk of becoming pregnant while still a teenager (Harari and Vinovskis 1993). The implication of this argument is that because more young people can conceive, and are, the increase in concern is related to an increase in incidence of teen-aged pregnancy (i.e. in the number of young women who conceive each year).

However, there is a major flaw in this argument, certainly both with regard to the United States and South Africa. At the same time as concern was increasing, so the rates of teen-aged pregnancy in the United States were actually decreasing from a peak in 1957 (Vinovskis 1988). In South Africa, interest in the social problem of 'teenage pregnancy' took off in the 1980s, with research and discussion continuing unabated in the 1990s. However, fertility rates among teen-aged women declined rapidly in the 1980s through into the 1990s (Makiwane and Udjo 2006). For example, in 1988, the annual birth-rate to women in the age category 15 to 19 years old was 116 per 1000 women. By 1996 this had decreased to 78 per 1000 women. This latter rate is similar to the US rate – although the United States has a relatively high rate in comparison to other developed countries (Bradshaw et al. n.d.).

A second possibility for the increase in interest in 'teenage pregnancy' is that previously births to teen-aged women in the United States occurred chiefly within the context of marriage. If the couple were not married at the time of conception, a quick wedding was organized (Davis 1989; Miller 1993). Thus negativity towards young women conceiving resulted not because the numbers of births were increasing, but because they were occurring, relatively more than before, among those who were younger, white and unmarried. Consider once again the textbook, *Life-span development*, in which Santrock (2002) admits, 'Despite the rise in the teenage birth rate in the 1980s, the rate is lower now than it was in the 1950s and 1960s. What is different now, though, is the steady rise in births to unmarried teenagers' (Santrock 2002: 359).

Arney and Bergen (1984) take a completely different tack. In their article entitled 'Power and visibility: The *invention* of teenage pregnancy' (my emphasis), they argue that 'teenage pregnancy' became a problem because of a shift in power relations and, consequently, in how women were treated. They show how, in the United States, prior to the late 1960s the morally loaded concepts of 'unwed mother' and 'illegitimate child' were used to describe young women who conceived. Young pregnant women were excluded from society, with the accompanying shame around the lack of proper conjugal arrangements. Thus, what was of issue was not the *age* of the person, but rather the conjugal status of the woman, and the 'legitimacy' of the child.

Sometime around the early 1970s the words 'unwed mother' and 'illegitimate child' disappeared from formal use and were replaced with the term 'teenage pregnancy'. Thus terms that implied moral judgement were removed and a more neutralized one used. The supposed neutrality of the term lent it scientific and professional credibility.

Arney and Bergen (1984) are, however, very sceptical of this shift (from using 'unwed mother' and 'illegitimate child' to using 'teenage pregnancy'). They do not believe that the shift took place because our understanding of the phenomenon was becoming more accurate or because the problem demanded more humane treatment. Rather, they state, it was because it allowed for these young women to become the objects of scientific scrutiny. Whereas previously young women who became pregnant were excluded from 'good' society and were implicitly chastised for their poor moral standing, they now became publicly visible, a social problem that required scientific understanding, research and intervention. In other words, social scientists, educators and health service providers could now study and intervene with young women who conceive on the basis of a neutral scientific interest in 'teenage pregnancy' that was not, at least ostensibly, judgemental about their marital status. Certainly, as noted above, there is currently a plethora of research about 'teenage pregnancy'.

A similar trend is evident in South Africa. Research conducted among black women in the 1940s, 1950s and 1960s repeatedly referred to the problem of 'illegitimate' births (Delius and Glaser 2002). It is only in the late 1970s and early 1980s that the term 'teenage pregnancy' emerged in the social science literature and became a serious field of study in and of itself.

The invention of 'teenage pregnancy' and the supposed scientific neutrality of the term do not, however, mean that concerns around the marital status of the young woman have suddenly disappeared. What the supposed neutrality of the term has done is mask or disguise this concern. In my analysis of the South African social science literature on 'teenage pregnancy' (Macleod 2003), I found a constant slippage between the terms 'teenage pregnancy' and 'unwed pregnancy' or 'extra-marital pregnancy'. Although the ostensible focus of many of the studies was on 'teenage pregnancy', the marital status of participants was frequently referred to.

Indeed, although the emphasis has supposedly shifted to a scientific stance, the ghost of the threat of degeneration implied by 'unwed' motherhood and 'illegitimacy' remains. Only what is being threatened, at least ostensibly, is different. Prior to the invention of 'teenage pregnancy', 'unwed' mothers were viewed as a threat to the moral fabric of society. They threatened the patriarchal order in which women were expected to become wives and mothers, and children were descendants of the patriarch or head of the family. Unwed mothers with their illegitimate children threatened the nuclear family, which was viewed as the correct and morally wholesome family formation in which children should be raised. The social climate of the 1960s in the developed world (anti-Vietnam war demonstrations, the Civil Rights movement, the hippie era) undoubtedly had an effect in making 'unwed mother' and 'illegitimacy' politically loaded terms. While these terms mostly (although not completely, as indicated above) disappeared from the lexicon in discussing young women and reproduction, the threat of degeneration has not. These women are no longer described as threatening the patriarchal order or the nuclear family (at least not overtly so). Instead, they are depicted as threatening degeneration in other ways: through perpetrating poverty, through contributing to health costs because of poor obstetric outcomes, through depending on welfare and thus increasing the fiscal load of decent citizens, and through contributing to population growth.

How 'teenage pregnancy', once invented, was taken up, and the implications of the term, were not, of course, uniform. Linders and Bogard's (2004) paper indicates how the invention of 'teenage pregnancy' in the 1970s took on different dimensions depending on the social and political climate. They compare Sweden and the United States. Currently, Sweden has a much lower rate of 'teenage pregnancy' than does the United States; it has what the authors refer to as a 'stable institutional apparatus' (including public agencies and schools who assist and educate young people) that keeps a vigilant eye on early pregnancy and responds accordingly if there are any changes in the rates of pregnancy or abortion. The authors attempt to understand the differences between the United States and Sweden, specifically in how the 'social problem' of 'teenage pregnancy' is spoken about and acted upon, by inspecting the 'institutional and interpretive configurations that preceded the modern approach to "teenage pregnancy" as a distinct social problem' (Linders and Bogard 2004: 4). By the 1970s, when the notion of 'illegitimacy' became a politically loaded term, a number of reforms in sex education, abortion, and public assistance to mothers had already taken place in Sweden. However, in the United States, no such action had been taken. Instead, the morally loaded remedial actions taken against young women who conceived remained intact right up to the 1970s, at which stage they basically collapsed as acceptable interventions. This allowed for the emergence of a 'crisis' with claims and counterclaims being made concerning the nature of the problem and the interventions to be taken to prevent and remediate it. It necessitated rapid changes in a number of areas including sex education, birth control, abortion and public assistance to mothers in need.

The social problem of 'teenage pregnancy'

By now, three or four decades down the line from the invention of 'teenage pregnancy', the concept has become firmly entrenched both in social science research and in the public lexicon concerning social problems. In a sense, 'teenage pregnancy' rolls off the tongue as a natural and self-evident signifier, generating much interest both in scholarly fields and in public debate.

Once 'teenage pregnancy' has become an established, supposedly self-evident signifier, it is easy to accept the associated research that points to a number of negative consequences resulting from 'teenage pregnancy'. This is because the signifier 'teenage', which precedes the 'pregnancy' signifier, foregrounds age as the most important aspect of a young woman's identity in relation to pregnancy. Research practices, including the assumptions underpinning the research, the ways in which the research questions and various measures are defined, and the methodologies utilized, simultaneously draw on and construct a discourse of 'adolescence as transition'. Age becomes the key variable, in isolation from other socio-economic and socio-cultural circumstances, and 'adolescence' is treated as a separable category of development.

In addition to unpacking some of the research practices associated with 'teenage pregnancy' as well as critiques of these practices, I shall trace, in the following, how the supposed scientific search for answers concerning the consequences of early reproduction feeds into a social concern around the threat of degeneration that teen-aged pregnancy brings with it. Fundamental to this is the 'adolescence as transition' premise with its associated imaginary wall in which the reproductive challenges facing young women are treated as separate to those of older women.

Readers should note that I am not implying that early pregnancy is not a problem for certain young people. Indeed, many young women who conceive and end up with unwanted pregnancies may find the situation intolerable. The fact that 12 per cent of the women presenting for terminations of pregnancies in South Africa are under the age of 18 (Department of Health [South Africa] 2006b) and that 17 per cent of termination of pregnancies in the United States are performed on teen-aged women (Guttmacher Institute 2008) indicates that a fair number of them do indeed find pregnancy to be severely problematic. However, the fact that 88 per cent of women presenting for terminations of pregnancy in South Africa and are over the age of 18, with 83 per cent being over the age of 20 in the United States, indicates that women of all ages find pregnancies, for a variety of reasons, problematic. Yet, we do not talk of adult pregnancy as a social problem.

The disruption of schooling and socio-economic disadvantage

The disruption of schooling that potentially accompanies 'teenage pregnancy' is seen as detrimental to the young mother, as it limits her future career prospects and, therefore contributes to a lower socio-economic status for her and her child (Chevalier and Viitanen 2003). Exactly how disruptive early pregnancy is on schooling, and its relationship with poverty are, however, a matter of debate. Greene and Merrick (2005) provide an overview of some of the findings from US research with regard to this issue. Research in the 1960s was unequivocal in stating that disadvantage emanated from early childbearing. In the late 1980s, the National Research Council declared, somewhat more guardedly, that teenagers who become parents are at more risk of social and economic disadvantage than those who delay childbearing. In the 1990s, however, researchers began to challenge this association, pointing to the methodological flaws of the studies conducted on 'teenage pregnancy', schooling and future economic outcome. They indicated that the effect of early fertility on disadvantage was greatly exaggerated.

School disruption is a complicated notion. Studies in the United States show that many young women who become mothers in fact dropped out of school before pregnancy (Brindis 1993; Manlove 1998). The same appears to be true in South Africa (Macleod 1999a; Manzini 2001). Some of the major reasons cited for dropping out of school in South Africa include poverty and a lack of motivation to complete school (schooling seen as useless or uninteresting) (Mokgalabone 1999; Crouch 2005). Indeed, the 2003 South African General Household Survey statistics indicate that of all the females who had dropped out of school, only 13 per cent cited pregnancy as a reason (Crouch 2005).

The lack of motivation of many young women to complete schooling has been referred to in the literature as school disengagement. In the case of young women, this may lead to withdrawal from school prior to conception, as discussed. However, some young women who conceive while at school may also experience school disengagement (Hosie 2007). School disengagement stems from factors such as, as cited by research in the UK, difficulties with specific teachers, bullying, boredom, difficulties with particular subjects or with work in general (Hosie 2007) and, as cited in South African research, frustration with the inexperience of teachers, lack of relevance of the curriculum, and need to care for siblings or sick relatives at home (Human Sciences Research Council 2007). It also indicates a (perhaps realistic) perception of the foreclosed opportunities available to women in the world of work, especially to those from lower socio-economic brackets. Disengagement from school has been mooted as a useful concept for understanding the school completion rates of both childbearing and non-childbearing young women.

An oft-cited American study is a seventeen-year follow-up study (Furstenburg et al. 1987) of the young mothers first studied in 1976, in which the authors concluded that while the women who had become pregnant in their teen-age years remained at a lower level of education and income than women who had delayed pregnancy, their education and income levels were far better than would be predicted by a straight deterministic model. In other words these women had fared better than the researchers had initially expected. This study has, however, been criticized for comparing young mothers with women who do not match the young women in a range of characteristics (Geronimus 2003). The implication here is that if the researchers had compared young and older women who were more similar, the differences found may have been even more minimal.

It is this exact issue – that women who conceive while teen-aged not only are pregnant but also live in a particular social and economic milieu – that some researchers have highlighted. These social issues, including socio-economic status, partner relationships, family structure, living conditions, health conditions and employment opportunities, form part of the complex context within which pregnancy is experienced and may very well be implicated in the educational disadvantage and poor economic outcomes these women experience. Research practices that foreground age mean that the social situatedness of young women is lost. These practices simultaneously draw off and assist in entrenching the 'adolescence as transition' discourse and the associated imaginary wall.

When the factors highlighted above are taken into consideration, the effect of early reproduction, *in and of itself*, on educational or economic outcomes is far less catastrophic than commonly assumed. Geronimus (2003: 881), in summarizing the conclusion of well-designed comparative studies, states that these outcomes are 'slightly negative, negligible, or positive'. To rephrase this in one of the key themes of this book, when the imaginary wall between adolescents and older women of similar social circumstances is removed, or when we compare women of similar socio-economic and socio-cultural circumstances, we find our basic assumptions concerning the negative educational and economic consequences of 'teenage pregnancy' beginning to break down.

Indeed, revisionists (researchers who dispute the simple 'teenage pregnancy = social problem equation') are suspicious of the arguments that ignore the gendered and classed environment within which many young women who conceive live. They argue that the one-to-one correspondence made between education and future advantage (if you have a better education you will earn better) hides a multitude of social inequalities. It is posited that the belief that 'if only women forbore from having babies while in their teens they would succeed in the educational and occupational markets and therefore not live in poverty' (Macintyre and Cunningham-Burley 1993: 60) rings hollow in many societies in which opportunities for emotionally and financially rewarding jobs for women are restricted. This argument seems to be supported by research in the United States in which it was found that when opportunities for employment increase (such as in a time of economic boom), the rate of early fertility decreases (Colen et al. 2006).

Thus, the main arguments with respect to pregnant young women and schooling have been the extent to which early childbearing disrupts schooling and what the nature of the association between education and future advantage is. What these arguments fail to acknowledge is that childbearing is costly to women at any age, both in terms of direct costs (clothes, nappies etc.) and in terms of opportunity costs (having to take time off school or work, having to be available for child-caring even if working, being unable to take on more responsible or better paid or full-time work because of domestic responsibilities). In other words, in concentrating on young women and the opportunity costs in terms of schooling, researchers are constructing an imaginary wall between teen-aged and older women, implying that somehow there are opportunity costs for young women in bearing children, but none for older women. Indeed, some revisionist authors have implied that early childbearing is a rational choice for many women in disadvantaged circumstances as the opportunity costs of child-bearing are fewer at this stage than when they are older. This, they state, is because these young women have greater access to familial support in caring for the child than they would have at a later stage (Geronimus 1991).

Health risks

'Teenage pregnancy' has been identified as a key public health issue. Dangal (2006), for example, has this to say:

Teenage pregnancy, which is detrimental to the health of mother and child, is a common public health problem worldwide. It is a problem that affects nearly every society – developed and developing alike. It is one of the key issues concerning reproductive health of women not only in developing but also in developed countries.

(Dangal 2006)

But exactly how detrimental is 'teenage pregnancy', per se, to the health of the mother and infant? There is some controversy concerning this, as elucidated below.

Some studies have shown increased health risks associated with teen-aged pregnancy and childbearing. These include pregnancy-induced hypertension, premature labour, anaemia, small-for-date babies, neonatal and infant mortality and neonatal morbidity (Gilbert et al. 2004; Chen et al. 2007). Most of these studies have been conducted in developed countries such as the United States. However, similar findings have emerged in studies conducted in South Africa (Boult and Cunningham 1995; Cameron et al. 1996).

Some researchers have disputed the health risk association, criticizing the methodologies of these studies in terms of the comparison groups used. In South Africa, Ncayiyana and Ter Haar (1989) compared the obstetric outcome of teen-aged women with that of an equal number of matched (in terms of number pregnancies and socio-economic status) adult women aged 20 to 29 years. This means that for each teen-aged woman, there was an equivalent older woman who came from the same socio-economic status group and who had had the same number of pregnancies. The researchers found no significant differences in the obstetric outcomes of these women. They concluded that the total obstetric population (in other words all older women giving birth) is an unsuitable group for comparison with teen-aged women. Age per se, they state, does not confer increased risk. Rather it is socio-economic status that accounts for the observed differences. This conclusion is supported by research conducted in Kenya (Taffa 2003) and Australia (Bai et al. 1999) where researchers have found no significant difference between teen-aged and older women of similar socio-economic, marital and lifestyle (e.g. smoking) circumstances in terms of obstetric outcomes. Bukulmez and Deren (2000) found in their study in Turkey that, among other things, level of prenatal care (rather than age) accounted for difference in obstetric outcome between younger and older women. They argue that, given adequate prenatal care, there are no increased obstetric risks for teen-aged women. In the words of Cunnington (2001: 36), who conducted a systematic review of the literature on the health consequences of teenage pregnancy, 'Critical appraisal suggested that increased risks of these [negative health] outcomes were predominantly caused by the social, economic, and behavioral factors that predispose some young women to pregnancy'.

Some American research has found that the health risk to the mother and child in fact increases with age among African American women. For example, in one study (Geronimus 1996), the risk of low-birth-weight infants increased three times between maternal ages of 15 and 34. This, the researcher suggested, was because of what she terms 'weathering' – the physical consequences of social inequities.

The problem of confounding variables (socio-economic status, ethnicity, marital status, lifestyle factors, parity, prenatal care etc.) in investigating the health consequences of 'teenage pregnancy' has been taken up by some researchers who continue to insist that age is the single most important factor (Chen et al. 2007). Geronimus (2004), however, brings a different angle to the question of 'teenage pregnancy' and public health. She argues that for young women who live in conditions of poverty, having children early in life represents an adaptive health response because of the shortened healthy life expectancy these women and their partners enjoy. In other words, these women can expect to spend more of their lives ill and to die earlier than women from the middle classes. The chances of being widowed, of their children being orphaned, or of illness interfering with childcare increases as they grow older. This shortened healthy life expectancy is largely owing to the conditions of poverty within which they live. We may hypothesise, also, that the HIV/AIDS epidemic provides even more impetus for these women experiencing a sense of foreshortened life-span and health expectancy, especially in places like South Africa.

Poor child outcomes

Some researchers believe that the nascent developmental status of the young caregiver increases the probability of poor outcomes for the child as a result of a maladaptive relationship between the mother and the child. It is suggested, among other things, that the children of young mothers will have academic difficulties owing to their mothers' vocalizing less often with them and providing fewer stimulating experiences than do older mothers (Barratt 1991; Hofferth and Reid 2002), and that they will have an increased risk of behavioural problems (Hofferth and Reid 2002) or of psychopathology as their mothers do not provide opportunities for affectional exchange, or else share emotions inconsistently (Osofsky et al. 1992). A link has been made between young parenthood and child abuse because the purported patterns of young parenting are akin to those described among abusive mothers. Furthermore, studies suggest that teen-aged mothers who were themselves sexually abused will go on to neglect and abuse their children (Becker-Lausen and Rickel 1995).

Various authors dispute the young mother/poor child outcome or abuse association, however. They postulate that the parent–child interaction is influenced by a range of factors such as the financial, social, emotional and social support resources available to the mother, and that these need to be accounted for before ascribing the negative interaction or child outcome to the mother's age. As Levine et al. (2007) indicate:

> It is equally plausible . . . that timing of parenting itself does not cause children's poor outcomes. Instead, background factors such as poverty that select women into early childbearing may also select their children into experiencing negative outcomes. Thus, correlations between early parenting and children's poor outcomes may be noncausal.
>
> (Levine et al. 2007: 106)

In studies that have attempted to take the above mentioned factors into account, the results have shown that the association between young parenthood and poor child outcomes is a lot more complicated than initially supposed. For example, Geronimus (2003) used a sample of sisters who had had their first children at different ages. The rationale for using sisters is to try to match older and younger mothers as much as possible in terms of background factors. Tests conducted on the pre-school and primary school children of these sisters showed that there was little difference between the children born to teen-aged mothers and those born to older mothers; where differences were found, the children of younger mothers usually fared better! In a longitudinal study, Shaw et al. (2005) studied the psychological, health and behavioural outcomes of teen-aged children born to teen-aged mothers in Australia. The authors claim that, because teenage pregnancy is not a prominent policy concern in Australia, they were able to study outcomes in an environment in which there is less stigma attached to early reproduction than in other comparable countries. They conclude that 'the associations between maternal age and psychological distress, school performance, and smoking and alcohol use were all largely explained by socioeconomic factors, maternal depression, family structure and maternal smoking' (Shaw et al. 2005: 2538). In other words, when adequate adjustment with respect to socio-economic status and other social variables is made, the effect of maternal age virtually disappears.

Welfare and demographic issues

Bonell (2004) conducted a systematic review of published research on 'teenage pregnancy' in the United States and United Kingdom between 1981 and 2000, analysing the justification used in each of the studies for the research. An interesting trend was observed. UK researchers justified their focus on 'teenage pregnancy' from a health perspective (although, as Bonell points out, few of them focused on very young teenagers in whom more health difficulties may be expected). US researchers tended to focus on 'teenage pregnancy' because of the potential for welfare dependency. To quote Bonell (2004):

> Many [studies] suggested that teenage fertility is a key mediator in the intergenerational transmission of worklessness, welfare uptake and out-of-wedlock birth and other 'deviant' social norms from one generation of such populations to the next. Such research did appear to be informed by a fear of a growing underclass.
>
> (Bonell 2004: 268)

This fear is racialized, with many studies concentrating on poor and black populations, citing the fact that young black women tend to use welfare in the United States for longer than do their white and Hispanic counterparts. It is to the 'fear of the growing underclass', expressed through, first, demographic concerns and, second, concerns about welfare dependency, that I turn to in this section.

In the early literature on 'teenage pregnancy' in South Africa, it was demographic concerns that featured rather than welfare ones. Various authors (Anagnostara 1988; V. De Villiers 1991) cited 'teenage pregnancy' as one of the contributory factors to population growth. In this understanding, the increase in population in developing countries represents a major obstacle to economic development. With a significant proportion of the population being younger than 20, the low ratio of workers to non-workers creates what is called a 'burden of dependency'. Clear racial overtones were evident in the rhetoric of population growth and explosion, with white South Africans being implicitly exempt from blame. As the language of demographic concern was fuelled by the Apartheid government's official position on population control, which ranged from encouraging white people to have more children to implicitly blaming black people for their poverty because they have too many babies, this type of rhetoric has receded in the post-Apartheid years.

This kind of position (the association of teenage pregnancy and population growth, and the racialization thereof) was not unique to South Africa, however. In 1987, a manpower report, entitled *The changing face of America*, had this to say:

> By the year 2000, the U.S. population will be less than 76 percent White and more than 24 percent minority. The minority student populations of Blacks, Hispanics, and Native Americans are rapidly increasing, especially in urban areas. Their school graduation rates remain low while their dropout rates continue to rise. The academic achievement of these minority students is well below that of most White students. The percentage of Blacks and

Hispanic students living in poverty is high. Unwed teenage pregnancies are rising, and a recent study links academic failure with teenage pregnancies.

(Lisack 1987: 1)

Nowadays the concern with the 'growing underclass' is expressed more in terms of welfare dependency. In South Africa a popular belief is that young women are deliberately conceiving in order to access the Child Support Grants (CSGs) available to mothers. The CSG was introduced in 1998, initially for children under the age of 8, but later extended to children up to the age of 14. The criteria for payment of the CSG are based on the personal income of the primary caregiver or spouse, and the area and type of dwelling in which the child is living. A means test is applied to these criteria in order to ascertain whether the applicant qualifies for the grant. The aim is to reach poor children. The amount paid is small (less than R200 or US$16 a month).

In response to concerns raised in the media with respect to a rise in 'teenage pregnancy' as a result of CSGs, the Department of Social Development commissioned research to investigate the matter. The report (Kesho Consulting and Business Solutions 2006) and another one from the Human Sciences Research Council (Makiwane and Udjo 2006) conclude that there is no evidence that the CSGs lead to an increase in welfare dependency. This is based on two observations. First, the rates of teenage childbearing were high prior to the introduction of the CSG with a decrease in fertility after its introduction. Second, only 20 per cent of teen-aged mothers are beneficiaries of these grants. Of those who would qualify for the grant, the proportion of teen-aged mothers taking them up is considerably lower than those in older age groups.

Of course, South Africa is not alone in the concern expressed over welfare. In an edited collection of papers from around the world on welfare and early childbearing, Daguerre and Nativel (2006) indicate that 'teenage pregnancy is stigmatised because of its association with welfare dependency' and that, 'in liberal welfare states, teenage pregnancy is analysed through the prism of welfare dependency' (Daguerre and Nativel 2006: 8). They single out the United States, New Zealand and to a lesser extent the United Kingdom in this respect.

Two issues arise with respect to the discussion of welfare dependency. The first is the very conceptualization of dependency. McLaughlin and Luker (2006), in their paper in the above-mentioned collection, indicate that our current understandings of welfare dependency are permeated by historical meanings of dependency – meanings that 'justified colonization, slavery and the exclusion of women from paid work, while at the same time made wage-earning men heroically independent' (McLaughlin and Luker 2006: 28). Dependency is thus a politically loaded and ideological term that positions poor people as 'dependent' on government assistance and housewives as 'dependent' on their husbands, and that renders all labour performed by 'dependants' invisible.

The second question in relation to dependency is how costly early reproduction is to the general fiscus. In an innovative study, Hotz et al. (1996, cited in Geronimus 2003) compared teen-aged mothers with teenagers who were pregnant but had a miscarriage (i.e. would have been mothers had the miscarriage not occurred). Their conclusions are startling, given the usual assumption in the United States that early reproduction contributes to welfare dependency. They state that if all teenagers delayed childbearing the total expenditure on public assistance would *increase* slightly and that the lifetime earnings of these women would *decrease*. This conclusion speaks to the point made earlier about childbearing being costly to women at any stage of their lives. The conclusion here is that early childbearing was less costly both personally and to the general fiscus.

Power relations in constructing a threat of degeneration

A teenager who becomes a parent is at a significant disadvantage in becoming a contributing adult, both psychologically and economically. . . . Children of teenage mothers are at increased risk of cognitive and psychological deficits. The combination of cognitive, emotional, academic and social problems amounts to 'massive school failure' for these 'children of children'. These problems are attributable to poor parenting, lower socioeconomic status and disadvantaged neighbourhoods. A few studies find a higher likelihood of abuse of children by teenage mothers.

(F. De Villiers and Kekesi 2004: 21)

This quote comes from the introduction of an article published in the journal *South African Family Practice* and entitled 'Social interaction of teenage mothers during and after their pregnancy'. The aim of the research was to investigate the social interaction of a group of young reproductive women. Although the article is about the social interaction of young reproductive women, and not about the negative consequences of teen-aged pregnancy, these authors choose to frame their article with a list of what can only be described as sensationalist depictions of the dire consequences of teen-aged pregnancy. These authors are not alone in this. Several articles on 'teenage pregnancy' and abortion *begin* by extolling the social problem that teenage pregnancy represents. In other words, this forms the basic foundation from which they proceed.

And yet, as we have seen above, these are not foregone conclusions. Given this, I turn to a question posed by Geronimus (2003), in an article aptly entitled 'Damned if you do: Culture, identity, privilege, and teenage childbearing in the United States'. Why, she asks, are we 'unaware that the scientific evidence on the consequences of teen childbearing, per se, is equivocal?'. 'In the light of actual scientific evidence [to the contrary], why does the conventional wisdom on the consequences of teen childbearing continue to be at once overstated and never in doubt?' (Geronimus 2003: 881 and 884)

Geronimus (2003) argues that researchers and broader society are selective in their attention to the issue, choosing to ignore the difficulties pointed out with regard to studies finding negative consequences across the board, as well as the real-life circumstances of many women who have children early. She believes that this 'selective focus helps maintain the core values, competencies, and privileges of the dominant group' (Geronimus 2003: 884). 'Teenage pregnancy' is used as a political tool to entrench ideas about race, responsibility, sexuality and family values. The message that early reproduction produces disadvantage under all circumstances is used by dominant groups to produce a social control message directed at their own youth to postpone childbearing – for whom, because of the structural advantages they enjoy (including access to health care, employed domestic help or daycare facilities, and better chances of employment), delaying childbearing is advantageous.

These comments have been made in the context of American politics. However, I argue that the same is true within South Africa and many other countries. The language of a threat of degeneration implicit in talk about the consequences of 'teenage pregnancy', in which the less developed undermine the stability and morality of good society through abandoning schooling, perpetuating poverty, contributing to health costs, producing less-than-adequate children, and relying on welfare, continues to dominate. The persistence, despite the work of critical public health and critical health psychology scholars, points to a political process and power relations that serve a particular purpose.

Geronimus (2003) concludes her article with the following, sentiments that apply equally well in many contexts:

> To acknowledge cultural variability in the costs and consequences of early childbearing requires public admission of structural inequality and the benefits members of dominant groups derive from socially excluding others. One cannot explain why the benefits of early childbearing may outweigh the costs for many African Americans without noting that African American youth do not enjoy the same access to advanced education or career security enjoyed by most Americans; that their parents are compelled to be more focused on imperatives of survival and subsistence than on encouraging their children to engage in extended and expensive preparation for the competitive labor market; indeed, that African

Americans cannot even take their health or longevity for granted through middle age. And one cannot explain why these social and health inequalities exist without recognizing that structural barriers to full participation in American society impede the success of marginalized groups.

(Geronimus 2003: 890)

The essential argument here is that our discussions on 'teenage pregnancy' are always already political and speak to racialized, classed and gendered power relations that are seldom acknowledged in the scientific quest to answer the question of the consequences of 'teenage pregnancy'.

Conclusion

'Teenage pregnancy' has become such a common signifier that it is difficult to believe that there was a time, relatively recently in fact, when it made little, or no, sense. As indicated in this chapter, 'teenage pregnancy' entered the public domain as an issue of common concern in the early 1970s, not because the rates of pregnancy among young women were increasing, but rather because of a shift in how young women and sexuality and reproduction were viewed.

The shift from 'unwed motherhood' and 'illegitimate child' to 'teenage pregnancy' has allowed for a slicing off of a segment of women, based purely on their age. As a result the lens of analysis in research has focused on age as the primary variable around which to investigate pregnancy. The social milieux within which women live, including socio-economic conditions, partner relationships, family structures, health status, employment opportunities, social support networks, health provision, social security provision and educational opportunities recede into the background.

The result is that much research points in the direction of negative consequences attendant upon teenage pregnancy, including school disruption, socio-economic disadvantage, poor health and child outcomes, and welfare dependency. However, once some of the conceptual and methodological issues related to research conducted on the consequences of early reproduction are sorted out, the picture that emerges is not as cut and dry as suggested by people like De Villiers and Kekesi (2004), cited in the previous section. When factors relating to the complex social milieux within which women live are taken into consideration, the effects of early reproduction, in and of itself, on the educational or economic outcomes of young women, the physical and psychological outcomes for the children and the health of both are, at worst, slightly negative, and may even be positive. Indeed, early reproduction may be an adaptive response in certain situations where healthy life expectancy is reduced and there is greater access to a familial care-taking nexus earlier in life. In considering these issues the cost of childbearing to women at various ages needs to be considered, which opens up the possibility of early childbearing have fewer opportunity costs for women in particular circumstances. Indeed, it is suggested that early childbearing may, for some women, be less costly financially both personally and in terms of the general fiscus.

Despite these arguments against the necessarily deleterious view of 'teenage pregnancy', pregnancy and childbearing among young women continues to be represented as a social problem. I argue in this chapter that this represents a sanitized version of the threat of degeneration. Scientific method is used to position young women as threatening social order and community stability.

5

YOUNG WOMEN AND LEGALIZED ABORTION

The new 'social problem'

Prior to the airing of the *Special Assignment* programme on termination of pregnancy among teen-aged women (mentioned in Chapter 1), the following appeared on the South African Broadcasting Corporation's website (www.sabc.co.za):

> In Duduza, a member of Doctors for Life, Dr Eva Seobi speaks out. She feels the medical profession has been raped: how can they be expected to protect life but on the other hand take life? She takes us through post-abortion complications such as smelly discharges, depression and scarred wombs. She believes child abuse happens because women have been hardened and don't care anymore.

On the actual programme, Dr Seobi says:

> Now with all the gadgets we have, we are going to dilate that cervix prematurely. The tendency would be to cause some lacerations. It could be the very muscles around that area they get damaged and that could lead to cervical incompetence. So you find that the mother at the time now when she wants to have the child, she can't have the child. There's also infection, you find now someone's being troubled by the recurrent infection [and] discharges, which are smelly, sometimes pussy. . . . When women have an abortion even their emotional make-up alters. They become harsh, very hard, they don't care. They are just hardened. That's why you find a woman can have an abortion once twice, three times, seven times and they tell you they feel nothing. Why? It's because their conscience is already seared, they can no more feel.
>
> (*Special Assignment* and SABC)

In this rendition, abortion among young women is cast in a similarly negative light to 'teenage pregnancy'. A termination of pregnancy, according to Dr Seobi, leads to terrible health consequences, emotional difficulties, psychological disruption and moral laxness. But the picture of negative consequences does not end with the individual. Negative social consequences are spoken of too. The medical profession is 'raped' by abortion and child abuse occurs because women are 'hardened' by abortion.

At one level of logic, abortion could be seen as the solution to the 'teenage pregnancy = social problem' equation. Abortion prevents the disruption of schooling, means that young women are not becoming (what some see as inadequate) mothers, ensures that young women do not access welfare, and do not contribute to poverty and population growth. The threat of personal and social degeneration implied by 'teenage pregnancy' could, in this logic, be solved by making termination of pregnancy freely and openly available to young women with unwanted pregnancies.

This logic is, however, seldom evident in discussions on young women and reproduction. Abortion among young women joins 'teenage pregnancy' as posing a threat of degeneration both personally and socially. There are a number of potential reasons for this. First, abortion obviously implies pregnancy, thus invoking the dominant 'teenage pregnancy = social problem' equation. Second, pregnancy implies sexual activity, meaning that the young woman has clearly been engaging in activities that rupture the 'adolescence as transition' discourse in which young people may practise at being adult, but not actually be adult. Third, abortion politics play a large role in any discussion concerning abortion, and obviously abortion among young women is no exception. Finally, and it is to this main point that I turn in this chapter, abortion is associated in the literature and in the popular media with negative medical and psychological consequences.

It is important to note here that I am referring specifically to legal termination of pregnancy. Many countries have extremely restrictive abortion laws, rendering legal terminations of pregnancies virtually impossible to attain. This leads to unsafe abortions being performed by individuals without the necessary know-how and in conditions that are medically suboptimal. Grimes et al. (2006) estimate that 19 to 20 million unsafe abortions are performed globally each year, resulting in the death of approximately 68,000 women, and in severe health complications for millions more. Whilst acknowledging this as an enormous problem, my focus in this chapter is on the manner in which *legal* termination of pregnancy, performed by trained personnel and under safe and hygienic circumstances, is spoken of in relation to teen-aged women.

The association of legal abortion and negative medical or psychological consequences turns abortion among young women into the new social problem. However, it is depicted as a social problem of different proportions to the 'teenage pregnancy' social problem. Instead of the social costs of welfare dependency, poverty and poor mothering associated with teen-aged childbearing, abortion among young women is depicted as having enormous personal health and psychological cost, which then is turned into social costs. Abortion, it is implied, will inevitably lead to health difficulties as well as some form of personal crisis, ranging from regret to full-blown psychiatric problems. Through the politics of abortion, these supposed personal crises are turned into social problems, thus extending the threat of degeneration to include not only pregnancy and reproduction among young women, but also abortion.

In the following, I review some of the research on the health and psychological consequences of abortion for women in general. This lays the framework within which debate about the consequences for young women takes place. As with any discussions around abortion, the scientific debate is quite acrimonious at times. Some researchers argue strongly that there are severe health and psychological consequences to abortion, while others are equally convinced that the consequences are no worse than for women in similar circumstances taking an unwanted pregnancy to term. Part of the debate centres on the manner in which the research is conducted, or put differently, on the research practices that allow the emergence of particular discursive constructions.

Following on from this discussion, I narrow the focus to discussions on the consequences of abortion specifically for young women. Here, in addition to the argument about whether abortion has negative consequences for women in general, the debate centres around whether abortion has a greater effect on young women than it does on older women owing to young women's developmental status.

The debate in the academic literature about the consequences of abortion is probably set to continue for some time yet. Leaving this aside, though, the question to which I turn in the final section of this chapter is how the suggestion that there are health and psychological consequences (i.e. that there is a threat of personal degeneration) is taken up in the anti-abortion lobby. Abortion has, since the early 1960s or so, been an issue that slips between the personal and public in interesting and complex ways. On the one hand, it is a personal issue –the individual woman's decision whether or not to terminate a pregnancy. On the other hand, it is an intensely political debate that draws on religious, medical, gender, cultural and, more recently, psychological discourses. In this section we see how the threat of personal degeneration is taken up by the anti-abortion lobby in ways that turns it into a threat of social degeneration.

As the chapter deals specifically with legal termination of pregnancy, the legal framework for termination of pregnancy in two countries will briefly be discussed below. Much of the research conducted regarding the consequences of abortion has taken place in the United States. Thus, by way of contextualizing this research, the legal situation will be outlined. And because much of the textual data utilized in this research is from South Africa, South African law will also be explained. South Africa represents an interesting case study in terms of abortion research in the sense that the

76

country went from having very restrictive termination of pregnancy legislation to allowing termination of pregnancy on request up to twelve weeks.

Abortion legislation in the United States and South Africa

Abortion was famously legalized in the United States through a landmark court case, *Roe v Wade*, in which the Supreme Court ruled that pregnant women had a constitutional right to obtain an abortion free from government interference. The court overturned the laws of Texas and other states banning abortion on the basis that: protecting a woman's health was no longer necessary owing to technological advances in abortion procedures; the right to privacy in the *Griswold v Connecticut* case which legalized the use of contraceptives by married couples extended to a woman's decision to terminate a pregnancy prior to viability; foetuses did not constitute 'persons' under the Fourth Amendment. A trimester system was established with abortion in the first three months being unregulated. During the second trimester, states could introduce laws to ensure the health of the woman was not jeopardized. In the third trimester, during which the foetus becomes viable, states may regulate abortion except when there is a threat to the woman's life (Dudley 2006).

Roe v Wade has, over the years, created substantial political controversy. It has been contested in more than twenty Supreme Court decisions, with some pro-choice advocates indicating that there is slow erosion of the gains made in *Roe v Wade*. Various regulations and restrictions have been upheld, and individual states have some leeway in the manner in which they implement abortion laws (Dudley 2006). For example, thirty-four states require minors either to notify their parents or to obtain their consent before having a termination of pregnancy. The constitutionality of these statutes has been upheld by the Supreme Court, although states are required to have mechanisms whereby approval may be obtained via the courts. This is called judicial bypass (Sanger 2004).

The legalization of abortion in South Africa took a very different route from that of the United States. Instead of a court judgment, legalization was through an Act of Parliament. Soon after the first democratic elections in South Africa in 1994, the Choice on Termination of Pregnancy (CTOP) Act of 1996, which legalized abortion for the first time, was passed. Women may now request abortions up to the twelfth week of pregnancy. After this, up to the twentieth week, abortions may be performed under specified conditions. After twenty weeks, termination may be performed only if two doctors (or a doctor and a registered midwife) determine that continued pregnancy would endanger the woman's life, result in severe malformation of the foetus or pose a risk of injury to the foetus. The Act also promotes the provision of non-mandatory counselling before and after abortions are performed.

Minors are counselled to notify their parents or guardian but do not require consent from their parents or guardian. This subsection of the Act has caused some controversy. The Christian Lawyers Association filed a suit in the Pretoria High Court in 2003 on the basis that the above-mentioned subsection was unconstitutional (previously, in 1997, several Christian groups failed in their court challenge to have the CTOP Act in its entirety declared unconstitutional). In this suit they argued that it was in the best interests of the pregnant teenager to obtain the consent of her parents or guardian in order to avoid the adverse effects of abortion. They claimed that there should be mandatory counselling before the abortion and a time for reflection, and that if consent was not obtained, the abortion should be refused (*Christian Lawyers Association v Minister of Health and Others* 2005). They failed in their application. This aspect of the legislation remains controversial.

Prior to the legalization of abortion in South Africa, a termination of pregnancy could be obtained only under very specified and restrictive conditions. Access to abortion was skewed along racial and class lines with virtually the only women managing to obtain legal abortions being white and middle class (Cope 1993). In a study conducted prior to the legalization of abortion, researchers found that unsafe abortion was a major cause of death and illness among women in South Africa (Rees et al. 1997). Later research confirmed that the legalization of abortion has had a major impact on mortality in women, particularly with regard to younger women (Jewkes et al. 2005).

Research on the health and psychological consequences of abortion

Although the negative health consequences of unsafe termination of pregnancy are reasonable clear cut, there is some controversy concerning the health consequences of legal abortion. Some researchers suggest that, even under medically controlled conditions, having an abortion is worse than carrying a pregnancy to term. Thorp (2003) conducted a review of a number of studies concerning the effect of abortion on a woman's health in the future. He concluded that having an abortion meant a greater risk for future preterm delivery and placenta previa (where the placenta gets implanted over or near the top of the cervix), and possibly for breast cancer. However, abortion was not associated with increased levels of difficulty with conception, spontaneous abortion or ectopic pregnancy. Other researchers argue, however, that abortion carries fewer risks than childbearing. For example, Adler et al. (2003) quote statistics from the United States showing that 9.2 per 100,000 women die as a result of pregnancy- or birth-related complications, while only 0.3 per 100,000 die as a result of legal abortions. This is confirmed by Grimes (1994) in which the health consequences of contraception, sterilization, abortion and childbirth were compared. Grimes (1994: 1489) conclude that 'For most women, fertility regulation by contraception, sterilization, or legal abortion is substantially safer than childbirth'.

In South Africa the maternal mortality ratio (the number of deaths per 100,000 women pregnant or bearing children) is much higher than in the United States, with current estimates placing it at 150 per 100,000 (Department of Health [South Africa] 2007). The 'big five' causes (those that account for 86.5 per cent of maternal deaths) are quoted as (in descending order): non-pregnancy related sepsis (including complications from HIV/AIDS), complications from hypertension in pregnancy, obstetric haemorrhaging, pregnancy sepsis (including sepsis relating to illegal abortion) and a pre-existing condition. According to the Department of Health, the majority of deaths due to abortions occur in the second trimester. These are usually the result of interference by the woman herself or a non-registered person, that is, illegal terminations of pregnancy (Ijumba and Padarath 2006). Despite an extensive search, I was unable to obtain any figures on maternal deaths owing to legal terminations of pregnancy in South Africa.

Turning to the psychological consequences of abortion, once again, there is controversy concerning this. A fair amount of research has been conducted on the psychological consequences of abortion, much of it pointing to negative effects, such as fatigue, guilt, depression, anxiety and sexual dysfunction (Bianchi-Demicheli et al. 2002). One of the major developments in this respect was the suggestion that the psychological consequences of abortion may represent a recognizable psychological disorder.

This suggestion was postulated by Speckhard and Rue (1992) when they published their conclusions from the meta-analysis that they conducted on a number of studies. All the studies analysed found some negative outcomes for at least a proportion of the women. On the basis of this, Speckhard and Rue (1992) suggested that the clinical literature as well as their experience with post-abortion trauma among some women suggest the need for a diagnostic category of post-abortion syndrome. They argued that abortion, as a psychosocial stressor, may cause mild distress through to severe trauma in some women, creating the need for a continuum of categories from post-abortion distress (PAD), post-abortion syndrome (PAS) and post-abortion psychosis (PAP). Their main focus was on PAS, which they described as a variant of post-traumatic stress disorder. They described the basic components of PAS as

(1) exposure to or participation in an abortion experience, i.e., the intentional destruction of one's unborn child, which is perceived as traumatic and beyond the range of usual human experience;

(2) uncontrolled negative experiencing of the abortion death event, e.g., flashbacks, nightmares, grief, and anniversary reactions;

(3) unsuccessful attempts to avoid or deny abortion recollections and emotional pain, which result in reduced responsiveness to others and one's environment; and

(4) experiencing associated symptoms not present before the abortion, including guilt about surviving.

(Speckhard and Rue 1992: 105)

Their desire clearly was to get PAS accepted as a diagnostic category in the American Psychiatric Association's *Diagnostic and Statistical Manual of Mental Disorders* (this is the manual used by psychologists and psychiatrists to assist in diagnosing mental disorders). It took over a decade, they pointed out, for post-traumatic stress disorder to be officially recognized. PAS, they felt, may be making a similar transition.

Despite PAS not being recognized as a separable diagnostic category, support from some researchers (e.g. Gómez and Zapata 2005) for its recognition continues. It has also been taken up by researchers in a range of settings. For example, in South Africa Van Rooyen and Smith (2004) administered a questionnaire relating to the symptoms of PAS to women presenting at the Family Medicine Clinic of Kalafong Hospital. These women had had a termination of pregnancy on request. Of the forty-eight women who participated, sixteen (33 per cent) fulfilled the criteria for PAS, with more than half having some form of emotional effect.

These kinds of studies are not without their difficulties, however. There are three main concerns with respect to research practices in relation to the psychological consequences of abortion (Stotland 2001). First, there is often a lack of meaningful comparison between women who undergo an abortion and women who are pregnant and give birth. Second, there is no indication of the women's functioning prior to the abortion. Third, the circumstances under which the abortion was performed are not considered. Each of these will be discussed below.

First, many studies fail to include a meaningful control group. The critical issue in designing research around the psychological responses of women to abortion is the validity of the control group. Comparing women who have undergone a termination of pregnancy with women in the general population means that you are really comparing apples and oranges. Women in the general population have not necessarily faced an unwanted pregnancy, whereas women who opt for an abortion are typically faced with an unplanned and unwanted pregnancy. Thus, the only reasonable control group for women who terminate their pregnancies is women *of similar social and material circumstances* with *unwanted* pregnancies who bear children and either keep them or put them up for adoption, or who miscarry. As stated by Stotland (2001: 28), 'Abortion is performed on women who are pregnant, and, for those women, abortion and childbearing are the only two alternatives'.

Without this kind of comparative data, there is the danger of ascribing experiences to an abortion when they may in fact have been the result of an unwanted pregnancy. Two articles have compared women with unwanted pregnancies who terminated their pregnancies with women with unwanted pregnancies who delivered a live baby. They used data from the US National Longitudinal Survey of Youth. The first one, written by Reardon and Cougle (2002) found that, among married women, those who carried their pregnancy to term were less likely to become depressed than those who terminated their pregnancy. There was no difference for unmarried women. The authors stated that the latter lack of difference may be owing to the stress of raising a child as a single parent or to the under-reporting of abortion among unmarried women. The publication of this article led to a flurry of letters being sent to the *British Medical Journal* in which the article appeared. Some of these raised concerns with the manner in which the research had been conducted. Three years later, using the same data as used by the first set of authors, other researchers, Schmiege and Russo (2005), reached very different conclusions. Schmiege and Russo (2005) argued that the manner in which Reardon and Cougle (2002) coded and analysed their data was flawed. In particular they accuse Reardon and Cougle (2002) of misidentifying unwanted first pregnancies and excluding women who were at the highest risk of developing depression following childbirth. Their (Schmiege and Russo's) analysis, they claim, used more precise coding and more appropriate selection of women. They conclude that terminating an unwanted pregnancy did not lead to more risk of clinical depression than carrying an unwanted pregnancy to term. Again the article led to a flurry of letters concerning their results and how they conducted their research.

The second issue with respect to research conducted on the psychological consequences of abortion relates to the psychological well-being of the participants prior to the abortion, or perhaps prior to the pregnancy. It has been suggested that women who opt for abortions may, to start with, have a range of mental health problems rendering them less capable of seeing a pregnancy through to term and caring for a child. For example, one study compared women who were admitted to hospital for a threatened miscarriage, women who were attending a routine outpatient antenatal class, and women who were about to undergo a voluntary termination of pregnancy. In comparison with the first two groups of women, the women who were about to terminate their pregnancies had higher levels of psychological distress related specifically to an underlying neurotic personality structure (Renzo et al. 1991). Thus, if particular women have pre-existing psychological problems and display psychological distress after an abortion, this may be owing to the pre-existing problems rather than to the abortion per se.

Certainly, it is well known that pre-existing psychological problems are a major risk factor for the development of psychiatric illness after childbirth (Stotland 2001), and the same may very well be true for abortion. Including data on what researchers call the baseline functioning of the women (i.e. before the abortion, or before the pregnancy) would help researchers to separate out how many of the symptoms seen post-abortion were due to the abortion or due to prior difficulties. How exactly to measure pre-pregnancy functioning is somewhat of a dilemma. One set of researchers (Reardon et al. 2003) used admission to a psychiatric hospital one year prior to the abortion as a criterion for exclusion from their study. In other words, they were attempting to sift out any women who had prior problems from the group they were studying. However, as pointed out by Major (2003), this does not account for other indicators of poor mental health or for episodes that may have required hospitalization prior to one year.

Finally, few studies that research the consequences of abortion consider the circumstances surrounding the abortion. Two broad sets of circumstances need to be considered. The first set of circumstances is those that surround the woman when making the decision. These include such factors as the level of support from partner and family, local social and cultural norms including gender relations, and the material conditions under which these women live. Studies that look specifically at the decision-making process stress the importance of these sorts of issues in women's decisions to terminate a pregnancy (Whittaker 2002; Puri et al. 2007). The second set of circumstances is the conditions under which the abortion itself is performed. Factors such as supportiveness and attitudes of the staff and local anti-abortion activity may affect the experience of women who terminate their pregnancies and may well affect their reactions afterwards; interestingly some research (Cozzarelli et al. 1994) indicates that whether a partner does or does not accompany the woman to the abortion has little effect on her reactions (i.e. does not affect her psychological responses to abortion).

One study that captures contextual elements was conducted by Remennick and Segal (2001) in which they compared the experiences of abortion of native Israeli women and recent immigrant women from the Soviet Union. The research aimed to explore abortion in the context of 'macro-level factors such as legislation, practice and public attitudes towards abortion and micro-level life contexts including reasons for the termination, relationship with the partner, material resources and social support' (Remennick and Segal 2001: 49). The researchers found that intense emotional reactions to abortion were rare. However, women's experiences of abortion, they conclude are 'shaped by both social context and concrete life circumstances' (Remennick and Segal 2001: 49).

The debate over the psychological consequences of abortion is probably going to continue for some time as it is deeply embedded in abortion politics. The weight of expert opinion over the years, however, points to legal abortion not posing a significant threat to mental well-being. In the 1990s a panel commissioned by the American Psychological Association (APA) to investigate the psychological consequences of abortion concluded that 'the weight of evidence from scientific studies indicates that legal abortion of an unwanted pregnancy in the first trimester does not pose a psychological hazard for most women' (Adler et al. 1992: 1194). Various researchers have reached the same conclusion, that 'the existing data point firmly to the conclusion that abortion has fewer existing psychiatric sequelae than childbirth' (Stotland 2001: 27) or 'the emotional well-being of women who abort an unplanned pregnancy does not differ from that of women who carry a pregnancy to term' (Major 2003: 1258). Most recently, the new APA task team on mental health and abortion had this to say:

> A critical evaluation of the published literature revealed that the majority of studies suffered from methodological problems, often severe in nature. . . . The best scientific evidence published indicates that among adult women who have an *unplanned pregnancy* the relative risk of mental health problems is no greater if they have a single elective first trimester abortion than if they deliver that pregnancy. . . . The prevalence of mental health problems observed among women in the United States who had a single, legal, first-trimester abortion for nontherapeutic reasons was consistent with normative rates of comparable mental health problems in the general population of women in the United States.
>
> (Major et al. 2008: 3–4, emphasis in the original)

Young women and abortion

It is against the backdrop of this debate concerning the consequences of abortion, as well as the extensive literature on 'teenage pregnancy', that research on young women who have undergone a termination of pregnancy is conducted. The standard 'teenage pregnancy = social problem' and 'abortion = possible medical and psychological consequences' equations (with the implied threat of social and health degeneration implicit in each) together with the discourse of 'adolescence as transition' set the scene for inquiries into this area.

We saw in Chapter 3 how proponents of compulsory parental consent in young women's decision-making regarding abortion argue their point based on the fact that abortion carries substantially more risks for young women than it does for adults. Therefore, the advice and counselling of an older and wiser person is required. But is this argument a sound one?

Very few studies compare the reactions of teen-aged women with other women. If we want to find out whether abortion is detrimental to the psychological well-being of young women, there are two important groups with whom young women who are terminating a pregnancy should be compared. The first is older women of similar circumstances (socio-economic status, partner support, marriage, number of previous pregnancies). The other is teen-aged women who bear a child and either give the baby for adoption or keep the child. In the latter, the first option (giving the baby up for adoption) is the most useful comparison group because this speaks to the wantedness of the pregnancy.

Some studies do compare younger and older women. However, there are often a number of problems with the research. For example, Franz and Reardon (1992) found that the young women in their study reported a greater degree of psychological stress, more dissatisfaction with their decision to abort and feeling forced by circumstances to have an abortion, than did the older women. However, the sample used was of women who report to support services post-abortion because of negative reactions to the abortion. Thus the study was not representative of the average woman's reaction to abortion. There are also other factors that may affect the relationship between abortion and emotional responses, one of which is marital status. According to Adler et al. (1998) unmarried women are more prone to negative responses following abortion than married women. Therefore, the negative effects that some studies have found among young women in comparison with older women may be owing to the fact that fewer young women are married than older women. If this is the case, then the issue is less one of developmental status and more a relational one.

Adler et al. (2003) report on studies that suggest that, where safe and legal abortion is available, there are no increased risks for young women, compared to adult women, who have undergone a termination of pregnancy. These studies measured the responses of teen-aged and adult women one month post-abortion, and two years post-abortion. While there was little difference between the two groups in terms of depression, self-esteem, anxiety, states of mind or emotional responses, the group of young women did express less satisfaction and benefit from their decision to abort than did the older women, although in absolute terms they were still generally comfortable with their decision (in other words, they were generally positive but less so than the older women). However, these differences decreased over time and in the two-year post-abortion measurement disappeared completely. In other words, the two groups of women expressed similar levels of satisfaction with their decision to abort at this stage.

Studies that compare groups of young women against each other are also few and far between, although the exception is Zabin et al. (1989) who followed 360 young women over two years after they had been interviewed when seeking a pregnancy test. These women were divided into three groups: those who had a negative test, those who were pregnant and carried to term, and those who were pregnant and aborted their pregnancy. Compared to themselves (i.e. from before the abortion to two years later), the young women who had an abortion were significantly less anxious, and had better self-esteem and sense of control over their lives two years after the abortion than before it. Furthermore, compared to the other groups (those who had a negative pregnancy test and those who carried to term) the young women who had an abortion were doing as well as, but usually better than, the other women (negative pregnancy test or carried to term) in terms of levels of anxiety, self-esteem, sense of control, educational and economic status. One possible reason for this is that those young women who abort are ones who actively consider their options and take a decision, whereas some of the young women who carry to term may do so basically by default. In other words, there is no active decision to continue with the pregnancy but rather an inactivity that leads to carrying to term.

Both these forms of comparative data are required if we want to answer the question of whether a termination of pregnancy is more detrimental for younger women than for older women (and therefore the decision requires parental input), and whether a termination of pregnancy is a more traumatic event than carrying an unwanted pregnancy to term. The difficulty with the relative lack of comparative data is that researchers may attribute effects to the age of the young woman when these effects may be owing to some other factor – for instance, degree of social support, number of previous pregnancies, or living in circumstances of poverty.

This lack of comparative data and the tendency to attribute effects to age without full consideration of alternatives rests on the dominant discourse of 'adolescence as transition'. It is exactly because this discourse is so dominant and because of the imaginary wall that it constructs between teen-aged and adult women that it is possible for researchers to continually presume that age rather than anything else is the main cause of young women's experiences of an unwanted pregnancy and abortion.

Indeed the 'adolescence as transition' discourse is taken as the unquestioned, fundamental starting point of much of the South African research on young women and abortion. For example, Geldenhuys and de Lange (2001), at the beginning of their article on black teen-aged women's experience of abortion, state:

> The adolescent's affective development is unstable and variable in nature because they find themselves between the child and adult world.
>
> (Geldenhuys and de Lange 2001: 92, translated from Afrikaans)

They go on to explain their view on 'adolescence'. It is, they state, a time in which the important developmental tasks of the formation of self concept, the development of relationships and responsibility, preparation for a career, emancipation from parents, and adjustments to various aspects of society are undertaken. Olivier et al. (2000: 213), and Olivier and Bloem (2004: 177), similarly state at the beginning of their articles that the teen-aged woman who terminates a pregnancy 'is merely an adolescent'; the adolescent is still 'en route' to, or on the threshold of, adulthood. Adolescents, they state, 'often find themselves belonging nowhere and floating in between childhood and adulthood' (Olivier et al. 2000: 214).

Thus, the understanding of the teen-aged person as going through a stage of transition is taken as a firm basis, the generally acknowledged universal truth, from which these studies proceed. The researchers then use this foundational understanding to intimate, first, that young people are, to start off with, unstable, and, second that abortion is a problematic experience for young people, despite the lack of comparative data.

PAS and the anti-abortion lobby: personal degeneration turned social

Despite the debate concerning research on the psychological consequences of abortion and evidence that points in a contrary direction to the inevitability of psychological consequences, the notion of PAS has taken root in much anti-abortion activism. Hopkins et al. (1996) analyse the ways in which the notion of PAS has assisted in anti-abortion activities in the United Kingdom. The foetal rights campaign, they state, was not winning large numbers of people over to the anti-abortion cause because it inevitably invoked the opposing rights of the woman, leaving a conundrum. This conundrum is resolved by the introduction of PAS into anti-abortion politics.

What PAS does is to construct not only the foetus as the victim but also the woman. The insinuations of therapeutic care in the talk of PAS allow anti-abortion activists to be portrayed as caring and respectful of the woman's experiences. Key to this, however, is the concept of denial contained within PAS. In other words, women who claim that there are no negative consequences are merely suppressing the painful experience. In this way anti-abortionists can declare that most women are adversely affected by abortion (Hopkins et al. 1996).

PAS allows anti-abortionists not only to declare that most abortions are traumatic, but also to construct the foetus as a person. In other words, although the shift from the rights of the foetus to the psychology of the woman appears to move the focus away from the foetus, the relationship that is assumed to exist between the woman and her foetus reintroduces the personhood of the foetus. Recall that Speckhard and Rue's (1992: 105) first component of PAS is 'exposure to or participation in an abortion experience, i.e., the intentional destruction of one's unborn child, which is perceived as traumatic and beyond the range of usual human experience'. 'One's unborn child' immediately assumes a relationship. This relationship is further concretized through the notions of denial and grief. Speckhard and Rue's (1992: 105) second component of PAS is 'uncontrolled negative experiencing of the abortion death event'. Essentially a whole range of experiences and emotions are reformulated as grief. Grief implies a person whose passing is being mourned. Thus the foetus becomes a person who may be grieved (Hopkins et al. 1996).

PAS has become so pervasive in talk about abortion that those dealing with women who have undergone a termination of pregnancy have to find some way of understanding it. Feminist therapists (Rubin and Russo 2004) in the United States have dealt with it in an interesting and subversive way. They argue that abortion, in general, has minimal effects but that some women may find it difficult. However, instead of seeing PAS as an individualized phenomenon, they place it within the social context of its usage. Thus, they recognize that abortion politics, including talk of PAS, makes abortion a more threatening, stressful and stigmatized event than it would otherwise have been. They use this approach in therapy to develop women's coping strategies when dealing with abortion.

The idea of the inevitability of psychological consequences and PAS has been taken up by anti-abortion groups in South Africa as well. The following appears on the Africa Christian Aid website. This organization, based in Cape Town, boasts under its 'Activities' list about organizing the first pro-life demonstrations in South Africa, publishing the first pro-life book in South Africa, and organizing events such as the National Day of Repentance to mark the passing of CTOP Act.

> The physical complications [of abortion], however, are over-shadowed by psychological effects. Guilt, regret, remorse, suicidal impulses, mourning, nightmares, lower self-esteem, anger, rage, hostility, child abuse, despair, helplessness, promiscuity and loss of interest in sex are all documented consequences of abortions. Teenagers (who are less emotionally mature) and those who are ambivalent about the abortion are most likely to suffer psychological consequences. Because of the immediate sense of relief (the 'problem' has gone away) and repression of feelings after an abortion, post-abortion effects often only show up years later when sparked by an incident like the birth of another child. Seeing babies, children, pregnant women and even baby goods advertisements can also trigger a surge of emotion.
>
> (Africa Christian Aid 2003)

Since the passing of the CTOP Act in South Africa, what are called Pregnancy Crisis Centres or Pregnancy Care Centres have sprung up around the country. These centres, often attached to Christian organizations, offer counselling for women who have an unwanted pregnancy, and post-abortion counselling. The counselling with respect to the unwanted pregnancy revolves chiefly around supposed informed consent to abortion. Here there is an emphasis on the (supposed) negative health and psychological consequences of abortion. As the website of the Neobirth Pregnancy

Care Centre (n.d.) states, 'Abortion is not an easy thing to do. It may appear as if it is, but many women find they simply exchange one set of problems for another'.

Despite the fact that the clear message is that abortion is detrimental either psychologically or medically, the fact that these centres do not use an overtly moralistic tone means that they are able to incorporate women who have undergone an abortion into their network of care. On the same Neobirth Pregnancy Care Centre website, we find:

> If you are suffering from the loss of a child from abortion, there is help for you – you don't have to be alone. Neo Birth offers free post-abortion counselling. It takes a lot of courage to come for help. You'll have the opportunity to see someone on a one-to-one basis. You'll be able to tell your story confidentially and gradually work through your feelings such as guilt and shame, grief, anger and depression. You'll be offered help to resolve these things in healthy ways, rather than struggle to keep everything under control.
>
> (Neobirth Pregnancy Care Centre n.d.)

Thus abortion has shifted (at least partially) in the anti-abortion lobby from something that is morally wrong. Although the language of murder and sin still appears in the writing and talk of these activists, there is also a strong emphasis on the inevitable personal degeneration that abortion brings with it. In this way, they (anti-abortionists) are no longer positioned as people opposed to women who find themselves with unwanted pregnancies (i.e. as opposing their rights), but rather on the side of this woman in protecting her from the inevitability of this degeneration or, alternatively, helping her to overcome it.

The supposed personal degeneration that these women undergo has been taken up by anti-abortion activists as a social issue. For example, at a conference held in 2001 by the National Alliance for Life, an umbrella body for twelve pro-life organizations in South Africa, the issue of PAS featured prominently. One of the keynote speakers had this to say:

> Abortion has only been legal in South Africa for a few short years, so you haven't experienced the other side of the coin that we have in America and that is Post Abortion Syndrome both in women and men. The issue of Post Abortion Syndrome has grown so big and so strong that it sometimes seems to eclipse the issue of abortion itself. We have tens of millions of hurting mothers and fathers who mournfully cry out for their wives and their unborn babies that are no more.
>
> (Mattes 2001)

However, some anti-abortion groups believe that South Africa has indeed 'experienced the other side of the coin'. In a call to the members to join the International Life Chain, the African Christian Democratic Party (ACDP) motivated in the following way:

> Since abortion-on-demand was legalized in 1997, over 600,000 pre-born babies have been murdered through abortion. Women are being exploited by being told that this 'right' will make their lives better. Thousands are now suffering from symptoms of Post-Abortion Syndrome such as guilt, grief, nightmares, depression and suicidal tendencies. Most women considering having an abortion are not being told of these possible after-effects or about their alternatives. Sunday, 1st October 2006, is International Life Chain Sunday. Over 1 million Christians in over 900 locations worldwide are expected to stand for the right to life of pre-born babies. Will you be part of this great chain of Christian love and concerns?
> (African Christian Democratic Party 2006)

Thus PAS or the psychological consequences of abortion are no longer a personal or private matter to be faced by an individual woman either in the privacy of her home or in counselling with a sympathetic counsellor at a Pregnancy Care Centre. Rather it becomes an issue affecting the population, a public health problem. When 'tens of millions' or 'thousands' of people are suffering from some ailment, the issue becomes a social one, a public health concern, one that requires some form of action (the action advocated by ACDP is joining the International Life Chain – protest action in the face of the unwillingness of government to take action in the intensely public problem). Abortion no longer poses a threat of simple personal degeneration, but an intensely social degeneration as well. The young pregnant woman poses a threat not only through being pregnant, but also through terminating her pregnancy.

Conclusion

Abortion has been, and in all likelihood will continue to be, one of the most controversial political issues globally. However, the terms of the debate do not remain the same. The early Western feminist concentration on a rights-based approach (emphasizing the rights of women to determine what happens to their bodies) has been criticized by feminists recently. This approach inevitably knocks up against the argument for foetal rights, setting up an unsolvable moral dilemma. Some feminists have argued that we should shift the framework within which we see abortion from one that focuses on 'rights and fairness' to one that emphasizes 'responsibilities and relationships'

(Smyth 2002: 335). In other words, our concern should be less about the masculinist notion of justice and more about care and relatedness.

Much of the lobbying around abortion has centred on public health issues. For example, in South Africa, the work of people like Helen Rees, Rachel Jewkes and colleagues (Rees et al. 1997; Jewkes et al. 2002, 2005) has concentrated on the public health consequences and costs relating to illegal abortion versus legal abortion.

In terms of health issues with respect to abortion, it is clear that legalizing abortion decreases the rates of mortality and morbidity associated with illegal abortion. What is more hotly debated is whether legal abortion has greater health consequences than carrying a pregnancy to term. Although some research points in the direction of greater risk for abortion in some areas, the general consensus is that abortion is in fact safer than carrying a pregnancy to term. The psychological consequences of abortion are, however, somewhat more difficult to pin down. There are vociferous debates in the literature on whether abortion carries the risk of psychological fallout.

Part of the debate concerning the psychological consequences of abortion centres on how the research is conducted. In order for us to say with any kind of certainty that abortion *itself* is the cause of psychological problems among young women, we need to compare young women who undergo abortions with, first, older women of similar circumstances who undergo abortions, and second, with other young women of similar circumstances who have unwanted pregnancies that they take to term. In addition, the pre-pregnancy personal and social functioning of the young women should be considered in making ascriptions of negative psychological consequences.

As we have seen in this chapter, examples of this kind of careful research that separates out the effects of abortion from the effects of an unwanted pregnancy, and provides valid comparisons between groups of women of similar circumstances, are extremely few and far between, in the case of women in general and in the case of teenagers. Where research that does take these issues into account is conducted, the results appear to point to the conclusion reached by the American Psychological Association, namely that legal abortion of an unwanted pregnancy in the first trimester is not psychologically damaging for most women, including teenagers.

Despite this, the idea that abortion will be psychologically traumatic and the proposal of a diagnostic category of PAS has held sway, particularly among anti-abortion groups. This is partially because of the virtual impossibility of designing research in a way that the question of psychological consequences can irrefutably be answered.

PAS allows anti-abortion lobbyists to frame their rhetoric as one of care and concern for the woman. No longer are they people opposing women's rights to terminate a pregnancy. No longer are they the moral police pointing out the moral laxness of abortion. Instead, they are people concerned with the psychological welfare of the woman, people who understand that abortion is intrinsically traumatic, people who care about the inevitable consequences a woman will face should she undergo an abortion. With this as their newfound armour, they are able to incorporate women into their network of care. They are able to point out to those considering abortion that abortion will cause distress and trauma. They are able to argue to those who have terminated a pregnancy that if they do not feel these emotions now, they will at a later date because at the moment they are merely in denial. They are able to position women who have had abortions as victims, as people who, unaware of the psychological consequences of abortion, were convinced by other arguments to proceed. They are able to argue that women will inevitably regret the decision. Finally, they are able to offer assistance, understanding and counselling to these 'victims'.

As stated at the beginning of this chapter, on one level of logic, termination of pregnancy provides the perfect solution to the 'teenage pregnancy = social problem' equation. Young women who terminate their pregnancies will no longer be disrupting their schooling, becoming inadequate mothers or contributing to a cycle of poverty. However, through the positioning of abortion among women in general and among young women specifically as necessarily psychologically traumatic, abortion becomes the new social problem. Although the difficulties are cited as personal ones – i.e. the woman becomes psychologically unstable as an individual – the implication among the anti-abortion groups that this is occurring on a large scale turns it into a public issue that requires political action. Personal degeneration as a result of abortion is turned into social degeneration, and the young woman represents the threat of this social degeneration not only through being pregnant, but also through the possibility of her terminating her pregnancy.

6

OTHERING

Race, culture and 'teenage pregnancy'/abortion

In Chapter 2, we saw how Stanley Hall, the person credited with the invention of 'adolescence' within the United States saw himself as a Darwin of the mind (Moran 2000). In other words, the type of theorizing that characterized evolutionary theory to explain biological phenomena (change over time, mutation and survival of the fittest) was transposed into the social world and used to explain a number of complex social features. In particular, social Darwinism was used to separate out the 'civilized' from the 'savage' races, and to explain why the 'savage' races were on a lower social evolutionary scale than the 'civilized' ones. Sexuality played a particularly important role in this theorizing. For example, Stanley Hall theorized that prolonged chastity was a factor in the evolution of the 'civilized' race while Victorian ethnographers argued that polygamy, promiscuity and incest were part and parcel of the sexual morality of the 'lower' or 'savage' races (Moran 2000).

This kind of social Darwinism was essentially a form 'othering'. Othering is a term utilized in postcolonial theory to describe the processes through which the 'excluded or "mastered" subject is created by the discourse of power' (Ashcroft et al. 2000: 171). Various discourses, such as primitivism, set up the possibility of a separation of the self as the colonizer and the other as the colonized. These discourses allow a number of binaries to operate between the self and other, setting the distinction up as natural, and reinforcing the power of the colonizer. Examples of the kinds of self/other binaries allowed through a discourse of primitivism include: progress/backwardness; rational/ child-like; civilized/primitive; Christian/heathen; developed/developing; sophisticated/savage; knowledgeable/ignorant; refined/barbaric.

Within the theorizing of social Darwinism, race took on a position of particular significance. Historically, 'race' surfaced as a signifier of difference in scientific and philosophical thought in the early nineteenth century. At this time, in which there was significant colonial expansion, the notion of humans representing distinct, primordial groups, characterized by specific physical traits emerged (S. Jones 1997). Race became the repository for representations of difference as biological variance was represented as natural, inherent and unalterable.

The 'scientific' claim of superior and inferior 'races' has largely disappeared. Because of its later unpopularity and the accusation of racism, attempts to scientifically prove differences between races diminished. However, this does not mean that processes of 'othering' diminished. With the disappearance of crude scientific racism, we have the emergence of explanations centred around culture and ethnicity. In the former, biological explanations were sought to explain the social differences between people. In the latter, cultural explanations do the work previously performed by biological explanations. In other words, instead of differences being explained in terms of biological inferiority/superiority, cultural and traditional patterns are used. Culture and tradition allow for particular collectivities to be essentialized and naturalized through an appeal to the past (the myth of origin), and to homogenized social practices (called culture), while at the same time masking the underlying process of 'othering'.

Also in Chapter 2 we saw how the concept of developmental time, and the linkage of 'adolescence' with the development of civilization (ontogeny recapitulates phylogeny) served to perpetuate colonial understandings of the nature of being human. Both 'primitive' societies and young people were implicitly represented as developing towards the desired end-product – the characteristics displayed by the rational, economically active, heterosexual white male. However, the labour that was implied in the movement from one to the other (primitiveness to civilization; childhood to adulthood) meant that there was always a danger of degeneration. The less developed, the more primitive, and especially those who were both primitive *and* immature (and female), were always in danger of disrupting or undermining the stability of those who are developed or civilized.

In this chapter, we shall see how, in discussions concerning 'teenage pregnancy', 'black' and minority group young women emerge as particularly problematic. (In South Africa 'black' people are not in the minority, but are still subjected to subtle (and not so subtle) 'othering' processes. In other parts of the world, such as the United States, 'blacks' (African Americans) do form part of a minority group, along with various 'cultural' groups such as Hispanics.) Despite the movement away from crude and scientific racism, the utilization of the notions of culture, ethnicity and tradition within the literature on 'teenage pregnancy' and abortion continue to position 'black' and minority group teen-aged people as a threat to themselves and to society. My use of examples from South Africa is, of course, particularly pertinent, given its deeply colonial and racialized past. As we shall see below, 'black' teen-aged women are depicted as being the repositories of culture, attitudes, traditions, values, ethnicity and behaviours, all of which are yoked into the explanatory framework of a problematized phenomenon such as 'teenage pregnancy' and abortion.

In these discussions of 'culture' and 'tradition', there is an unstated standard or backdrop against which these 'cultural' patterns are viewed.

'Whites' have a 'way of life', while 'blacks' and minority groups have 'culture'. The rate of 'teenage pregnancy' is low among 'whites', and when it does occur, psychological explanations are invoked. The rate of 'teenage pregnancy' is, on the other hand, high among 'black' and minority group people, with cultural patterns (either direct practices or, contradictorily, the breakdown of culture) being used to explain the occurrence. Thus, although 'black' people are no longer depicted as 'primitive', they are 'cultural'; although 'white' people are no longer depicted as the 'civilized' ones, they are the taken-for-granted standard for correct living. And as these cultural patterns (or the breakdown thereof) lead to the occurrence of the social problem of 'teenage pregnancy' and abortion, the implication of 'degeneration' hangs about like a ghost in the halls of our understanding of young women and reproduction among 'black' people.

In the following, I discuss some of the trends noted concerning race and 'teenage pregnancy' and abortion. This forms the backdrop against which an exploration of how 'race' and social degeneration are connected with respect to 'teenage pregnancy' and abortion. I initially trace the slipperiness of racialized boundaries using the South African context as an example. This is followed by a discussion of how culture is used as an othering process. I indicate how culture is used in contradictory ways to explain social degeneration. In the first instance, culture is viewed as a direct contributory factor in promoting the occurrence of 'teenage pregnancy'. Second, it is the absence or breakdown of culture or acculturation that is seen as causing the problem.

Race and 'teenage pregnancy' and abortion

'Race' is frequently cited as an issue in the research literature on the rates, causes, and consequences of 'teenage pregnancy', teen-aged childbearing and abortion, as the following examples (briefly) illustrate. Writing in the United States, Bryant (2006: 133) declares that, 'With a disproportional rate of Black adolescents becoming pregnant, there is a need to examine factors related to the high adolescent pregnancy rate among the Black community'. The *South African Demographic and Health Survey 2003* (Department of Health [South Africa] 2007) breaks down the rates of 'teenage pregnancy' by what is termed 'ethnic group'. Rates are reported as follows: African: 12.5 per cent; Coloured: 11.7 per cent; Indian: 2.2 per cent; White 2.4 per cent (teenage pregnancy was defined here as women in the age range 15 to 19 years old who had ever been pregnant). Thus, 'race' becomes a key signifier in understanding rates of 'teenage pregnancy'.

The social circumstances of early reproduction are seen as differing depending on race. For example, Forste and Tienda (1992) used the *National Survey of Families and Household* to indicate that 'black' teenage mothers in the United States are less likely to marry and more likely to complete school than are 'white' or 'Hispanic' teenage mothers. Wiemann et al. (2006) found significantly lower levels of support were provided by the fathers of babies born to African American teenagers in comparison to that provided to Mexican American and Caucasian teenagers.

Various explanations regarding the noted 'racial' differences have been proposed. These explanations tend to fall into two distinct camps: one structural and the other cultural. Structural explanations emphasize contextual issues such as socio-economic status, and access to health and education. Thus, for example, early childbearing may be seen as a life-affirming choice or alternative life course for African American and Latina teenagers in the United States in the context of violence, foreshortened healthy life expectancy and economic strain (Jacobs 1994; Geronimus 2003). Cultural explanations tend to emphasize the normative expectations of a group, showing how the general assumption that 'teenage pregnancy' is deleterious may not hold universally. Thus, for example, it is argued that the appropriate age for sexual relations and parenthood are a matter of cultural definition attached to particular socio-historical conditions (such as the history of slavery), with culturally specific normative expectations being transferred intergenerationally (Rhode 1993).

In South Africa, Preston-Whyte and colleagues, who have attempted to understand 'teenage pregnancy' in context, take a cultural approach, suggesting, for example, that the cultural emphasis on fertility among African 'black' people means that early reproduction is not met with the same negative response as it would in the 'white' community. Although theirs is mostly a cultural understanding, they also acknowledge structural constraints. For example, they state:

> Childbirth confers on girls the valued status of motherhood and it may be the pathway to adulthood in cases where marriage is delayed by lack of money, suitable accommodation or the necessity of amassing bridewealth. By having a child a girl realises an important aspect of her femininity.
>
> (Preston-Whyte and Zondi 1991: 1391)

Thus cultural constraints are acknowledged (value of motherhood in achieving adulthood, system of bridewealth) as well as structural ones (economic difficulties and shortage of accommodation). In a later section, I discuss the difficulties potentially (although not necessarily) associated with a 'cultural' approach. But before this, I explore the complexities of the notion of 'race'.

Racialized boundaries

Despite the clear-cut manner in which much social phenomena, including early reproduction and abortion, are spoken about in terms of race, racial categories are, in fact, very slippery. 'Race' is not self-evident, not a contained and easily identifiable taxonomy of difference. Instead 'race' is a slippery and dynamic term that has been used in a range of ways over the years, with the boundaries around particular categories changing.

Take, for example, Apartheid definitions of 'race'. The Population Registration Act (Act No. 30 of 1950), together with Proclamation 123 of 1967, introduced nine categories into which people in the country had to be classified. The main divisions were 'White', 'Black' and 'Coloured'. 'Asians' (who were further subdivided into 'Chinese' and 'Indians') were the main subdivision of 'Coloured'. In terms of the Group Areas Act (Act No. 41 of 1950, as amended), each group was to live in separately allocated areas.

The definitions of the various groups seemed clear cut, and was accepted by many as a realistic means of distinguishing between the various groups in South Africa. However, there were always a significant number of people who defied classification or who were reclassified into a different category. The efforts by Apartheid officials to find the correct category for people became legendary. Deborah Posel (2001) describes some:

> Some officials read racial differences into the texture of a person's hair, the notorious pencil test being used to determine the boundary between 'white' and 'non-white' [the pencil test consisted of inserting a pencil into the hair of the person; if the pencil fell out, the person was declared 'white'; if it did not, then they were 'coloured' or 'black']. Appeal boards adjudicating requests for reclassification sometimes called barbers to testify as to the texture of the person's hair. For others, it was a matter of the pallor of a person's skin 'a shiny face being the emblem of continuity of race', or the feel of an ear-lobe ('softer in natives than in Coloureds') or the appearance of the cheekbones (high cheekbones being seen as a sign of a Coloured). One official insisted he could 'tell a Coloured with absolute certainty by the way he spits'. . . . At other times, various 'stigmata' of race were invoked as in 'the eyelid test' or 'the nail test', or in the examination of genitalia. . . . All in all, almost any aspect of a person's size or shape was potentially a signifier of race, in unpredictable and idiosyncratic ways.
>
> (Posel 2001: 59)

One of the dominant ways in which race was spoken about during Apartheid was in terms of 'white' and 'non-white'. Those old enough will remember the infamous signs posted on various public amenities indicating that the use of the amenity in question was for 'whites only' or for 'non-whites only'.

These distinctions were used in the early literature on 'teenage pregnancy' in South Africa. For example, De Villiers and Clift (1979: 196) report on a study conducted on what they called 'non-white girls' and Prinsloo (1984: 699) states that 'Illegitimacy rates remain high in the non-White groups'. Thus, 'white' (the self) was what all else was defined against. All 'others' were homogenized into a non-specific (and in South Africa denigrated) 'non-white' form.

The homogenization of 'other races' against the backdrop of 'whiteness' is not unique to South Africa. For example, Henshaw (1993) reported on the rates of pregnancy, birth and abortion among US teenagers by race, using the categories of 'white' and 'non-white' as signifiers. Henshaw (1993: 125) states that, 'For the United States as a whole, the pregnancy, birth and abortion rates among women aged 15–19 were two or more times as high among nonwhites as among whites'. Thus, not only are 'non-whites' homogenized against 'white', but also what is 'white' is taken as the benchmark against which the rates of pregnancy of the 'other' is measured.

Despite forming the backdrop against which the 'non-white' is defined, 'white' has not always been considered a single race. In Europe's history those currently defined as 'white' were previously categorized as belonging to different races (Miles 1989). The construction of 'white' as a separable race had much to do with colonialism and, in South Africa, Apartheid. The emphasis on being 'white' in South Africa represented a move to politically unite Afrikaans- and English-speaking people of European descent (Stadler 1987).

Other than the Indian, Coloured and African distinctions that were made with respect to the 'non-white' in South Africa, a further gradation of racial categories was introduced with the notion of ethnicity. The concept of ethnicity gained currency in political and academic language in the 1950s and 1960s. In South Africa the 'African' population was no longer seen as one race comprising of different tribes, but rather, as stated in the *South African Yearbook of 1976*, as 'separate ethnic groups, each with its own language, legal system, life-style, values and socio-political identity' (cited in Sharp 1988: 112). Academically, there was an increase in the number of international journal articles and index entries concerned with ethnicity (S. Jones 1997). The surge in interest in ethnicity represented a shift in classificatory terminology because of the increasingly pejorative connotations of the existing taxonomic categories which centred chiefly on race.

The shift to describing patterns in terms of ethnicity instead of race is evident in the South African literature on teenage pregnancy. For example, Garenne et al. (2000) describe the participants in their study as belonging to the Shangaan ethnic group. Eaton et al. (2003) summarize research conducted on the sexual behaviour of youth in South Africa. In a table in which the social demographics of participants used in the various studies are described, they use signifiers such as 'White', 'Black', 'Indian', 'English', 'Afrikaans', 'Xhosa', 'Coloured', 'Asian' and 'Zulu'. As this is a summary of other research, one assumes that the signifiers used are those specified by the researchers whose studies are included in the table. What is interesting in the context of this discussion is that Eaton et al. (2003) specify under some of the studies: 'all ethnicities included' or 'ethnicity not specified'. Their analysis of the table leads them to conclude that 'Black (African) youth are more likely to start sexual activity in their teens than are other ethnic groups' (Eaton et al. 2003: 151). 'Ethnicity' thus becomes the dominant signifier in terms of describing groupings of people and their sexual and reproductive behaviour.

Again this is not unique to South Africa. As discussed above, Henshaw (1993) reported on the rates of pregnancy, birth and abortion among teenaged women in the United States in 1988 in terms of 'white' and 'non-white'. Some time later, Henshaw and Feivelson (2000: 272) reported on similar statistics collected in 1996, but in a slightly different manner: 'Teenage abortion rates according to state of residence, race and ethnicity were calculated'. Thus a level of refinement was introduced into the analysis through the notion of ethnicity. However, the authors were then forced to grapple with the slipperiness of the categories they invoked: 'Racial categories other than black and white are not shown separately because of the small size and heterogeneity of these populations. Hispanics may be of any race, and the figures for whites include the majority of Hispanics'. Their solution is to assign race and ethnicity differentially, as in: 'Teenagers having abortions were distributed by race and Hispanic ethnicity' (Henshaw and Feivelson 2000: 272 and 273).

The type of racialized boundary shifting described above has to do with social politics of the time. What remains constant, however, is how, as Rattansi (1994) states, the drawing and redrawing of these boundaries take place chiefly within 'minority' communities in relation to 'white' groups. In other words, the categories within the 'non-white' get further and further refined, with 'white' remaining as the backdrop, the normalized landscape against which the peculiarities of other 'ethnic' groups are etched.

The reproduction and maintenance of racialized and ethnicized boundaries (albeit in slippery ways) against the backdrop of 'white' normalcy allows for 'race' or ethnicity to be used as an explanatory tool in the investigation of medical, psychological or social deviance. Consider, for example, the following extracts, taken from a research report on teenage pregnancy in South Africa:

> The apparent association between race or ethnicity and [the] tendency for teenagers . . . of African descent to give birth to smaller infants than their counterparts of other ethnic origins is well documented but not satisfactorily explained.

> A higher frequency of contracted or inadequate pelvis among Black patients was found by Off et al. (1985) . . . They contend, on

the basis of forensic data that, '. . . a narrower pelvic girdle (for equivalent body size) is a racial characteristic of blacks' . . . before qualifying that this need not imply greater risks as Black women tend to have smaller neonates than White women.

(Boult and Cunningham 1993: 52 and 22)

The anatomical identity of the 'black' woman is defined in these extracts as deviant. Her pelvis is contracted or inadequate, the implicit comparison being the white woman's pelvis, which presumably is adequate. Note how these adjectives stand despite the anatomical identity of small pelvis not meaning any greater danger in birth. The 'black' woman gives birth to smaller babies than women from 'other ethnic' groups. The assumption is that 'other ethnic' group babies are normal-sized, making 'black' babies small (if black babies were normal, other babies would be large).

Later in this chapter we shall see how this tendency – defining 'blacks' or minority groups against the normal backdrop of 'whites' – is taken up in the language of culture. We see how 'whites' have a 'way of life' and 'blacks' and minority groups have 'culture', in the same way that 'whites' have normal pelvises and babies, and 'blacks' have inadequate ones. I argue that it is precisely this (the definition of the 'black' or minority groups against the backdrop of the 'white') that allows for the ghost of the threat of degeneration to continue to plague our understandings of 'teenage pregnancy' and abortion in relation to young 'black' women.

Culture, young women, 'teenage pregnancy', abortion and degeneration

As noted earlier, what has been termed scientific racism has largely disappeared from academic discussions. Instead, social scientists tend to concentrate on culture, attempting to understand the influence of culture on social phenomena. However, 'culture' is a difficult concept, defying easy definition, and being used in a number of ways in theorizing about people and their world. In the first part of this section I trace some of the ways of looking at culture, utilizing the discipline of psychology as an example. Although there is potential for culture to be studied in a dynamic and complex manner, much work in the area of 'teenage pregnancy' and abortion treats culture as a static and homogenous entity.

Following on from this I explore how, in discussing 'teenage pregnancy' and abortion, 'black' and minority group people are foregrounded as having 'culture' while 'white' people are the taken-for-granted, the backdrop against which the exotic practices and ways of being of 'blacks' and minority groups are etched. In this 'culture' is treated in two ways. In the first, 'culture' is seen as having a direct influence on promoting conditions that lead to the social problem of 'teenage pregnancy' and abortion and to the negative consequences thereof. In the second, it is the breakdown of culture, its lack, that is responsible for the degeneration of teenagers and society into a poor state of affairs.

How we understand 'culture'

'Culture' has proved to be a complex and slippery term in the social and health sciences. In the following I trace some of the ways in which 'culture' has been dealt with in psychology as a discipline by way of example of some of the difficulties that may arise. Of course these difficulties and complexities are not unique to psychology (see, for example, Harding's (2006) discussion of the theorization of culture in sociology).

One of the first ways in which 'culture' featured in psychology was through what is called cross-cultural psychology. The aim here was (and is) to test and interpret differences between various populations in the performance of psychological tests and tasks. In other words, cross-cultural psychologists are interested in measuring the internal processes and mechanisms of individuals and making a comparison between populations of different cultures. Thus, 'culture' is treated as a bounded entity, a variable in the search for similarities and differences in the performance of particular tests. People belonging to a certain 'culture' are seen as being clearly discernible, and applying tests or measures to a number of people within this 'culture' is viewed as revealing tendencies or patterns within the 'culture'. 'Culture', thus, was first used in psychology as a static and homogenizing concept.

This understanding of 'culture' as a bounded entity is in evidence in some of the research on 'teenage pregnancy'. For example, Russell et al. (2004) state:

> Research on Hispanic cultural values, attitudes and behaviours that influence sexual and contraceptive behaviour has shown that sexuality is often a taboo subject and that parental communication regarding sexuality is often lacking in Hispanic homes. At the same time, Hispanic culture supports early and high fertility, as well as the belief that early motherhood and continued education are incompatible. These cultural values may explain why Hispanic women desire marriage and children at a younger age than do blacks, Southeast Asians and whites. In addition, Mexican Americans are more likely than whites to believe that marriage affirms one's womanhood. Although Hispanics have more conservative attitudes toward sexuality than whites or blacks, they are more likely to enter sexual relations at a young age.
>
> (Russell et al. 2004: 142–143)

We see here the clear delimitation of various cultural groups: Hispanic, black, white, Southeast Asian, Mexican American. The delimitation of these into specific bounded entities allows for the measurement of values, attitudes and behaviours among these various groups. Comparison of the results allows for particular groups (in this case Hispanics) to be positioned as lacking or as engaging in problematic practices.

The difficulty with this rendition of 'culture' – as a bounded entity, the characteristics of which may be measured and described – is that the boundaries are slippery (in much the same way as the boundaries around racial categories are slippery). For example, the above-mentioned authors concede that 'the experiences and expressions of these dimensions of traditional Hispanic culture vary significantly according to country of origin, economic status, immigrant status and acculturation; traditional Hispanic values are strongest among those who are least acculturated in the United States' (Russell et al. 2004: 143). Thus, despite the delimitation of a specific cultural group, the authors admit that within this group there are multiple variations.

Cultural psychologists, who distinguish themselves from cross-cultural psychologists, have attempted to rescue the concept of culture from this static, bounded version. 'Culture', they believe, is useful in understanding the various ways of being human, but not if it is conceptualized in the way described above. They argue that culture is a dynamic, complex phenomenon. In the words of Shweder (1991), one of the leading cultural psychologists:

> Cultural psychology is the study of the ways subject and object, self and other, psyche and culture, person and context, figure and ground, practitioner and practice, live together, require each other, and dynamically, dialectically and jointly make each other up.
>
> (Shweder 1991: 73)

In this way the interaction between self and culture is recognized. Culture is seen as being constructed through the ways in which people make meaning, use resources and interact. On the other hand, individuals, in the process of making meaning within a particular cultural setting, will come to understand and interact with the world in particular ways. What should be highlighted here is the dynamic and changing nature of culture and people's intersection with it. Cultural psychologists view the dialectical relationship referred to above as a complex one that is fluid, and variable across time and place.

Of course, there is substantial debate about the most useful way of theorizing this dynamic interaction. As Bhatia and Stam (2005: 419) state in a special edition of the journal *Theory and Psychology* devoted to 'Critical engagements with culture and self', 'Theorizing the relationship between self and culture remains both a vexing and relevant question. . . . Both "self" and "culture" are contested topics'. One of the vexing problems within cultural psychology is to account for the power relations implicit in the range of social asymmetries (such as gender and class) that permeate our lives.

The careful reflection evident in cultural psychology is frequently absent in psychology texts. Frequently, a split between 'self' and 'culture' is assumed, with culture being something out there, something in the public domain that has its own set of rules and properties. The self, on the other hand, is seen as a private entity with internal processes that are not immediately discernible and that are separate from the outside world (McHoul and Rapley 2004). The result of this is that culture takes on the status of an explanatory tool. In other words, 'culture' can start doing things, causing certain things to happen. This, together with the tendency of culture to be used exclusively when describing minority groupings or, in South Africa, 'black' people (in other words as a code-word for race), allows for concerns around racial of cultural degeneration to covertly slip into discussions on issues such as 'teenage pregnancy' and abortion.

Indeed, in my analysis of the South African literature on 'teenage pregnancy' and abortion, I found that 'culture' was frequently treated in exactly the manner described in the last paragraph. 'Cultures' are seen as neatly bounded entities which are self-contained and self-regulating. They are attributed subject status with the power to influence or even determine events. For example:

> Cultural as well as peer group pressures also *play a role* in teenage pregnancies.
>
> (Ntombela 1992: 12, emphasis added)

> This difference does not necessarily mean that the boyfriends' support [for the pregnant teenagers] is weaker than girlfriends', but this aspect is also culturally *determined*.
>
> (Tanga 1991: 88, emphasis added)

> Pregnant adolescents are not *supported* in the black culture because a girl that has never given birth may not socialise with pregnant girls because she may teach the other girls how to fall pregnant.
>
> (Jali 2006: 12, emphasis added)

'Culture' is portrayed in these extracts, written fourteen years apart, as something that exerts pressure, determines outcomes, excludes and supports. It is rendered real by the ascription of a wholeness which affects people's actions and beliefs. It is held accountable for teenagers becoming pregnant, for differences in social support, and for lack of social support. However,

102

'culture' is not only something that does things, something that performs actions accountable for certain social problems, but also something that minority groups or 'black' people possess, rather than 'white' people.

Minority groups and 'blacks' have culture and 'whites' a way of life

In their work in Aotearoa/New Zealand, Wetherell and Potter (1992) found a difference of how the term 'culture' was deployed in talk by Pakeha (people of European descent) concerning Maori politics and affairs. Pakeha were portrayed as having 'civilization', a 'mundane, technical and practical outlook' (Wetherell and Potter 1992: 135), but not culture. When they were depicted as having culture, it was the 'high' culture of operas, novels and art. On the other hand, 'culture' was referred to in two senses with respect to the Maori. The first was culture as 'heritage': a set of traditions, rituals and values passed from one generation to another. The second concerned culture as 'therapy', in which it was suggested that young Maoris needed to rediscover their culture in order to become 'whole' again.

This rendition of culture is evident in the South African literature on 'teenage pregnancy' and abortion. For example,

> It is however with much disgrace that the cultural values of the African people were perceived to be inferior and on the other hand the western way of life which was seen to be superior did not bring a substitute for the social structures that were broken.
>
> (Mkhize 1995)

Thus 'Africans' have 'culture' whereas the 'westerners' have a 'way of life'. 'Westerners' constitute society, the common sense against which the cultural peculiarities of 'Africans' are etched. The above statement draws on the 'therapy' construction identified by Wetherell and Potter (1992) above. In other words, it is a valorization of African practices that are held in contradistinction with Western practices.

There has been some debate in the postcolonial literature concerning the notion of the 'indigenous'. It is recognized by many that the concept of a pure, indigenous African identity was essential to much of the anti-colonialist and anti-Apartheid movement. However, its shortcomings have also been pointed out, in particular the myth of origin and the essentialization and homogenization of African culture (as seen in the above quote).

While this debate is interesting, what interests us here rather is how, in positioning Maori or African 'culture' against the supposed neutral background of 'whiteness', certain suggestions of degeneration are made. Geldenhuys and de Lange's (2001) article on the 'black' teen-aged women's experience of abortion provides a good example. They interviewed a small sample of women presenting at a Termination of Pregnancy Clinic. In their results, they identify an inadequate parent–child relationship and an inadequate relationship with the 'baby's father' as features of the young women they interviewed. What they fail to do is to spell out exactly what an 'adequate' relationship is – the standard against which these young women may be evaluated as lacking. It is the taken-for-granted, something that Geldenhuys and de Lange (2001) presume the reader understands. It needs no further explication.

This may sound like a reasonable conclusion based on the data. However, what does become clear is the racialization that infuses this judgement. Following an extract from two of the participants, in which they (the participants) express concern about their parents hearing about the pregnancy, Geldenhuys and de Lange (2001) state:

> Viljoen (1994:82) [who investigates the strengths and weaknesses in the family life of black South Africans] asserts that this [inadequate relationships] can point to black parents' poor involvement in the primary socialization of their children and also to poor support of their children's personal problems.
> (Geldenhuys and de Lange 2001: 94, translated from Afrikaans)

From a sample of nine young women, Geldenhuys and de Lange (2001) suddenly jump to the entire black population. In this statement (whether or not it is an accurate reflection of what Viljoen did actually say), black parents become pathologized – people who are (en masse it would appear) not involved with the primary socialization or support of their children. Apart from the manner in which this homogenizes all black people, there lurks in the background a particular (white) standard of involvement in child socialization and provision of support which, it is implied, is normal. Also in the background stalks the ghost of degeneration – if 'black' parents are not involved in socializing their children and if they provide poor support to their children, what can be expected of the next generation of 'black' people? And what does this mean for our 'normal' (white) standard of living?

Culture, or lack of culture, as directly linked to difficulties

'Culture' is used in contradictory ways in the explanation of the 'social degeneration' that 'teenage pregnancy' implies. On the one hand, it is implicated directly in the problem: cultural ways of doing things contribute to the social problem of 'teenage pregnancy'. On the other hand, it is rather the lack of culture or the breakdown thereof that is held accountable for difficulties.

In the following quotes from the South African literature, we see how 'culture' is implicated in contributing to the social problem of 'teenage pregnancy':

> This last objection [to contraceptives] . . . deserves attention. It is an inherent part of a set of interlocking cultural values which we have already met in this chapter. These are: the love of, and desire for, children, either within marriage or outside it; and the emphasis on, indeed approval and encouragement of, active male sexuality. Both derive from the paramount importance which is placed on fertility. . . . This value underlies, and makes understandable, the refusal of parents to allow young girls access to easy contraception.
>
> (Preston-Whyte and Zondi 1992: 236)

> The high value placed on children in African culture further increases the risk of teenage pregnancy.
>
> (Hann 2005: 34)

> The 'fertility conundrum', whereby girls have to demonstrate their fertility before marriage, is evident in many African cultures, and further perpetuates the early age of sexual activity among youth.
>
> (Frank et al. 2008: 394)

'Cultural' values such as an emphasis on fertility and active male sexuality are invoked in these extracts as reasons for pregnancies among young women. This ascription is not unique to South Africa, however. Recall, for example, Russell et al.'s (2004: 142) statement cited above that 'Hispanic culture supports early and high fertility'.

In contrast to this, it is the 'breakdown of culture' that is used to explain the difficulty of 'teenage pregnancy' or the accompanying lack of marriage.

> Rapid urbanization and westernization has eroded many of the traditional norms and values of the black family in Africa and South Africa. The percentage of out of wedlock births has grown steadily during the past 30 years in South Africa.
>
> (Boult and Cunningham 1992: 161)

> The overwhelming behavioural cause identified by most analysts for increased fertility is modernization. This has caused both an erosion of traditional values and controls and the introduction of new values and norms, such as equal sex roles, postponement of early marriage and non-virginity prior to marriage.
>
> (Preston-Whyte 1991: 10)

> In the traditional African culture, when young girls fell pregnant, they would be expected to marry immediately to avoid any humiliation for the family. In all participants' cases nothing was said of plans to get married as a result of the pregnancies.
>
> (Temba 2007: 76)

In these extracts, it is the breakdown or 'erosion' of 'traditional' culture, through such things as urbanization, modernization and Westernization, that is seen as contributing to social degeneration. Traditional values and norms are juxtaposed with urban, modern and Western ones, with the assumption that they are mutually exclusive and that movement towards the urban or the modern necessarily entails an erosion of the social cohesion implied by the 'traditional'. The erosion leads to social degeneration of two types. First, it leads to increased early fertility through lack of the normative function of 'traditional' values and control. Second, it contributes to the problem of out-of-wedlock pregnancy and childbearing, as stated very straightforwardly in the third extract above.

Seeing culture as being eroded or broken down is, of course, possible only when culture is viewed as a static entity, as something that homogenizes people into a particular group and gives them identity. What is interesting about this rendition is that it is seen as 'erosion' rather than 'progression' (i.e. to a more civilized state). Progression or development implies forward or positive movement. The manner in which 'culture' and 'tradition' are depicted here (as protecting or preserving good values that exclude the possibility of early fertility) precludes the implication of forward movement.

It seems that this notion of the erosion of culture through Westernization, urbanization and modernization is enabled in colonialized contexts such as South Africa. In my reading of the literature I have not come across such a notion outside of these sorts of contexts. However, the idea of 'acculturation', while possibly more subtle, has similar implications.

Acculturation has been utilized in the American literature to explain, among other things, the onset of sexual intercourse (Adam et al. 2005), birth outcomes and family planning compliance (M. Jones et al. 2001). Exactly how acculturation is measured differs. For example, Adam et al. (2005) utilized language as a proxy for acculturation, with Hispanic participants who indicated that they spoke English most of the time being seen as acculturated. Jones et al. (2001) utilized the Acculturation Rating Scale for Mexican Americans II (ARSMAII). This scale consists of two subscales of Anglo Orientation and Mexican Orientation. Participants' scores are ranked on five levels: 1 = very Mexican oriented; 2 = Mexican oriented to approximately balanced bicultural; 3 = slightly Anglo oriented bicultural; 4 = strongly Anglo oriented; 5 = very assimilated, Anglicized.

These studies draw on an established field of acculturation psychology. This domain of study fits neatly with the cross-cultural psychology paradigm described above. Cultures are treated as definable, measurable entities. Critique from within the paradigm deals with refining the concepts used in the field as well as the rating scales (Rudmin and Ahmadzadeh 2001).

Three problems arise with the notion of 'acculturation'. First, culture, because it can be measured and people assigned into categories based on performance on a scale, is seen as a bounded and static entity that changes only when in contact with other definable cultures. Given this, people possess a certain culture or mix of cultures like they own clothes or a house. Second, there is an implicit assumption that the dominant culture (e.g. Anglo Orientation) remains static or unintegrated. It is the 'others' who assimilate or acculturate to the assumed dominant culture, rather than the other way around. The infiltration of cultural metaphors and under-standings from the assumed 'other' culture into the assumed dominant culture is overlooked. Third, the multiplicity of and contradictions con-tained within cultures (in particular the assumed dominant one) are, for the most part, ignored.

Acculturation is used as an explanation for difficulties noted among young people with respect to sexual and reproductive health. In South Africa, Ntombela (1992: 4) notes, 'It appears that acculturation is also a factor contributing to teenage pregnancy'. Adam et al. (2005: 261) argue from the United States that, 'Low acculturation emerges as a significant protective factor [for early onset of sexual intercourse]'. This rendition draws on the 'culture as therapy' discourse as discussed above. For example, Jones et al. (2001: 84) state that, 'As they [Mexican Americans] become fully acculturated to US cultural values and norms, which include increased tobacco and alcohol use and nonnutritious food consumption, they exhaust Mexican cultural assets that support health'. Thus 'traditional' culture (something that the 'others' possess) is seen as protective and as an asset that, once lost, leads to problems.

Conclusion

In previous chapters we saw how the invention of 'teenage pregnancy' led to the possibility of young women's reproduction being seen as a social problem suitable for scientific investigation. The invention of 'teenage pregnancy' is possible only in the context of 'adolescence' being viewed as a period of transition between childhood and adulthood. With this under-standing of the less developed moving to a more developed state, comes the possibility of a threat of degeneration – the less developed, through their actions threaten the developed. In this chapter, we have seen how this threat of degeneration is not colour or 'culture' blind. It is particular teenagers who actually pose the threat – to be specific 'black' or minority status teenagers, people who, owing to their status of 'other', are easy to position as outside of the framework of 'self' or 'normality'.

The research on 'teenage pregnancy' and abortion is not neutral with respect to how young women are treated. Explanations for the occurrence of 'teenage pregnancy' among 'whites' are usually psychological in nature, while socio-cultural explanations are invoked for its occurrence among 'black' or minority group teenagers. This is because of the manner in which 'culture' is frequently dealt with in the social science and health literature. Using a static, homogenizing understanding of 'culture', much work positions (mostly without intent) 'whites' or 'Anglos' as the taken-for-granted, the backdrop against which the practices of 'black' or minority group people are to be viewed.

Despite the fact that there are contradictions in the manner in which 'culture' is treated (on the one hand, culture is the cause of the problem; on the other hand, it is the lack of culture or acculturation that is the cause of the problem), attributing 'culture' or tradition to 'black' people allows for the intersection of the primitive/civilized, child/adult to reassert itself. The threat of degeneration centres on the primitive threatening civilization and the less developed in age-threatening developed adult society. In the ascription of 'culture' to 'blacks' or minority group people, with 'whites' as the taken-for-granted, the intersection of these two planes of threat of degeneration reconnect, creating a double difficulty for young women who are categorized as 'black' or as minority group.

7

MANAGING THE THREAT OF DEGENERATION

Towards the beginning of the SABC's *Special Assignment* programme on young women and abortion, a pre-termination of pregnancy counselling session between a nurse and a 17-year-old woman is featured. According to the CTOP Act, the state should provide counselling both before and after a termination of pregnancy, but this counselling should not be mandatory nor should it be directive. The camera is placed strategically so that the identity of the young woman requesting the termination of pregnancy is not revealed. What one does get is an excellent view of the nurse, including her facial expressions and body language. The following is a written rendition of the session, focusing on the language and bodily expressions of the nurse (N stands for nurse, W for the young woman and Nar for narrator):

N: What can I do for you today?
W: I'm about 17 and I'm pregnant. I didn't plan it. I need help. I need an abortion.
N: Were you using contraceptives? [The camera zooms in on a couple of packets of contraceptive pills followed by a poster on how to use a condom]
W: Yes, I was using condoms. When I fell pregnant, I was using condoms and it burst.
N: The constitution allows you to terminate at any time you wish but it is your responsibility to look after yourself because, you know, these days with this pandemic of AIDS and HIV you've got to look after yourself. So, still, on that note, we don't just start by advising you just to terminate. Maybe you can start by considering other options, e.g. adoption. How about that? [At this point the nurse leans forward, smiling and raising her eyebrows in encouragement]
W: I don't think I can opt for adoption. The problem is I don't think I can take being pregnant. I'm still young. No, I don't think I can do that.
Nar: *TOP is a process. This pre-counselling session is the first step.*

N: You can still study and still there are grants, the government is giving grants. How about that? [Again the encouraging look which disappears on the young woman's refusal]

W: I do understand all these things, but my problem is being pregnant at this age. I didn't plan this. I'm not ready to hold it.

N: Okay.

Nar: *This girl is 17, she is doing her second year at Limpopo University [there is probably some error here as being 17 in the second year of university seems unlikely]. It seems nothing the nurse says will get her to change her mind.*

N: There could be perforation of the uterus whilst we do the procedure. Maybe we might pierce through your uterus and then that would warrant you to be hospitalized, *ne?* And I'm afraid if you're a minor and you didn't involve your parents, what are they gonna say? Do you think it is now the time when you have to involve them?

W: I do see that but if I can involve the parents it will be a big problem.

N: [The nurse capitulates, although her body language indicates that this was not her preferred option] Okay, seeing that you have a right and the constitution allows you, I have no choice.

Nar: *The TOP Act says that medical staff must advise a minor to consult her parents before a pregnancy is terminated. It also says that an abortion can't be refused if a minor chooses not to consult them.*

N: You are ready to sign. [Young woman signs documents]

Nar: *With the signature the girl has sealed her fate. It's time to insert the pills that will force her womb open and cause bleeding. Visible blood is a sign that abortion is taking place, that the girl won't have to see her pregnancy through.*

(*Special Assignment* and SABC)

Later, while the camera pans in on an abortion procedure in which groans from the young woman lying on the bed are audible, the narrator states:

Nar: *Sisters just don't seem to have time to talk about complications that may arise during the procedure. In fact it is debatable whether short counselling sessions can empower girls to make such life changing decisions.*

This interaction is obviously a staged performance for a camera, and should not be taken as an example of everyday counselling sessions. What the transcript does tell us, however, is the taken-for-granted assumption by the presenters of the programme that a service provider's task is to manage risk. The narrator laments the fact that the counselling sessions are so short, that the space for the presentation of 'complications' and persuasion is truncated. In the staged performance, we see how the nurse lectures the young woman on her responsibilities, assumes that she had not thought through the decision to terminate her pregnancy, attempts to cajole her into options other than a termination of pregnancy and uses scare tactics in an attempt to get the young woman to involve her parents. Termination of pregnancy is presented as a negative occurrence that requires some kind of intervention in order to avert the risk of medical and psychological damage.

It is easy, perhaps, to judge this rendition of a counselling session. The nurse in the scene possibly goes a bit overboard. But we must recognize that she and the presenters of the programme are operating within the dominant discourses of, first, the threat of degeneration caused by 'teenage pregnancy' and termination of pregnancy, and second, of 'adolescents' as in need of assistance owing to their going through a transitional stage. Nurses are charged, through their positioning as health experts, with managing the risk of this young woman engaging in an activity that she will later regret, and the possibility that she has made the decision without proper forethought.

Nurses are not alone in this. There are a large number of experts, in the form of educators, health service providers, social workers and psychologists, whose task it is to manage risk in relation to the sexual and reproductive habits of young people. It is to this management of risk that I turn in this chapter.

One of the components of the management of risk is the expert calculating the possibility of a negative occurrence. For example, in the case of young women, sexuality and reproduction, the expert may calculate, based on her developmental status, that, first, when engaging in sex, the young woman may be careless about contraception (negative occurrence); or second, if she is a mother, she may neglect her children (negative occurrence); or third, if she decides to have an abortion, she may feel traumatized (negative occurrence). As seen in this book, the calculation of negative occurrences is easy to make with regard to young women and reproductive issues based on the young women's developmental status as an 'adolescent'. This is not because these calculations (that young women are at higher risk of negative occurrences with respect to reproductive issues than older women) are necessarily accurate – as we have seen younger and older women in similar social circumstances tend to have similar outcomes in terms of reproduction. Rather it is because the dominant discourse of 'adolescence as transition' predefines young people as vulnerable and as potentially engaging in behaviour that threatens self and society.

Having calculated the possibility of negative occurrences, experts are tasked with instituting interventions that reduce the possibility of the negative occurrence. They must prevent the negative occurrence by assisting the vulnerable individual in avoiding particular events and by creating circumstances that protect the vulnerable individual. In the place of the negative occurrence, they must promote well-being. To do this, they must identify vulnerable individuals – the ones likely to succumb to external or internal forces that lead to the negative occurrence.

In the following, I discuss the various components of the management of risk, namely managing a vulnerable person (component one) who potentially will be exposed to or engage in an event (component two) that results in a negative occurrence (component three). I explore how the calculation of risk infuses the talk of health service providers whose task it is to assist young women in sexual and reproductive matters. Finally, I discuss interventions aimed at managing the risk of young people engaging in risky sexual behaviour. To do this, I turn to the recommendations made by some South African authors with respect to sex education. These authors researched abortion among young women, and made these recommendations in order assist in preventing abortion among young people.

The management of risk

'Risk' has become an increasingly popular word in public health discussions (Moreira 2007). Public health is an approach to health that considers the overall health of a population. It analyses illness and disease patterns within a community and institutes measures to reduce the prevalence (numbers of cases) and incidence (number of new cases) of an illness in that community. As part of the analysis of illness patterns, public health specialists analyse the possibility of an illness occurring, i.e. the risk factors. On the basis of this calculation (the probability of some illness or negative health event occurring), measures to manage the risk are suggested.

There are a number of aspects to risk. First, risk clearly is associated with threat. A threat of some difficulty arising is identified. The threat is not the actual illness, but is rather attached to a potential event that may lead to the health problem. Second, there is a vulnerability or susceptibility on the part of a person to succumb to the threat. Third, the actual occurrence of the threat will have an impact on not only the vulnerable person's life but also on the common good.

Let us make this more specific to the case of 'teenage pregnancy' and abortion by citing a number of examples that illustrate the risk scenarios. First, there is the threat that an ill-informed teenager (vulnerable person) will engage in unprotected sex (event) that will lead to pregnancy, which in turn will lead to obstetric difficulties (individual risk) that need to be cared for in state hospitals (public risk). Second, there is the threat that a pregnant teenager (vulnerable person) will decide without the assistance of her parents to have an abortion (event) leading to psychological problems (individual risk) and the need for counselling (public risk). Third, there is the threat that a childbearing teenager (vulnerable person) will not return to school (event), thereby becoming poorer herself (individual risk) and contributing to cycle of poverty in the country (public risk). Fourth, there is the threat that the young mother's child (vulnerable person) will be neglected or under-stimulated by his/her mother (event) thereby leading to later behavioural and learning difficulties (individual risk) that require remedial assistance in school (public risk).

Once a potential risk has been identified and the likelihood and impact thereof analysed, the next step in the process is to institute procedures to manage the risk. For example, in the examples cited above, sex education may be implemented to assist the ill-informed teenager in avoiding the occurrence of the event. When pregnancy does occur, regular antenatal visits are encouraged to avoid the risk of obstetric consequences. When abortion is being considered, counselling is instituted to assist in ameliorating any negative psychological effects. When the young woman bears a child, input on parenting skills, and encouraging her to return to school are seen as offsetting any negative economic or emotional impact for her and her child.

Two people stand out in the implementation of strategies to manage risk. One is the expert who implements the interventions and the other is the vulnerable person as the target of the interventions. The expert, in monitoring the possibility of risk and in implementing interventions that ameliorate the risk, becomes the protector of both the individual and the common good. Thus, his/her actions are instituted as a matter of national as well as individual concern. The expert becomes the insurer of the physical, emotional and social well-being of the 'adolescent' and her child, as well as the protector of the common good.

As Ewald (1991) points out, the experts' task, however, is not merely to passively register the existence of risk, and then to offer programmes to avert the risk. Instead, they 'produce risks' (Ewald 1991: 199). Because experts in risk management must identify *potential* problems rather than problems that are actually in existence, it becomes possible for them to prescribe prophylactic programmes across a range of people. All you need to do in order to be subjected to a programme of risk prevention is to possess the characteristics which specialists consider to be risk factors. The possibilities for intervention become endless, for 'what situation is there of which one can be certain that it harbours no risk, no uncontrollable or unpredictable chance feature' (Castel 1991: 289).

Thus the site of intervention is no longer the ill, pathological, dangerous or deficient person, but rather the normal person at potential risk. Normality turns to constant potential vulnerability. For example, sexuality education programmes are not instituted for sexual 'deviants' only. Being a teenager is considered sufficient grounds for being subjected to the prophylactic intervention that sexuality education is considered to be.

The 'adolescence as transition' discourse sets up all teen-aged people as always already vulnerable. Their very nature ensures that they are at risk for a number of difficulties that must be averted through the institution of programmes such as sex education. For example, in 2002 the US National Institute of Mental Health funded a research project entitled, 'Parents, peers and health risk behaviour in adolescence'. The opening sentence of the proposal summarizes much of the thinking in developmental psychology concerning 'adolescence': 'Health risk behaviors are particularly salient during adolescence, which is not surprising given the specific developmental challenges faced during this time (for parents and adolescents)' (Schettini 2002: 1). The author attributes risky behaviour to the developmental status of the teenager. In other words, by their very definition all teen-aged people are prone to risky and irresponsible behaviour.

Health service providers: calculating risk

Since the late 1990s when I began researching discourses concerning 'teenage pregnancy' and abortion, I have interviewed a number of health service providers who work in antenatal clinics, termination of pregnancy clinics, maternity wards and school health programmes (Macleod 2006a; Macleod and Luwaca, in press). In the following, I present a few extracts from these conversations. These extracts illustrate how the service providers view the personalized and collective outcomes of 'teenage pregnancy' and abortion. In this talk, health service providers are 'calculating' the possibility of negative occurrences or calculating risk. Of course, this calculation is not formal. However, it reflects quite closely the consequences elucidated in the research on 'teenage pregnancy' in which these kinds of calculations are more formal. (In the following extracts, A, B, C, D, E and F represent various respondents, while R represents myself as interviewer. Various transcription conventions are included, as follows: pauses in speech are indicated with seconds in parentheses (round brackets), e.g. (1), with (.) indicating a pause of less than a second; authorial clarification is in square brackets, e.g. [inaudible]; noises of assent, e.g. /hmm/, /yes/, go between slashes.)

A: Well (.) it [pregnancy during teen-aged years] starts them off on a lifetime of reproduction and probably single motherhood, because, you know, once it has happened once *it is very likely to happen again*. It also means that there are a lot of children who are being brought up by the *Gogos* [grandmothers]. You can argue that the nuclear family is a European concept, but they are not getting the [inaudible] that they should. Their mother is not there, and the grandmother is old, sometimes not (.) well (.) things are relatively unstructured, undisciplined / hmm/. But I think that the main concern is that these kids are being brought into families where there is stress financially already (.) and then there is the problem of schooling etcetera [my emphasis].

A: And then there is a higher medical risk as well, a higher risk of pre-eclampsia, a higher risk of maternal death, more difficult pregnancies.

A: I think that what happens if a girl gets pregnant, you know, under the age of 16, it cuts short her teenage years (1) which means that she misses out on a certain amount of growing up. She now has this responsibility which really never leaves you (1) and I think it leads to a less developed woman than it would have, had she had the chance to go through her education (.) training, whatever. Instead she's having to be responsible for a baby from the age of 16.

A: [T]hey think it's okay to have multiple sexual partners. It really doesn't matter too much who you sleep with. The consequences you will think of later. The fact that there may be (.) I am not sure if I am being racist in saying this, but it may be a Zulu phenomenon, that they don't really think about tomorrow (.) in general.

B: Because teenagers (.) even if you talk to them (.) they always think that even if I do it for the first time I will not fall pregnant.

B: They can sleep with you today, the following day with somebody else.

C: [M]ost of them, after delivery, we find that they have maternal psychosis, sort of mentally disturbed, after delivery due to the problems that were not solved during antenatal care.

D: So I find that one tends to be a lot more lenient with teenage pregnancies and we do do them [perform a termination of pregnancy] right up to twenty weeks. Unfortunately not after twenty weeks but we do them right up to twenty weeks. Because you find that with a teenage pregnancy they have been traumatized already. Because they don't know what to do. They don't want their parents to find out /hmm/. You know, there are so many issues with a teenage pregnancy.

Participant A intimates that reproductive young women are at risk in terms of repeating the mistake ('a lifetime of reproduction and single mother-hood'), obstetric difficulties, becoming less developed people by mothering rather than completing their education, having to take on responsibilities prematurely, and poverty. He suggests that young women conceive because of a lack of forethought (he racializes this as specific to Zulus). The children of these young women, he states, are at risk of growing up in an undisciplined and unstructured environment. Participant B, similarly to participant A, ascribes a lack of forethought to young women who conceive, but also accuses them of creating risk through promiscuity. Participants C and D invoke a psychological discourse in positioning young pregnant women as at risk for trauma and mental health problems as a result of either the pregnancy or by childbirth. Similarities in these responses to the consequences elucidated in the literature, as outlined in Chapter 4, are clear.

In each of the above extracts, concern is expressed with respect to the risk to individual well-being. However, risk is never seen as merely individual.

Donzelot (1993) talks of the socialization of risk. This has two aspects to it. The first is that the collective – society if you will – has the responsibility of ensuring that individuals take responsibility for their actions in order to avert difficulties occurring in the individual's life. Thus, individuals are no longer left to their own fate, but rather the collective ensures that steps are taken to ameliorate the potential difficulties arising from individuals' vulnerability to certain events. The second aspect is that various individuals' risks are aggregated into risks involving the population or the collective. The second aspect is evident in the following extracts.

E: And the economy is affected.

R: The economy, what?

E: The economy of the country, because you find that there are so many teenagers who have got children. They become dropouts from school. They don't have work to do because they are not trained, they are not skilled, you know.

F: I don't see anything positive [about young women conceiving], especially for the overpopulation (1)

R: You think that is part of the problem, that they are contributing to the overpopulation?

F: Hmm. Why should you have children when you don't need (1) and you are also not working. They should have children when they know that they can see for those children. []

R: In what way is the overpopulation a problem?

F: Ai, it is a problem because now all these shacks that they build next to our houses [] Because people run away from the rural areas. They're starving. People are working in town. They don't bring money home then they build these shacks next to our houses.

We see here how participant E does not position the young women as experiencing personal misfortune owing to their lack of skills. Instead, it is the country, the collectivized economy, which is affected.

Underlying this socialization of risk is a finer gradation in terms of those who bears the brunt of troublesome behaviour. Participant F intimates that it is not the pregnant young woman who carries the burden, or rural people, or people living in shacks. Rather the people living in houses, those implicitly defined as decent, hard-working and caring properly for their children, are the ones most affected. It thus falls to these kinds of people to implement mechanisms for the management of risk.

These calculations of risk occur within the discursive environment concerning, for example, the nature of adolescence, of good mothering, and of welfare dependency. This is well documented by Breheny and Stephens (2007a, 2008), who present results from interviews with health service providers in New Zealand. Breheny and Stephens (2007a) found that these service providers deployed what they call a 'developmental' discourse and a 'motherhood' discourse to position teen-aged mothers as problematic. The 'developmental' discourse, which is similar to the 'adolescence as transition' discourse I have described in this book, sees 'adolescence' as a stage of transition between childhood and adulthood in which 'adolescents' are naive, distracted and self-centred. The 'motherhood' discourse attributes certain behaviours as indicative of the 'good mother'. Taken together, these discourses paint a picture of the 'adolescent' mother as irreconcilable with the 'good' mother. Breheny and Stephens (2008) describe how the service providers talk of 'adolescent' mothers who are on welfare as transgressing social norms, in particular appropriate family structures and the sexual practices legitimized within these structures. In this, the work of mothering is underplayed and instead a 'life of ease and plenty on welfare' (Breheny and Stephens 2008: 257) made visible. These kinds of constructions are what enable and make concrete the calculations of risk referred to in this section.

Sex education, school counselling and the management of risk

Clearly, in terms of the management of the various risks calculated with respect to young women and reproduction, the optimal is to avert the occurrence of the primary event that leads to a series of events. In the talk and writing of health service providers and researchers on 'teenage pregnancy' and abortion, returning to the primary preventive measure of sex education is stated as the best solution, as evidenced in statements made by participant D (a nurse working in a Termination of Pregnancy clinic):

D: Ja, I feel good when, when the teenagers come forward and we ter- minate them. I don't have a problem at all. Um, I just think that they need more education and that there needs to be more, um (1) education given in the schools although I believe that it has increased quite a lot.

It is to this most optimal of risk management or preventive mechanisms that I now turn. We have already encountered sex education in this book in Chapter 3. There I indicated how the rise of sex education was linked to the instrumentalist goal of contributing to the future good of the individual and of society. I discussed the inherent contradiction of sex education in terms of the 'adolescence as transition' discourse: exposing the child/not adult to adult material in order to prevent future problems for the adult. This contradiction was illustrated through analysing two sex education manuals.

In the following I continue to analyse sex education, but this time I locate the discussion within an understanding of the management of risk. In order to illustrate the issues, I take an in-depth look at the recommendations made by some South African researchers with regard to sex education and the role of the teacher as counsellor in high schools. The researchers in question (Olivier et al. 2000; De Lange and Geldenhuys 2001; Geldenhuys and de Lange 2001; Varga 2002; Olivier and Bloem 2004) investigated the issue of abortion among young women (some investigated teachers' under-standing of and approach to abortion among teen-aged women; others researched young women's experiences of abortion). These researchers present their research results and then on the basis of these results make a number of recommendations in terms of interventions that can assist in ameliorating the problem.

Although it is often not at all clear how the results that the researchers present led to the particular recommendations that they put forward, the recommendations themselves provide an interesting insight into the under-lying assumptions made about young people and how the necessity of managing risk infiltrates our interventions with young people. In the fol-lowing, I explore how the 'adolescence as transition' discourse and the implication of the need for the management of risk that the vulnerability of the developing 'adolescent' implies informs the educational recommenda-tions made by these researchers. As Luker (1997: 4) puts it, 'people deemed incapable of making meaningful moral choices often find themselves the targets of those who would make choices for them'.

While recommendations and what actually happens in the classroom are not necessarily the same thing, an analysis of these recommendations allows us some insight into the philosophies and understandings of education educators are exposed to when studying at tertiary level. The people writing the recommendations in research articles are the same ones lecturing to cohorts of students who later become educators.

We saw in Chapter 3 how the way in which sex education is viewed and the methodologies employed are not universally the same. In this chapter we see how the basic educational philosophy underlying the recommenda-tions concerning sex education made by these researchers also differs. However, despite these differences in approach there are basic similarities. We saw in Chapter 3 how the inherent contradiction of sex education inhabits two very different sex education manuals. Here we see how the 'adolescence as transition' discourse and the management of risk underlie two very different philosophical approaches to sex education.

An understanding of the nature of being human underpins the approach educators take to the task of educating young people. The philosophy and practices of education rest fundamentally on conceptions of the person and, in particular, of the child or the 'adolescent'. The 'adolescence as transition' discourse dovetails very neatly with two of the educational philosophies that have been used in South Africa, namely fundamental pedagogics and the child-centred approach. Although these two approaches were initially seen as quite disparate, the popularity of the liberal notions inherent in the child-centred approach means that these have been taken up by and infused with fundamental pedagogics understandings. In the following, I trace how these two philosophies underpin the recommendations made by the researchers in question, and how these recommendations and the fundamental educational principles on which they are based dovetail with the imperative to manage risk among young people.

Fundamental pedagogics and the teacher as 'guide' through the transition of adolescence

Olivier and Bloem (2004), who studied educators' views on abortion among young people, argue that:

> The task of the teacher demands much more of him/her than mere instruction. He/she has to face the daily challenge to deal with the child in a variety of situations where the child is in need of meaningful accompaniment with regard to the complex world, characterized by changes in all spheres of life, fleeting contacts, superficial relationships, inadequate socialization and insecurity in which the child is growing up.
>
> (Olivier and Bloem 2004: 181)

In this quote, the relationship between the educator and learner is set, a priori, through the positioning of the learner as child and the educator as the one who accompanies the 'child' through the vagaries of 'the complex world'. The learner, thus, is the deficient one, the one in need of accompaniment, the one requiring input, the vulnerable one whose life is characterized by inadequacy and insecurity. The educator, it is implied, is rational, in control, able and mature, the one who, through gentle guidance and persuasion, helps the learner make his/her way through the dangerous waters of growing up, and is instrumental in managing the risk that merely being young implies (although, as discussed later, the educator may also fall short and require further assistance by experts higher up the ladder of expertise).

The basic philosophy underlying the relationship between the educator and learner envisaged by Olivier and Bloem (2004) is what is known in South Africa as fundamental pedagogics. Fundamental pedagogics was the educational philosophy that dominated in the Apartheid years, certainly in many Afrikaans-speaking universities and the so-called 'bush colleges' (historically black universities set up during Apartheid to provide separate tertiary education to 'black' people). It provided the foundation for the system of Christian National Education, the educational policy of the Apartheid regime (Higgs 2003).

Fundamental pedagogics was seen by its proponents as a science that set out to describe the universal characteristics of education. It defined education as the process of the child being accompanied into adulthood by

119

the adult or educator (similarities to Olivier and Bloem's (2004) language is clear). It claimed to evaluate educational procedures according to fundamental pedagogical principles. Those procedures or doctrines that did not match up to these so-called universal standards would, it was argued, have disastrous effects. In the words of one of the proponents of this approach: 'children educated in this manner will have their adulthood impaired' (De Vries 1986: 121). In other words, the universal principles of education have to be implemented in order to avert the risk of impairment that would follow if the child was not meaningfully accompanied into adulthood by an educator.

Fundamental pedagogics draws very strongly on the discourse of 'adolescence as transition' with the implication of the need for the management of risk. As the adult is the person who must accompany the child to adulthood, a clear separation between adult and child is created, with the adult taking on the rational, mature and knowing position – the manager of risk – and the child the recipient of the wisdom of the adult. The following excerpt from Olivier and Bloem's (2004) article highlights this:

> It becomes evident therefore that the accompaniment of the adolescent, who is dealing with abortion, is one such responsibility of the teacher. Adolescence is seen as a phase of life between being a child and being an adult, when radical developmental changes take place and various challenges are faced to bring forth maturity, an own identity and full-blown adulthood.
>
> (Olivier and Bloem 2004: 177)

The vulnerability of the teenager is emphasized here: she faces radical changes and various challenges. The teacher, on the other hand, must manage this situation by taking responsibility and accompanying the young person to a state of maturity, identity and 'full-blown adulthood' (whatever that means). The assumption, of course, is that the teacher is her/himself a 'full-blown adult' (and the 'adolescent' is in the process of becoming, i.e. has some signs of adulthood, but these are not yet fully developed).

There has been much criticism of fundamental pedagogics in South Africa (Chrisholm 1992), and it is no longer seriously espoused by theorists in education. However, its legacy continues, as seen in the quote by Olivier and Bloem (2004) above. It is beyond the scope of this book, however, to engage in a full critique of fundamental pedagogics.

Child-centred education and the teacher as 'facilitator' of development

Although there are remnants of a fundamental pedagogics approach to be found in the research articles under discussion, the main thrust of the educational recommendations made by these researchers concerning sex education and abortion counselling are child-centred in nature. The central idea of child-centred education is that teaching should take the child as the starting point. In other words, the child is seen as the ultimate agent of his/ her own learning. If the child is allowed to be active in constructing the learning process, then learning will take place naturally. The child does not need to be instructed, directed or moulded but rather facilitated in her/his natural tendency towards emotional, social, mental, behavioural and sexual growth. In addition, the child must be seen 'holistically'. In other words, her full capacity as a human being must be acknowledged (rather than just her learning abilities), and the environment in which she is located must be considered.

The teacher's role thus is one of facilitator, who provides the space and opportunities within which the natural unfolding of learning will take place. Certain words are frequently utilized in describing the process of education in a child-centred approach. These include relevance, discovery, under-standing, problem-solving, creativity.

In the following quotes we see the infiltration of these ideas into the recommendations made by the researchers under question:

> The teacher must see to it that a learner-friendly atmosphere is created. This can be done by helping the learners to become more familiar with, caring for, and supporting of one another through co-operative learning and group work.
>
> (Olivier and Bloem 2004: 181).

> From an intervention viewpoint, such diversity points to the need to tailor the content of information, education, and communication efforts and other interventions to meet age, sex, and location requirements.
>
> (Varga 2002: 294).

> Regarding the complete ecosystem, the school could assist by introducing a psycho-education programme which will encourage interaction between the systems in the adolescent's life. Such a programme would enable adolescents to discuss problems they are experiencing within a structured and contained environment, as well as teach them skills to improve their social relations, family relations and formal relations at school. The family should be encouraged to participate in certain sections of the programme. Community members should talk to the adolescents about their heritage ('rites of passage') and their experiences of adolescence.
>
> (De Lange and Geldenhuys 2001: 256).

> The presentation and teaching methods of these programmes [sex education] are just as important as the content thereof. It is thus

recommended that a participatory teaching method is used and that sufficient time for questions and discussion is allowed.
(Geldenhuys and de Lange 2001: 97, translated from Afrikaans)

We see here how educators are invoked to provide an environment that suits the learner, and that is friendly to the learner. Instead of the teacher as the focus of learning, the learners are now expected to cooperate in the unfolding of a natural learning process. In this, diversity must be catered for. The educator must recognize that there are individual differences between students based on a number of factors (age, sex, location). The educator must tailor the intervention to the particular needs of individual learners. Learners are expected to be active in their learning and therefore a participatory approach is recommended.

As the child is placed at the centre of this kind of education, the nature of that child and how he or she develops becomes pertinent. Child-centred education is, to a large extent, based on the premises of particular strands of developmental psychology. The strands referred to here are 'organismic' approaches. These approaches to development see the development of the child as following a natural developmental blueprint. There are a set of internal forces (cognitive, emotional and social) that will unfold naturally, provided that a nurturing and facilitating environment exists for that development. Development is seen as proceeding through invariant stages. In other words, children (and some theories extend this to adults) will progress through a number of stages of development. These stages follow one from the other, and each person must go through each stage. The mastery of particular skills required in a stage is necessary before moving on to the next stage. Failure to master the skills of a particular stage will have implications for the development of later stages.

Child-centred education, and the associated assumptions regarding the nature of personhood and the developing child, dovetails very neatly with the 'adolescence as transition' understanding. Organismic developmental theories are utilized to understand the nature of 'adolescence' as a stage of transition to adulthood. In the organismic view of development, 'adolescents' need to master particular cognitive, emotional or social tasks (such as establishing an identity) in order to move successfully to adulthood. Consider, for example, Olivier et al.'s (2000) statement that precedes their recommendations to educators concerning the life-skills with which young people need to be equipped in respect of sexuality, pregnancy and abortion:

Adolescents nowadays require a *new kind of competence to cope*. Adolescents find themselves in a life period during which they must master specific tasks on their road to adulthood and they face challenges to maturity all the time.
(Olivier et al. 2000: 220, emphasis in the original)

Risk, thus, includes the possibility that teenagers will not master the specific tasks required of their developmental stage. As they are 'on their road to adulthood', but not quite there, a number of 'challenges' lead to the risk of their not completing the basic tenets of development in their developmental stage.

This organismic, stage-oriented understanding of development, together with the implication of the risk of not mastering the required developmental tasks, impacts on the practice of teaching. Teaching must be individualized, with careful observation of the individual child taking place in order to ascertain whether he or she has reached all the necessary milestones within a particular stage so as to move on to the next one. The role of the educator, therefore, becomes not only facilitator, but also observer and monitor. The educator must carefully watch the child's progress, judging whether it measures up to the predefined norms of a particular stage. If the child is not meeting the requirements for that stage, a variety of remedial steps must be taken in order for the child to reach the set milestones; disaster must be averted and risk must be managed.

It is exactly this aspect of child-centred education that has been the target of criticism. Walkerdine (1989) argues that the shift from the more authoritarian chalk-and-talk method, in which the authority of the teacher is made clear (as in fundamental pedagogics), to the child-centred approach, in which the teacher becomes the facilitator of the child's natural developmental processes, is a shift from overt to covert regulation. This regulation takes place through two mechanisms. The first is the manner in which children are monitored to ascertain whether they are meeting the requirements of the norms of a particular stage. The second is through what has been called 'technologies of the self', where young people internalize the messages given to them and self-monitor their behaviour in order to meet the norms and expectations set for them. Each of these will be discussed below.

Teachers in the child-centred approach observe and monitor the progress of learners. This observation and monitoring is not neutral, however. Learners' progress and adaptation is measured through a particular lens, through a particular understanding of what they should (and should not) be doing at their age or stage of development. If learners are not displaying the characteristics assumed to be the norm for their age, they are seen as at risk for educational and occupational failure, for psychological or emotional damage, and for illness. If this is the case, further measures to ensure that they attain these characteristics need to be put in place.

Consider, for example, the following recommendation made by Olivier and Bloem (2004):

The teacher must equip the adolescent with life-skills, such as a positive self-concept, decision-making, problem-solving and crisis management. This will enable the adolescent to handle difficult life situations with greater ease.

(Olivier and Bloem 2004: 181)

The norms set by Olivier and Bloem, thus, are positive self-concept, decision-making, problem-solving and crisis management. The teacher is responsible for creating the (participatory, cooperative etc.) environment in which these can develop. But what if particular learners fail to develop these competencies? In this model, extra effort should be expended to ensure that the learner does, indeed, engage in positive decision-making, and is, indeed, able to problem-solve. More, perhaps better, life-skills training would be required, or, in the case of individuals who flout the norm, counselling, as recommended by Olivier and Bloem (2004: 181–182): 'the teacher should encourage the adolescent who has had an abortion to join a support group and also to receive professional therapy'.

In this process, it is the educator (informed by his/her own cultural background as well as the professional training that he or she has undergone) who decides exactly what a positive self-image is, or what adequate decision-making or problem-solving is. Young women who portray the self-image of, say, punk rocker or hip-hop artist, may not meet with the educator's idea of a positive self-image. The decision of a young woman to engage in sexual intercourse, or to terminate her pregnancy without consulting her parents may be viewed as poor decision-making. The norms underlying judgements concerning adequate development and mastery of particular tasks are not neutral.

The second way in which regulation is effected in child-centred education is through inciting the learners to self-monitor their behaviour. In other words, the teacher no longer has to use authoritarian methods to gain compliance with particular norms. Instead, young people are convinced to monitor their own behaviour, to constantly check whether they are meeting the characteristics of the normal, balanced person. They are, as the sociologist Nikolas Rose (1996) points out, incited to manage their own lives in order to avert risk, harm or damage. Managing their own lives (or what Rose calls 'technologies of the self') involves knowing the self, mastering the self and caring for the self.

Consider, for example, the statement by Olivier et al. (2000) in which teenagers are encouraged in these tasks:

They [teenagers] need to be enabled to exercise better control over their own lives . . . and to adapt to changing circumstances with greater ease. . . . Regarding their sexual behaviour and an unwanted pregnancy they also need skills that will enable them to know how to be positive about and believe in themselves, communicate effectively, form, maintain and end a relationship, be

assertive, manage a crisis and conflict, consider options, find information and advice, use community networks, think logically and
creatively, adapt to life situations, make good decisions, solve a
problem, be self-reliant, take responsibility for themselves, be pro-
active, be tolerant, manage transitions successfully, live according
to a personal value-system for life, set personal goals, be an entre-
preneur and plan for their futures.

(Olivier et al. 2000: 221)

Thus, teen-aged people are incited to labour on themselves, to take control
of their lives. This is followed by a remarkably long and detailed set of
competencies that the young person should acquire. They must know
themselves (e.g. 'know how to be positive and believe in themselves'),
master themselves (e.g. 'take responsibility for themselves') and care for
themselves (e.g. 'live according to a personal value-system').

Although these kinds of skills may seem quite reasonable, what are
missing from the long list are the implicit, underlying qualifiers. As Rose
(1996) points out, 'technologies of the self' are always practised in relation
to some underlying 'truth' or ideological position. For example, in the
above quote, the young person is invoked to consider options. Obviously,
this is a good idea, but in considering options, the range of options and the
associated consequences of choosing a particular option presented to the
young person are not neutral. In the same article in which Olivier and
Bloem (2004: 217) state that teenagers need to consider their options, the
authors refer to 'the fact that the adolescent is facing medical risks and may
even lose her life terminating a pregnancy'. They, perhaps inadvertently,
refer to young women who have undergone a termination of pregnancy as
'victims' and state that, 'The experience of terminating a pregnancy appears
to be similar to the bereavement process' (Olivier and Bloem 2004: 217).
Thus, although abortion is presented as an option, it certainly is not presented, via this rendition of abortion, as the optimal or preferred one – it is
not a 'good decision' (as specified in the list of competencies listed above) or
an adequate solution to the problem. Furthermore, this rendition of abortion is, of course, not factual because, as we saw earlier in the book, the
medical consequences of terminating a pregnancy are in fact fewer than
carrying a pregnancy to term, and the psychological consequences are far
from clear-cut.

Continuing on this tack, teenagers are incited in the above quote to 'find
information and advice'. From whom? There is an implicit understanding
that some sources of information and advice would be good sources, and
others not. When a young woman seeks information or advice from a
person offering to perform an abortion outside a designated site, would she
be practising the life-skill recommended here? What if she spoke only to her
close friends and no adult? In the article by Olivier and Bloem (2004: 181) it

is stated quite clearly that although young people 'find it easier to open up to their equals than to authority figures . . . not all adolescents are mature enough to give guidance and support'. So perhaps this would not be considered an adequate attempt at finding information and advice.

A spiral of expertise

One of the interesting aspects of both fundamental pedagogics and child-centred education is the creation (in different ways) of hierarchies that are, in a sense, never ending. In fundamental pedagogics the teacher is the authority over the child, while in child-centred education, the teacher monitors the child and facilitates development. In both approaches there is the potential for a spiral of expertise to be created. In fundamental pedagogics, a higher authority than the teacher may need to inform the teacher of the correct attitude and approach. In child-centred education, the teacher must seek further development and growth him/herself, to be facilitated in his/her development of a better understanding of educational processes.

This spiral of expertise is invoked in the research articles under discussion. For example, in Olivier and Bloem (2004), the educator is, on the one hand, the wise adult accompanying the deficient learner on the correct path towards adulthood. On the other hand, the educator him/herself is in need of expertise. In the conclusion to their article Olivier and Bloem (2004) state that:

> The teachers must themselves be equipped with life-skills, otherwise they cannot convey them to the learners and cannot serve as an identification model. They can improve their own life-skills by inviting professionals to address them, by doing some reading of relevant literature on the topic or by doing a short in-service course on life-skills.
>
> (Olivier et al. 2004: 181)

And so a spiral of expertise and risk management is created. The learner, of course, is on the bottom rung. Although the educator is more advanced than the learner, he or she must defer to 'higher' professionals, inviting them to speak to them, reading their literature or undergoing their training. Olivier and Bloem (2004: 181) set themselves up as just such professionals. They provide a long list of 'guidelines for teachers to assist them in their accompanying and handling of the adolescent who has terminated an unwanted pregnancy'.

Olivier and Bloem (2004) suggest in the above quote that educators should serve as an identification model. Exactly what that identification model should act like, dress like, or speak like is not made clear but is implicit in the general tone of the article. The fact is that certain educators may not make the grade; they may be deficient in managing the risk implicit in 'adolescence as transition' discourse. This is made explicit in Geldenhuys and de Lange's (2001) article in which they suggest:

> Attention must also be paid to the teacher/educator's qualifications to offer sex education as well as his or her age, maturity, personality characteristics and life's philosophy. Selected teachers can be trained in counselling skills, thus empowering schools to support pregnant adolescents in their decision to either continue with the pregnancy or terminate it.
> (Geldenhuys and de Lange 2001: 97, translated from Afrikaans)

Thus, it is recommended by these authors that certain educators – those who are seen as immature, with an inappropriate personality characteristics or life philosophy – are excluded from offering sex education or counselling pregnant young women concerning their options. Once again, these recommendations may seem quite reasonable. After all, perhaps not everybody is suited to counselling. But also, once again, the exact personality characteristics or life philosophy that is required in order to fit the bill of an appropriate person to conduct these activities are not spelt out. Would a young, vivacious woman who dresses in bright clothes and who is explicitly pro-choice be acceptable? What about a reserved middle-aged man who dresses formally and who believes that men should be the head of the house? Who gets to manage the risk of young people engaging in inappropriate sexual activities or making inappropriate decisions when pregnant? And, furthermore, who gets to decide which the better personality characteristics and life philosophy are and who the better person is? Who gets to do the 'selection' referred to in the quote above? Who manages the risk of teachers engaging in inappropriate sex education or advising pregnant women inappropriately?

Geldenhuys and de Lange (2001) suggest that selected educators receive training in counselling skills. Thus, these particular people are inducted into the realms of psychologized expertise. In order to do this, they must learn the language of counselling, the professional talk of psychology. As Parker and Shotter (1990) point out, to be trained as an expert requires of a person to learn a set of vocabularies, a way of speaking, in which the everyday world is transformed into the professional rhetoric of counselling and psychology. This includes talk of the causes of particular behaviour (for example, the causes of 'teenage pregnancy') and the effects of particular events (for example, the psychological effects of abortion). It involves categorizing behaviour into symptoms and disorders (such as the post-abortion syndrome spoken of in Chapter 5) that reduces behaviour and interactions to medical conditions.

127

This world of psychology and counselling has become influential in not only the 'developed' countries, but also in 'developing' countries such as South Africa. Increasingly, there are calls for people to be trained in counselling skills at various levels. The effect is 'the construction of a world in which only the voice of the professional has currency, while the voices of those outside are rendered silent' (Parker and Shotter 1990: 9). The educators selected for training in Geldenhuys and de Lange's (2001) recommendations get to be the ones who are qualified to discuss young women's situation with them and who, owing to their training and experience, may proclaim on particular topics (such as the psychological risks attached to abortion).

Conclusion

In Chapters 4 and 5 we saw how 'teenage pregnancy' and abortion among young women are viewed as social and personal problems. A range of consequences are attached to both, extending from intensely personal difficulties to overtly social problems. In this chapter I have explored some of the implications of these equations in terms of interventions that occur in young people's lives. Because young women conceiving, bearing children or terminating a pregnancy are viewed as carrying personal and social risk, the management of these risks or the threat of degeneration becomes a priority. Experts must calculate the possibility of certain negative occurrences, must identify events that lead to the negative occurrences as well as individuals who are at risk of being exposed to or engaging in these events. With the calculation of these risks in place, the expert is then tasked with implementing interventions that must manage or ameliorate the risk.

Risk takes on two specific characteristics in the recent turn to the management of risk. First, interventions are not targeted at those who display the symptoms of abnormality or dangerousness. Rather, the notion of vulnerability makes it possible for the average person to potentially be at risk for a number of negative occurrences. 'Normality' becomes inhabited with the constant potential for disaster. Thus, risk prevention must be instituted across a broad range of people. All teen-aged people, it is argued, need to undergo sex education, with the implication that merely being a 'teenager' creates the grounds of vulnerability for negative occurrences. Second, there is the socialization of risk. It is no longer the bad luck of an individual or fate that leads to poor outcomes. People are no longer left to their own devices in terms of dealing with these issues. Instead, risk becomes a problem with which the collective must deal. Negative occurrences in individuals' lives are aggregated into social problems affecting the population. We saw how the health service providers whom I have interviewed over a number of years position young reproductive women not

128

only as suffering personally but also as contributing to social difficulties such as economic depression.

Sex education is mooted by many experts as the most optimal of risk management strategies. In this chapter, I reviewed the writings of some South African researchers who, having researched abortion among young women, make recommendations with respect to sex education and abortion counselling. Recommendations concerning how risk is to be managed differ. Recommendations drawing off fundamental pedagogics see it at the task of the teacher-as-guide to direct the young person on the correct path (and accompany them along the way). Those drawing off a child-centred approach enjoin the teacher to facilitate the natural unfolding of competencies in the young person that will lead to a positive result.

However, although these recommendations draw on two very different fundamental educational philosophies, they have many features in common. The first is the acceptance of the 'adolescent in transition' discourse, and the second, an injunction to manage risk around sex and reproduction among young people.

8

FROM 'TEENAGE PREGNANCY' TO UNWANTED PREGNANCY

At the beginning of this book, I stated that my focus will not be on individual young women and their experiences of pregnancy or abortion. The aim of this book was not to understand the individual factors that may lead young women to conceive, or to decide to terminate a pregnancy or to carry to term. I did not turn to interviews with young women in order to understand pregnancy, abortion and childbearing among young women. Instead, what I have tried to achieve in this book is an understanding of the public discursive context within which young women conceive and decide what to do about their pregnancy. I have tried, through a social constructionist theoretical framework, to understand the macro-social and cultural environment of public discourse and practice within which these young women will experience their lives. I have argued that the dominant discourse of 'adolescence as transition', and the ideologies attached to this discourse (the imaginary wall, the ghost of the threat of degeneration, and embedding the transition to adulthood within the individual) are implanted in our public understandings of 'teenage pregnancy' and abortion, as well as our research practices that foreground age as the single most important feature of a young woman's life.

Not only do these public discourses and social practices have implications for debates around 'teenage pregnancy' and abortion, but also they potentially have implications in terms of the personal lives of young women who conceive: the way that they feel about themselves and the decisions that they make; their interactions with significant others such as parents, peers and partner; their reactions to the pregnancy and abortion or childbirth; and the processes that they go through in order to reach a decision about the pregnancy. This is because discourses not only operate at a public level, but also are modes through which we live our personal lives. Indeed, through discourses, the internal and the external world become intricately interweaved. As social and cultural beings, we are inducted into particular discourses through a range of social processes, including parenting practices, schooling, reading, rituals and everyday interactions. Of course, these are complex processes and the range of discourses and social practices to which we are exposed will be multiple and, in many instances, contradictory. Thus, public discourses that circulate in formal texts, such as newspapers, articles, textbooks, television programmes and websites will intersect with local knowledge, discourses and practices that operate at a more micro-level in complex ways. In all of this we stand as individual agents, investing in particular discourses and discounting others, through complex psychological processes. For example, investing in particular discourses may afford us emotional or interpersonal benefits (Hollway 1998).

Young women live in a public discursive context in which the 'adolescence as transition' discourse is dominant. It is thus not surprising that many young women who conceive will see themselves as 'children having children'. Not because this is a fact that transcends all time and is true universally, but because at this particular point in time, the 'adolescence as transition' discourse has taken firm root and defines our public understanding of young people and how they should behave.

The entrenchment of the 'adolescence as transition' discourse in our discussions of young people and reproduction will have a number of implications for young people. Teasing out what these implications are, and how young women and those around them take up or resist such public representations, is not the brief of this book, however, and will have to wait for further work.

What I have covered in this book is, first, an indication of how this discourse infuses our public understandings of, research concerning and interventions with young people, and second, a questioning of the necessity of this discourse. In the following, I provide a brief summary of the key points of the book. I then go on to suggest that our focus should shift from 'teenage pregnancy' to 'unwanted pregnancy' in order to adequately address the situation in which some young women (and women in general) find themselves, namely carrying a severely problematic pregnancy. I argue that we should revoke the blanket term 'teenage pregnancy' (that homogenizes women around their age and invokes the imaginary wall). Instead we should concentrate on unwanted pregnancies, a move that undoes the artificial separation between young and older women who find themselves in the predicament of a conception that is severely problematic for a variety of reasons, and allows us to concentrate on the conditions under which pregnancies become a burden for women. This shift has implications in terms of research and intervention practices, some of which I shall address below.

The key points of this book

'Teenage pregnancy', the key focus of this book, has become such a common term, a taken-for-granted self-evident signifier, that it is difficult to imagine that it is, in fact, a recent invention. The media and social policy debates in the United States started referring to 'teenage pregnancy' in the early 1970s. The term entered common parlance in South Africa in the early 1980s. Previously words such as 'illegitimacy' and 'unwed motherhood' were used to describe young (and older) women who had children out of wedlock. With increasing concerns about the moral implications of such words, the focus shifted to the supposedly more scientific term 'teenage pregnancy'. What this shift introduced was a separation of the possibilities and constraints facing young reproductive women from those facing older women. While the term 'unwed motherhood' casts a net around women of all ages in its moral injunction, 'teenage pregnancy' slices off a segment of women, opening them up for further investigation and allowing for their age to become the prime suspect in the range of difficulties noted in their pregnancies, their terminations of pregnancies, and their bearing children.

The slicing off of a segment of women with the term 'teenage pregnancy' is made possible by the notion of 'adolescence'. 'Adolescence', as a stage of development, is seen as a transitional stage between childhood and adulthood. And yet, as indicated by social and historical analyses, the 'adolescence as transition' discourse is not something that reflects a trans-historical reality. 'Adolescence' is not something that occurs because of inevitable internal, biological forces. Rather it is something that was 'invented' just over a century ago. A number of sociological changes in the West (age segregation, the rise of mass schooling and the outlawing of child labour) together with the publication of Stanley Hall's (1904) text on 'adolescence' led to the emergence of a category of developmental stages called 'adolescence'. Colonial processes, such as schooling, Christianity, a monetary-based economy and urbanization, ensured the importation of a discourse of 'adolescence as transition' into Africa and South Africa, together with the implicit ideologies contained within the discourse. Transition to adulthood is no longer, in this rendition, a matter of social events (such as various rituals, rites of passage or initiation) taking place over a defined, usually brief, period of time, but rather an internalized, long-term affair of approximately eight years.

The first of the implicit ideologies of 'adolescence' is the threat of degeneration, a threat that is enabled by the connection that was made in early writings on 'adolescence' between the transition that young people go through in order to move from childhood to adulthood and the transition that humankind went through to in order to move from primitiveness to civilization (with the implication that some societies have not undergone this movement from primitiveness to civilization). Although the overt language of a threat of degeneration has disappeared, the manner in which 'teenage pregnancy' is seen as a severe social problem suggests that the ghost of a threat of degeneration continues to linger in our discussions of young people and reproductive issues. The fact that those who are pregnant are women, and that there is a double-bind implicit in the definition of 'adolescence' with regard to women – they are simultaneously the quintessential adolescent and excluded from the ideal end-point – allows for an intensification of ascriptions of a threat of degeneration.

'Teenage pregnancy' continues to be seen as a social problem despite the fact that there are questions concerning the research that points to negative consequences resulting from early reproduction, and despite the fact that 'revisionist' authors have argued that early reproduction is a rational choice for particular young people. The conclusions that pregnancy and child-bearing among young women leads to school disruption and economic disadvantage, to increased health risks, to poor child outcomes, and to welfare dependency have all been thoroughly critiqued. In particular the ascription of various consequences to the woman's age alone is prob-lematic. Young women who conceive not only are pregnant, but also have a range of other characteristics. For example, they occupy a certain socio-economic level, with the accompanying living conditions, health care possi-bilities, quality of schooling and employment opportunities. They live in particular family structures and have particular partner relationships. When research is conducted, thus, on the consequences of early reproduction, these sorts of factors should be taken into account. Research that does take these sorts of factors into account generally points in quite the opposite direction to the standard 'teenage pregnancy = social problem' idea. Thus, for example, women of similar socio-economic status and social circum-stances, whether teenagers or older women, have similar health risks in pregnancy, and their children have similar educational outcomes.

The question that I posed earlier is why, given the fact that the scientific evidence of the negative consequences of 'teenage pregnancy' are far from conclusive, does the 'teenage pregnancy = social problem' equation persist. The conclusion reached is that it has to do with power relations. Geronimus (2003) argues that the 'teenage pregnancy = social problem' notion main-tains the values and principles of the dominant (white) group. It allows for certain understandings around sex, responsibility, race and family values to be perpetuated. I agree, but argue further that the persistence of the equa-tion has to do with the manner in which we conceptualize 'adolescence'. Because 'adolescence' is a 'transition' that implies a state of 'less developed' and 'more developed', when the less developed engage in activities seen by the more developed as not fitting, then it is easy for the more developed to feel threatened by the less developed. They (certain young people) are engaging in activities that threaten degeneration of their (certain older people's) ideas of the civilized, rational and useful living.

Indeed, it is at the intersection of the concepts of 'race', 'culture' and 'adolescence' that we begin to see, in full detail, the way in which the threat of degeneration operates. The threats that the less developed in terms of age and the less developed in terms of 'civilization' pose, meet in mutually reinforcing ways, serving to construct 'black' and/or minority group women who are pregnant as the 'other' on dual levels. In Chapter 6 we saw how the peculiarities of 'black' and/or minority group people – their bodily functions, their reproductive trends, their cultural habits, their ways of bringing up their children – are etched against the unstated, normalized backdrop of 'white' bodies and ways of being. In this rendition, 'race' and 'culture' (or the lack thereof) are treated as unproblematic categories that are easily definable and may be used to explain problematic social issues like 'teenage pregnancy' among 'black' or minority group people. This, despite the fact that racial boundaries are, in fact, incredibly slippery and that culture is a dynamic and complex phenomenon that does not occupy people or place them within defined limits.

A certain kind of logic would have it that abortion among teenagers would solve the problem of 'teenage pregnancy', at least on the level of inadequate mothering, the disruption of schooling and the perpetuation of poverty, if not on the level of teenagers engaging in sex. However, abortion among young people has become the new social problem. The 'social problem' of abortion among teenagers takes a slightly different tack to the one of 'teenage pregnancy'. While 'teenage pregnancy' is cast as threatening social degeneration through poverty and poor child outcomes, abortion among teenagers is spoken of as threatening personal degeneration. Abortion is cast as necessarily psychologically traumatizing, with those who state that they do not experience negative consequences dismissed as merely being in denial. These assertions stand despite robust critique of the research that finds psychological distress following abortion among women in general and specifically among teenagers. The persistence of these assertions is largely due to the political mileage that anti-abortion lobbyists manage to glean from such a narrative concerning abortion. And it is in this move, in the supposed benign concern of anti-abortion activists, that the threat of personal degeneration turns into a social and public issue. The threat of degeneration is no longer cast as merely personal but also as intensely social because of the large numbers of women who will inevitably experience post-abortion distress.

The second ideology that infuses the 'adolescence as transition' discourse is the imaginary wall created between young women and older ones. The assumption here is that the social trends we see among young women are somehow separate from those that we see among older women. This allows for a certain pathologization of young women as they, or rather their developmental status, is seen as responsible for these difficulties.

An example of this is the research that has been conducted on young women who have undergone a termination of pregnancy in South Africa since the legalization of abortion. The design of these studies meant that the experiences of these women were studied in isolation, with the perhaps unintended implication that the results that they found were owing to the developmental status of the young woman. However, the question that arises is whether, given a similar set of circumstances older women who have undergone termination of pregnancy would not have the same experiences (Macleod 2008).

Further examples of this abound in the literature on 'teenage pregnancy' and childbearing. The mothering practices of young women are frequently viewed in isolation. When comparison is made with older mothers, this is frequently to mothers who do not live in circumstances similar to the ones that the teenagers being studied find themselves. The health risks attached to early pregnancy provide another example. Many studies find increased obstetric risk among young pregnant women. However, when research matches the younger and older samples in terms of socio-economic status and lifestyle choices, the differences suddenly disappear. In other words, women in similar circumstances face the same degree of complications during pregnancy and childbirth, no matter what their age. A third example is the assumption that bearing children during 'adolescence' has opportunity costs for young women which somehow magically disappear as women get older. In fact, women face opportunity costs in having children at any stage their lives and indeed, for some, having children earlier may have fewer (although not no) opportunity costs.

The internal contradictions implicit in the 'adolescence as transition' discourse, while somewhat contained by the notion of 'transition', are painted in stark relief under particular circumstances. The examples I used in this book were sex education, 'teenage pregnancy' and decision-making in the context of abortion.

Sex education, aimed at producing the good sexual citizen, defines teen-aged people as different to the end-product (the good sexual citizen). And yet, to get to that end-product, images, graphics, facts, stories and examples of sex must be introduced. All of this threatens the innocence of the 'not-yet-adult', with concerns about increased experimentation among teenagers as a result of sex education being expressed. Sexual desire, an adult emotion, although not spoken about directly, may be inappropriately awakened in these young people. The internal conundrum of 'adolescence as transition' (adult/not adult and simultaneously child/not child) inhabits sex education programmes despite differences in approach, as seen in Chapter 3.

Teenagers who become pregnant provide, in physical relief, the paradox stalking our definition of 'adolescence'. These are, as people literally talk about them, 'children having children'. Of course, this cannot be but is, and so a number of mechanisms to maintain our basic understanding of 'adolescence' must be put into place. One of these is to define mothering among young women as a skill rather than as natural. This means that we can describe the adult activity that these young women are performing (mothering) as something that they struggle to do adequately (because, of course, they lack the necessary skill, not being adult). However, when research that compares younger mothers with older mothers takes the social circumstances and context within which the mothers live into account, it is found that age plays no role at all in contributing to poorer mothering practices. Instead, things like the child's temperament, number of children cared for, family income and family structure are implicated in making mothering a difficult task.

Debates around decision-making in the context of abortion highlight the conundrum of the 'adolescent' as transitional being. Proponents of compulsory parental consent in a young woman's decision to terminate a pregnancy argue that because abortion is more traumatic for teenagers than it is for adults, and because teenagers have poorer cognitive abilities to make informed decisions, adult supervision is required. Both of these premises rest on a notion of lack. Young women lack the resilience and the cognitive skills of older people. Opponents of parental consent dispute the fact that abortion is more traumatic for young women, stating that there is no evidence (based on good sound research that compares younger and older women from similar circumstances) to support this. They also state that the decision-making abilities of young people, when viewed specifically in relation to abortion, do not differ substantially from older people. Thus the attempt here is to dislodge the essential 'imaginary wall' constructed by proponents of parental consent between young women and adults by showing that they (young women) are in fact more similar to adults than initially supposed.

The continued dominance of the 'teenage pregnancy = social problem' and 'abortion among young people = disastrous personal consequences' equations, despite research that suggests that the consequences of either are no different for women of all ages in similar social circumstances, has allowed for the implementation of strategies to manage risk. Risk in this sense is 'socialized'. In other words, an early pregnancy is no longer merely a personal crisis or a matter of fate. Rather, it is a something that the collective must insure against both for the sake of the individual and for the sake of the collective. In the management of risk, the expert calculates the possibility of a vulnerable person (e.g. young woman) engaging in or being exposed to an event (e.g. unprotected sex) that will lead to a negative occurrence (e.g. pregnancy) that has consequences for both the individual (e.g. not continuing with education) and the collective (e.g. contributing to economic decline). Procedures to manage risk are then put into place in order to prevent the problem from occurring and to ameliorate the effects should it occur.

In the case of young women, a number of interventions are recommended to manage risk. These include sex education in order to avoid pregnancy and sexually transmitted diseases, regular and specialized antenatal classes during pregnancy (in public health sector in South Africa all pregnant teen-aged women are automatically referred to the high risk clinic, no matter their health status), and pre- and post-abortion counselling with the recommendation that young women consult their parents. One of the most talked of interventions, in light of its potential to nip the 'problem' in the bud, is sex education. In Chapter 7 we saw how, for the most part, sex education, even when drawing from different theoretical understandings of education, relies on the 'adolescent as transition' discourse to justify the intervention of the expert educator in managing the risk of young people engaging in inappropriate sexual behaviour.

From 'teenage pregnancy' to unwanted pregnancies

Readers may rightly ask, 'So, what about those young women who land up with an unwanted pregnancy?' 'What about those young women for whom pregnancy does indeed mean difficulty in pregnancy, or increased chance of poverty, or psychological difficulties?' 'Should we not try to prevent this from occurring?' 'Should there not be services to assist them in their difficulties once they are pregnant?' The answer to the latter two questions clearly has to be, 'Yes'. But once having provided this answer, the question arises as to how we view these efforts at prevention and assistance. I argue that the focus should shift from 'teenage pregnancy' to unwanted pregnancies.

We know that a number of young women who are pregnant do not want to be pregnant from the mere fact that they present at Termination of Pregnancy Clinics. These young women have reached the conclusion that continuing their pregnancy will be deleterious to them in some way. However, teenagers are not the only ones presenting at Termination of Pregnancy clinics. If termination of pregnancy is taken as a clear indicator of the unwantedness of a pregnancy, then it is clear that women of all ages find themselves in the situation of carrying a severely problematic pregnancy. For example, in South Africa, minors account for only 12 per cent of people presenting at TOP clinics. That means that 88 per cent of these women are over the age of 18 (Department of Health [South Africa] 2006b). In the United States, teenagers account for 17 per cent of legal abortions, with 33 per cent of abortions being obtained by women in the age range 20 to 24 years old (Guttmacher Institute 2008). In England and Wales, the rates of legal termination of pregnancy per 1000 women in 2006 are presented in Table 1 (Department of Health [United Kingdom] 2007).

Thus, in England and Wales, more women in their early twenties find themselves with an unwanted pregnancy that ends in abortion than women in their teen-aged years or in their late twenties.

In what follows I unpack some of the implications of shifting our attention to unwanted pregnancies. But before this, three caveats around the word 'unwanted pregnancy' are needed. First, I have not called the pregnancies unplanned or unintended. While most unwanted pregnancies will have been unplanned, not all unplanned pregnancies are unwanted. This is clearly indicated by some data collected in the *South African Demographic and Health Survey 2003* (Department of Health [South Africa] 2007). In this, researchers made a distinction between pregnancies that were

137

Table 1 Rates of legal abortion per 1000
women in England and Wales, 2006

Age range	Rate of abortion per 1000 women
15–19	24
20–24	33
25–29	24
30–34	15
35–39	10
40–44	4
44–49	0

Table 2 Fertility planning status (percentages)

	Wanted then	Wanted later	Wanted no more	Missing	Total
Aged less than 20	20.8	42.6	34.4	2.2	100
Total across age range	50	24.1	23.2	2.7	100

Source: adapted from Department of Health [South Africa] 2007

'wanted then' (i.e. wanted at conception or planned), 'wanted later' (i.e. unplanned but not unwanted) and 'wanted no more' (i.e. unwanted). The results, as illustrated in Table 2, paint an interesting picture in terms of the wantedness of pregnancies.

Although, in this survey, a smaller percentage of teen-aged women planned their pregnancy than older women, for a substantial percentage (42.6 per cent) the pregnancy was unintended but not unwanted. The percentage of teen-aged women who found their pregnancy and childbearing problematic (i.e. 'wanted no more') is higher than for women across the age range. What is of interest, however, is that the percentage of women in the 40–44 year age range who indicated the status of their pregnancy as 'wanted no more' (not shown in Table 2) is similar to those of teen-aged women (34.9 per cent).

The second caveat concerning the term 'unwanted' is that while there does not seem to be any useful alternative, there are also problems with its use. 'Want' is associated with a state of desire. In other words, we 'want' something, but this thing may not really be necessary. It is not a need. Thus, a child may 'want' sweets, but what he or she 'needs' is nutritional sustenance for his or her survival. I may 'want' my morning cup of coffee, but what I need is some form of liquid. In line with this, then, 'unwanted' takes on the suggestion of choice. The pregnancy is 'unwanted' because you have other desires or wants. You have chosen something else over bringing the pregnancy to term and bearing a child. This is clearly not the implication that feminists using the term 'unwanted pregnancy' wish to convey.

We thus need to understand the term 'unwanted' pregnancy in a contextual and social sense. A pregnancy is unwanted not because a woman, through personal processes of choice given a range of options, decides against being pregnant. Instead, it is something that, for a range of social, interpersonal and contextual reasons, is simply an impossible situation. Indeed, it has been suggested to me that the term 'crisis pregnancy' more accurately captures this state of affairs. However, I have resisted utilizing this term because of its association with pro-life organizations that have set up what they term 'Pregnancy Crisis Clinics' across South Africa. Through its deployment within this context, the signifier has taken on undertones that do not suit the general understanding of unwanted pregnancy that feminists would want to espouse, an understanding that sees unwanted pregnancy as severely problematic and that fundamentally respects the rights of a woman to terminate a pregnancy.

The third caveat is that 'unwanted' is a relative term. The question 'Unwanted by whom?' may be posed. The potential conflict of interests that may arise around pregnancies is evidenced by the phenomenon of men opposing their sexual partners having an abortion. In this case, the woman feels that the pregnancy is unwanted, while the man wants the pregnancy. While the question of the power relations around the wantedness of pregnancies (not only within sexual partnerships but also within families and communities) is an interesting avenue of investigation that should be followed, it is important, especially from a feminist perspective, to retain the woman as the central focus of reproductive decision-making. In the same way that feminists have fought for the decision to terminate a pregnancy to be the woman's alone, so our understanding of the wantedness of a pregnancy should foreground the woman's relationship with the pregnancy, and the social power relations within which the woman is located.

Unwanted pregnancies

Shifting our attention away from 'teenage pregnancy' to unwanted pregnancies potentially has significant implications in terms of our social, research and intervention practices. This is because the two terms signify the event of pregnancy in very different ways. The signifier 'teenage pregnancy' foregrounds the young woman who is pregnant: the 'adolescent' who breaches (middle-class, white) developmental norms. The signifier 'unwanted pregnancy' reintroduces the fact that pregnancy is possible only within a gendered relationship, and that it occurs within a set of social circumstances. A pregnancy is 'unwanted' because a woman is located within a particular nexus of conditions (ranging from interpersonal relations and local context to macro-level structural and policy issues) that make the possibility of childbearing extremely difficult.

139

This shift in fundamental signification in terms of pregnancy means that our understandings of, and practices with respect to, women and reproduction can start aligning themselves to the social and gendered space within which women are located. In defining unwanted pregnancies as the key issue, we cease pathologizing young pregnant women merely because they are young. We undo the imaginary wall between younger and older women, thus opening up the space for understanding how women in similar social circumstances face similar dilemmas, difficulties, barriers and possibilities around reproduction.

Having said this, however, we must also acknowledge that this is a possible, but not inevitable, shift. For example, anti-abortion groups argue that women who terminate a pregnancy for any reason other than rape, incest or the endangerment of life do so for selfish reasons or for convenience. This foregrounds the 'deficient woman' in understanding unwanted pregnancies. In other words, the individual woman and her inadequacies, rather than the social and gendered circumstances which make the pregnancy deleterious, are the locus of explanation for women deciding that a pregnancy is sufficiently unwanted to have an abortion.

That concentrating on the individual woman's personal characteristics is misleading with respect to understanding termination of pregnancy (and thus unwanted pregnancy) is confirmed by Finer et al. (2005). In their analysis of the reasons women in the United States terminate a pregnancy, they conclude that responsibility to others and resource limitations (e.g. financial constraints and lack of partner support) were recurring and cross-cutting (across race, income and education category of the women) themes. Thus, pregnancies are unwanted in the context of structural, social and gendered relations. As Santelli et al. (2003) indicate, we need to pay attention to

> how contextual factors such as poverty, racism, gender inequality and the structure of health services might constrain women's life options and access to contraceptive methods . . . at both the micro level (e.g., how power disparities between patients and reproductive health service providers shape contraceptive choices and behaviors) and the macro level (e.g., how the reproduction of certain groups over time has been cast as socially desirable or undesirable).
>
> (Santelli et al. 2003: 97)

In the following I explore some of the possibilities around research and intervention practices that utilize unwanted pregnancies as a focus point rather than 'teenage pregnancy'. This discussion must, of necessity, be somewhat circumscribed through space limitations. There are, of course, implications beyond research and service provision (such as for media representations and for policy), which are not discussed here.

Research practices

Much of the discussion in this book has centred on how particular research practices have created fertile ground for the construction of an imaginary wall between teen-aged and adult women. In these practices, age is fore-grounded as the major factor around which we can explain particular problems, with the gendered, economic, cultural, geographical, familial and social circumstances of women receding into the background.

Some may argue that what is required in this case is more sophisticated research, better multivariate research that is able to account for multiple factors and that can tease out the relative weighting of each in terms of its contribution to poor health, psychological or child outcomes in the repro-ductive cycle. And, indeed, there may be a case for this, if only to counter the taken-for-granted assumption that 'teenage pregnancy' is necessarily deleterious or that abortion is necessarily psychologically damaging, as various researchers' work carefully designed research does(such as the work of Arline Geronimus or Brenda Major). The problem, however, with merely increasing the sophistication of this kind of research is that the object of study, and the kinds of research questions that may be asked, do not change fundamentally. The characteristics of the individual woman (albeit more complex now) remain the defining feature in accounting for particular outcomes; research questions remain focused on outcomes and on causes that may be traced back to individual traits.

The use of the signifier 'unwanted pregnancy' advocated here means that the focus shifts from the individual woman defined by her particular char-acteristics to the micro- and macro-level interactive spaces which women occupy. Gendered relations, familial support, access to services (such as health care, antenatal care or child daycare), policy environments, living conditions, employment possibilities etc. shift to the foreground in terms of our research attention. Questions shift from 'What are the causes of "teen-age pregnancy"?', 'What are the outcomes of "teenage pregnancy"?', and 'What interventions reduce the incidence of "teenage pregnancy"?' to 'How do women reach the point in which they experience "unwanted pregnan-cies"?', 'What social spaces (at a micro- and macro-level) make it possible for women to experience 'unwanted pregnancies'?', and 'What micro- and macro-level social spaces are required to promote reproductive freedom across the age range?'

Of course there are a myriad of ways in which these sorts of questions can be explored. Public health research is particularly interested in epi-demiological surveys in which population patterns are analysed. Depending on how these are conceptualized, useful social indicators may be revealed. In South Africa, for example, there has been an increase in the quantity and quality of national surveys. These have highlighted social inequities (for example around rural or urban location) and discriminatory service practices (for example, the *South African Demographic and Health Survey 2003* revealed that on all components of antenatal care women below the age of 20 receive poorer care than older women). Similarly, in the United States, Gold (2006) remarks on the 'gross disparities' evident in reproduction among women in the United States. She notes that, compared with higher-income women, women of low socio-economic status are four times as likely to have an unplanned pregnancy, three times as likely to have an abortion and five times as likely to have an unplanned birth. Gold (2006) concludes that 'much more attention should be paid to the constructive role society and public policy might play in better supporting people as they try to exercise 'individual responsibility' in their sexual and reproductive lives'.

Clearly information of this nature is useful in terms of understanding social patterns. But careful inspection of the taken-for-granted assumptions underpinning this research is always required. As illustrated in this book, the discourse of 'adolescence as transition' frequently becomes the bedrock upon which research questions are formulated and investigations launched. Revealing this discourse's historical and cultural roots and its linkages to neocolonialist understandings calls its easy assumption into question and hence the manner in which research that draws on such a discourse is conducted.

Furthermore, in an area as fraught with politics as reproduction and abortion is, the ideological underpinnings of research should be clearly spelt out. The feminist principle of transparency around position while retaining research rigour is important. This has, for the most part, been discussed under the rubric of reflexivity, about which there is substantial debate. I have suggested elsewhere (Macleod 2006b) that researchers need, in addition to being vigilant and reflective in terms of self, other, context, process, assumptions and theory, to engage in an analysis of the 'politics of location' and the 'politics of representation'. Mohanty (1995: 67) defines the politics of location as the 'historical, geographical, cultural, psychic and imaginative boundaries which provide the ground for political definition and self-definition for contemporary . . . feminists'. In the politics of representation, it is recognized that researchers are engaged in an active process of translating the lives of others into marks legible by the academic community. This translation process may be effected, and may be read, in various ways. Acknowledging this, rather than assuming that research directly reflects the reality of young women's lived experiences, is important.

Other than population level analysis that (critical) public health research allows, a range of methodologies are useful in highlighting the micro- and macro-level interactive spaces within which unwanted pregnancies occur. One particularly useful development since the 1970s has been the turn to discourse analysis, narrative analysis and conversation analysis heralded by the increasing popularity of social constructionism and post-structuralism. This has enabled researchers to highlight the manner in which a variety of gendered issues are constructed in local and national contexts. Complex and interweaving power relations and modes of regulation are illuminated, as well as the intersection of personal narratives or experiences with dominant social discourses. These methodologies provide the opportunity to obtain a rich, nuanced and in-depth understandings of the phenomenon of unwanted pregnancies, an opportunity that so far is under-explored (although there is some discursive work in the area of abortion, such as that conducted by Mitchell et al. (2006) in Kenya and Maleck-Lewy and Ferree (2000) in the former German Democratic Republic).

Service provision practices

The primary health care response to health problems is to develop comprehensive prevention strategies. Primary prevention implies preventing the health problem from developing in the first place; secondary prevention involves detecting the problem early in its development so that treatment may be effected from the outset; tertiary prevention refers to reducing the negative effects of the health problem. With respect to unwanted pregnancies, this would translate into strategies that prevent the occurrence of unwanted pregnancy, that empower women to detect pregnancy early on and to make informed decisions regarding the outcome of the pregnancy, and that provide support for women with unwanted pregnancies either through the provision of accessible and affordable termination of pregnancy services, or through providing health, welfare, legislative and social support for those carrying the pregnancy to term. In the following a few of the implications of such an approach, specifically in terms of primary and tertiary prevention, are outlined.

Primary prevention of unwanted pregnancies

The impact of publicly funded contraceptive services in terms of the prevention of unintended, and potentially unwanted, pregnancies is well documented, with the Guttmacher Institute estimating that some 1.3 million unintended pregnancies are prevented in the United States through federally funded contraceptive services (Cohen 2006). This is well recognized by many governments. For example, the provision of and information about contraception and family planning services is one of the cornerstones of the South African Department of Health's reproductive health strategies, resulting in a reported national contraceptive usage is about 62 per cent of women (Smit et al. 2004).

While the accessibility and availability of contraceptives are extremely important factors that should form the bedrock of any service provision, they are, in and of themselves, insufficient. The assumption of the rational woman availing herself of accessible contraception hides the fact that unwanted pregnancies occur for a range of complex sociological and personal reasons, understandings of which need to be incorporated into service provision. The need for this is clearly articulated by two sets of researchers in different locations, the first from South Africa and the second from Canada:

> All too frequently, health promotion interventions fail to acknowledge sexual encounters as sites in which unequal power relations between women and men are expressed. It is these power relations which determine women's ability – or inability – to protect themselves against sexually transmitted disease, pregnancy and unwelcome sexual acts.
>
> (Wood and Jewkes 1997: 41)

> Empirical public health research . . . has attempted to account for mostly negative sexual health outcomes . . . by examining individual characteristics and risk-taking behaviour. Public health practice has followed suit, focusing primarily on modifying sexual risk behaviour and lifestyle 'choices'. In doing so, we may be unwittingly committed to an unarticulated and unrealistic set of assumptions about the level of agency and control that is afforded to many young people.
>
> (Shoveller and Johnson 2006: 47)

Given these insights, it is imperative that primary prevention efforts begin to grapple with both micro- and macro-level power relations within which women are located.

An example of where this is beginning to emerge is in the acknowledgement of sexual coercion as a key concern in sexual and reproductive health in a range of countries. In South Africa, Dunkle et al. (2004) found in their sample of women attending antenatal clinics in Soweto that over half of the women aged 15–30 had experienced physical and/or sexual violence from male intimate partners, with nearly one-third reporting incidences in the last twelve months. Research in other sub-Saharan Africa countries (Moore et al. 2007) and India (Jaya and Hindin 2007) reveals similar levels of sexual coercion. Much the same picture also emerges in more economically developed contexts. In the United States, Silverman et al. (2004) utilized the National Youth Risk Behavior Survey data to explore what they call dating violence. Just less than one in five of the teen-aged women surveyed reported being physically hurt by a date in the previous year. In the United Kingdom, a survey of 13 to 17 year olds revealed that one-quarter of young women and 18 per cent of young men experienced physical intimate partner violence, and one in three young women and 16 per cent of young men experienced sexual intimate partner violence (Barter et al. 2009).

The link between these patterns and unwanted pregnancy is clear. For example, Silverman et al. (2004) found, in the United States, that those young women hurt by a date were more vulnerable to sexually transmitted diseases and were more likely to have been pregnant. In South Africa Jewkes et al. (2001) compared pregnant and never pregnant young women of similar background. The pregnant women experienced significantly more violence in their relationship and were more likely to have been forced to have sex for the first time.

Understanding the ways in which sexual coercion manifests is of vital importance to primary preventive service provision. Wood et al. (1998) found in South Africa that on the weaker side of the spectrum of sexual coercion there are particular constructions of love in which having penetrative sex is viewed as an essential aspect of love. In other words, 'If you love me, you will have sex with me'. The coercion here is verbal and emotional, drawing on expectations of what is 'normal' and how others will see the couple. On the other side is assault or the threat of assault. Wood et al. (1998: 237) report that 'violent practices described [by the young pregnant women] included forcing legs apart, tearing off clothes, punching with fists and locking the door'. In between are activities such as pleading or persuading. These kinds of encounters are maintained by an understanding among young women that silence and acquiescence are the best strategies to avoid further violence. For example, refusal to engage in sex is viewed as a sign that a woman has other sexual partners, an accusation that potentially is accompanied by extreme violence and gang-rape. Furthermore, general leisure activities are defined by men, which then gives them the opportunity to create situations in which they can demand sex (Wood et al. 1998).

Foregrounding the gendered nature of (hetero)sexual interactions, and particularly the potentially coercive nature thereof, would be an essential feature of dialogues that occur under the rubric of sexuality education. In their analysis of sexuality programmes in developed and developing countries, Rogow and Haberland (2005) note that where gender does feature, it is usually dealt with in a superficial manner, concentrating quite obviously on male behaviour. Other issues such as homophobia, female sexual pleasure and, significantly, gender discrimination in the social sphere receive virtually no attention. The promotion of critical thinking skills relating to gender norms is also basically absent.

A critical pedagogical project would involve raising questions and holding dialogues concerning the power relations that fix possibilities for young women in terms of, among other things, (not) engaging in sex, choosing to terminate a pregnancy or carry to term, opportunities to continue with education and raise a child. For example, it would involve asking the kinds of questions posed by Wood and Jewkes (1997):

• How, why and when are decisions made by individuals to have sex, and to engage in specific sexual practices?

- How are gender inequities played out and resisted in the community? For example, how far are practices such as condom use and female sexual refusal negotiable and negotiated between individuals in different settings?
- How is individual control asserted when there is conflict?

(Wood and Jewkes 1997: 44)

Tertiary prevention

Tertiary prevention in terms of unwanted pregnancies implies, in the first instance, the provision of accessible and affordable termination of pregnancy services. However, simply having legal abortion available in a country is insufficient. A range of factors, including anti-abortion activity, anti-abortion rhetoric, social stigma, unwilling service providers, parental consent laws and subtle narratives (such as the inevitability of psychological fallout following abortion) place barriers in the path of women accessing abortion. Continual advocacy around ensuring that abortion is an option that is freely available to women experiencing an unwanted pregnancy is required.

Other than termination of pregnancy services, a range of intervention practices could reduce the chances of unintended pregnancies being 'unwanted' and could prevent negative fallout should a woman choose to take an unwanted pregnancy to term. In relation to pregnancy among young women, Breheny and Stephens (2007b) indicate:

> Disadvantage associated with adolescent motherhood can be understood as mediated through social structures such as access to education, employment, and childcare facilities. The difficulty in combining early motherhood with successful adult life may contribute to levels of disadvantage. . . . [D]ifferent social support structures could support motherhood occurring at any point in the life course. This could enable motherhood to be successfully combined with education and employment in any order.
>
> (Breheny and Stephens 2007b: 344)

Interventions that improve the chances of women being able to access education, adequate health care, employment and childcare, and that make motherhood a feasible option at any point in a woman's life course, would assist in reducing the possibilities of women experiencing unwanted pregnancies, and the associated possibilities of negative outcomes.

One particularly pertinent issue is childcare. Many studies, using different techniques to measure household work and childcare work, have come to the same conclusion – domestic labour continues to be primarily women's work. Coltrane (2000), in his review of over 200 scholarly American articles, concluded that although men have slightly increased their participation in household work, women still routinely do about twice the amount of housework that men do. Other American authors have found that when children are born, men's share of domestic activities remains the same, while their hours of employment outside the house increase. Mothers, on the other hand, find their share of domestic responsibilities increasing, their hours of employment outside the house decreasing and their dependency on men increasing (Sanchez and Thomson 1997). There is no equivalent South African research, but there is little to suggest that the patterns noted above are any different in South Africa.

Other than promoting greater gender sensitivity among men, and insisting that they engage in primary care-giving on an equitable basis, interventions that assist in ameliorating these gendered set of circumstances include generous family leave for women (and for men), and the provision of adequate daycare and early childhood development centres in order to allow women to return to work or to school.

While, in some countries, progress has been made in terms of employers and the state providing these kinds of benefits and services, this is not always the case in terms of education. Indeed in some cases additional barriers are placed in the way of young women returning to school. In South Africa, for example, the Department of Education (2007b) developed a document entitled *Measures for the Prevention and Management of Learner Pregnancy*. This document states, among other things, that

> [Pregnant] learners may be required to take leave of absence from school to address pre- or post-natal health concerns and to carry out initial child-care duties. No predetermined time is given, but it is suggested that a period of absence of up to two years may be necessary. No learner may be re-admitted in the same year that she left school due to a pregnancy.
>
> Before returning to school the learner must produce a medical report stating that she is fit to resume schooling; she must also demonstrate that proper child-care arrangements have been made.
>
> (Department of Education 2007b)

These requirements are at loggerheads with the provisions made for women in the workplace, where, according to legislation, four months of paid maternity leave must be provided, with a further two months being possible. No woman in the employ of companies or the state need produce a medical certificate or proof of adequate childcare arrangements on returning to work.

If we are to start breaking down the imaginary wall between younger and older women, if we are to recognize that women in similar social circumstances face similar possibilities and difficulties in relation to sex and reproduction, if we are acknowledge that childbearing has opportunity costs for women of all ages, then there is a need for interventions that create educational environments that are sufficiently inclusive to facilitate the completion of schooling for those young women who have decided to carry their pregnancies to term and keep the child. For example, in the United States, some secondary schools have daycare facilities for high school students who have children (Luker 1997).

This having been said, it is important that women are sufficiently supported so that they can choose to not return to school or work but rather to concentrate on childcare. Austerberry and Wiggins (2007) report on the Sure Start Plus programme, a pilot project aimed at supporting pregnant and parenting young women as part of the UK government's inclusion initiative. They note that the government targets for return rates to school are at odds with the expressed interests of the young women who wanted to have the same choices as older mothers in terms of work–life balance. The authors conclude that

> [Government] policies toward motherhood and employment are inconsistent: they promote flexibility for middle-class mothers living in households with one or more members in regular employment while being prescriptive towards unwaged mothers, who are dependent on state benefits. The Government has extended paid maternity leave and rights to flexible hours for parents in paid work in recognition of the difficulties of combining such work with nurturing a baby (Employment Relations Act 2004). At the same time it encourages unwaged parents, many of whom are single mothers of infants, into work, and has reduced child benefit to single parents in real terms.
>
> (Austerberry and Wiggins 2007: 12)

Policies, interventions and practices that are supportive of women's and men's productive *and* reproductive roles, and that enable women (and men) to move between the private domain of childcare and domestic responsibilities as well as the public domain of work and education with ease are important in terms of creating the conditions in which pregnancies are viewed as possibilities rather than constraints.

Conclusion

I have argued in this book that the signifier 'teenage pregnancy' is fundamentally premised on an 'adolescence as transition' discourse, a discourse that is grounded in colonialist understandings of development, that enables the construction of a threat of degeneration to infuse our understandings of young women and reproduction, that constructs an imaginary wall between younger and older women, in which age is understood as the primary distinguishing feature between women, and that locates the transition to adulthood within the individual rather than social processes. In this chapter I have argued for a shift from 'teenage pregnancy' to 'unwanted pregnancy'. In this way the lens of inspection changes from the individual's characteristics and deficiencies to the gendered and social space within which reproduction occurs. The possibilities and constraints that women experience in terms of (hetero)sexuality and pregnancy may be laid bare, and intervention practices oriented towards the ameliorating the circumstances that place women in the invidious position of carrying an unwanted pregnancy. Analyses can become fine-tuned to understand cross-cutting issues as well as the local contexts within which women live and the specific challenges that particular groups of women face.

REFERENCES

Adam, M. B., McGuire, J. K., Walsh, M., Basta, J., and LeCroy, C. (2005). Acculturation as a predictor of the onset of sexual intercourse among Hispanic and White teens. *Archives of Pediatric and Adolescent Medicine, 159,* 261–265.

Adler, N. E., David, H. P., Major, B. N., Roth, S. H., Russo, N. F., and Wyatt, G. E. (1992). Psychological factors in abortion. *American Psychologist, 47,* 1194–1204.

Adler, N. E., Smith, L. B., and Tscahnn, J. M. (1998). Abortion among adolescents. In L. J. Beckman and S. M. Harvey (eds), *The new civil war: The psychology, culture and politics of abortion* (pp. 285–298). Washington, DC: American Psychological Association.

Adler, N. E., Ozer, E. J., and Tschann, J. (2003). Abortion among adolescents. *American Psychologist, 58*(3), 211–217.

Africa Christian Aid (2003). *Pro-life: Hard choices.* Retrieved 12 July 2007 from www.christianaction.org.za/articles/hard_choices.htm

African Christian Democratic Party (2006). *International Life Chains Sunday.* Retrieved 2 March 2007 from www.acdp.org.za/press/releases.asp?show=press 334.txt

Ambuel, B., and Rappaport, J. (1992). Developmental trends in adolescents' psychological and legal competence to consent to abortion. *Law and Human Behavior, 16,* 129–154.

Anagnostara, A. (1988). The construction and evaluation of a scale for assessing the sexual attitudes of black adolescents. Unpublished masters thesis, Rand Afrikaans University.

Anglin, J., Artz, S., and Scott, D. (1998). Rites of passage and child and youth care: An overview of the special issue. *Child and Youth Care Forum, 25*(7), 301–303.

Arney, W. R., and Bergen, B. J. (1984). Power and visibility: The invention of teenage pregnancy. *Social Science and Medicine, 18,* 11–19.

Ashcroft, B., Griffiths, G., and Tiffin, H. (2000). *Post-colonial studies: The key concepts.* London: Routledge.

Austerberrry, H., and Wiggins, M. (2007). Taking a pro-choice perspective on promoting inclusion of teenage mothers: Lessons from an evaluation of the Sure Start Plus programme. *Critical Public Health, 17*(1), 3–15.

AVERT (n.d.). *Sex education that works.* Retrieved 10 March 2007 from www.avert.org/sexedu.htm

Bai, J., Wong, F., and Stewart, H. (1999). The obstetric and neonatal performance of teenage mothers in an Australian community. *Journal of Obstetrics and Gynaecology*, *19*(4), 345–348.

Barratt, M. S. (1991). School-age offspring of adolescent mothers: Environments and outcomes. *Family Relations*, *40*, 442–447.

Barter, C., McCarry, M., Berridge, D., and Evans, K. (2009). *Partner exploitation and violence in teenage intimate relations*. University of Bristol and National Society for the Protection and Care of Children. Retrieved 13 November 2009 from www.nspcc.org.uk/Inform/research/Findings/partner_exploitation_and_violence_summary_wdf68093.pdf

Basu, K. (1998). Child labor: Cause, consequence, and cure, with remarks on international labor standards. *The World Bank, Policy Research Paper*. Retrieved 4 June 2007 from www.wds.worldbank.org/servlet/WDSContentServer/WDSP/IB/2000/02/24/000094946_99031911111649/Rendered/PDF/multi_page.pdf

Becker-Lausen, E., and Rickel, A. U. (1995). Integration of teenage pregnancy and child abuse research: Identifying mediator variables for pregnancy outcome. *Journal of Primary Prevention*, *16*(1), 39–53.

Bhatia, S., and Stam, H. J. (2005). Critical engagements with culture and self: Introduction. *Theory and Psychology*, *15*(4), 419–430.

Bianchi-Demicheli, F., Perrin, E., Lüdicke, F., Bianchi, P. G., Chatton, D., and Campana, A. (2002). Termination of pregnancy and women's sexuality. *Gynecologic and Obstetric Investigation*, *53*(1), 48–53.

Black, C., and Ford-Gilboe, M. (2004). Adolescent mothers: Resilience, family health work and health-promoting practices. *Journal of Advanced Nursing*, *48*(4), 351–360.

Bonell, C. (2004). Why is teenage pregnancy conceptualized as a social problem? A review of quantitative research from the USA and UK. *Culture, Health and Sexuality*, *6*(3), 255–272.

Boult, B. E., and Cunningham, P. W. (1992). Black teenage pregnancy: A sociomedical approach. *Medicine and Law*, *11*, 159–165.

Boult, B. E., and Cunningham, P. W. (1993). *Some aspects of obstetrics in black teenage pregnancies: A comparative study of three age groups*. Research paper C28, University of Port Elizabeth.

Boult, B. E., and Cunningham, P.W. (1995). Some aspects of obstetrics in black teenage pregnancy: A comparative analysis. *Medicine and Law*, *14*(1–2), 93–97.

Bradshaw, D., Masiteng, K., and Nannan, N. (n.d.) *Health status and determinants*. Retrieved 7 July 2007 from www.healthlink.org.za/uploads/files/ chapter4_00.pdf.

Breheny, M., and Stephens, C. (2007a). Irreconcilable differences: Health professionals' constructions of adolescence and motherhood. *Social Science and Medicine*, *64*(1), 112–124.

Breheny, M., and Stephens, C. (2007b). Individual responsibility and social constraint: The construction of adolescent motherhood in social scientific research. *Culture, Health and Sexuality*, *9*(4), 333–346.

Breheny, M., and Stephens, C. (2008). A life of ease and immorality: Health professionals constructions of mothering on welfare. *Journal of Community and Applied Social Psychology*, *19*(4), 257–270.

Brindis, C. (1993). Antecedents and consequences: The need for diverse strategies in adolescent pregnancy prevention. In A. Lawson and D. L. Rhode (eds), *The politics of pregnancy: Adolescent sexuality and public policy* (pp. 257–283). New Haven, CT: Yale University Press.

British Broadcasting Corporation (2002). *Teaching plans for sex education.* Retrieved 10 March 2009 from http://news.bbc.co.uk/1/hi/education/ 1842053.stm

Bryant, K. D. (2006). Update on adolescent pregnancy in the Black community. *The ABNF Journal,* Fall, 133–136.

Buccholz, E. S., and Korn-Bursztyn, C. (1993). Children of adolescent mothers: Are they at risk for abuse? *Adolescence, 28,* 361–382.

Bukulmez, O., and Deren, O. (2000). Perinatal outcome in adolescent pregnancies: A case control study from a Turkish university hospital. *European Journal of Obstetrics, Gynaecology, and Reproductive Biology, 88*(2), 207–212.

Burman, E. (2008). *Deconstructing developmental psychology,* 2nd edn. Hove: Routledge.

Burr, V. (2003). *Social constructionism,* 2nd edn. New York: Routledge.

Caldwell, J. C., Caldwell, P., Caldwell, B. K., and Pieris, I. (1998). The construction of adolescence in a changing world: Implications for sexuality, reproduction, and marriage. *Studies in Family Planning, 29*(2), 137–153.

Cameron, N., Richter, L., McIntyre, J., Dhlamini, N., and Garstang, L. (1996). Progress report: Teenage pregnancy and birth outcome in Soweto. Unpublished report: University of the Witwatersrand.

Cassim, F. (1998). It's winter baby season as more teenagers get in the family way. *Saturday Star,* 18 July, 3.

Castel, R. (1991). From dangerousness to risk. In G. Burchell, C. Gordon and P. Miller (eds), *The Foucault effect: Studies in governmentality* (pp. 281–298). Chicago, IL: University of Chicago Press.

Chen, X., Wen, S. W., Fleming, N., Demissie, K., Rhoads, G. G., and Walker, M. (2007). Teenage pregnancy and adverse birth outcomes: A large population based retrospective cohort study. *International Journal of Epidemiology, 36*(2), 368–373.

Chevalier, A., and Viitanen, T. K. (2003). The long-run labour market consequences on teenage motherhood in Britain. *Journal of Population Economics, 16*(2), 323–344.

Chrisholm, L. (1992). Policy and critique in South African educational research. *Transformation, 18,* 149–160.

Christian Lawyers Association v Minister of Health and Others (Reproductive Health Alliance as Amicus Curiae) 2005 (1) SA 509 (T) 2005 (1) SA.

Cohen, S. A. (2006). Toward making abortion 'rare': The shifting battleground over a means to an end. *Guttmacher Policy Review, 9*(1). Retrieved 12 November 2009 from www.guttmacher.org/pubs/gpr/09/1/gpr090102.html

Colen, C. G., Geronimus, A. T., and Phipps, M. G. (2006). Getting a piece of the pie? The economic boom of the 1990s and declining teen birth rates in the United States. *Social Science and Medicine, 63*(6), 1531–1545.

Coltrane, S. (2000). Research on household labor: Modeling and measuring the social embeddedness of routine family work. *Journal of Marriage and Family, 62*(4), 1208–1233.

Comaroff, J. (1989). Images of empire, contests of conscience: Models of colonial domination in South Africa. *American Ethnologist, 16*(4), 661–685.

Cope, J. (1993). *A matter of choice: Abortion law reform in apartheid South Africa.* Pietermaritzburg: Hadeda Books.

Coren, E., Barlow, J., and Stewart-Brown, S. (2003). The effectiveness of individual and group-based parenting programmes in improving outcomes for teenage mothers and their children: A systematic review. *Journal of Adolescence*, *26*, 79–103.

Cozzarelli, C., Karrasch, A., Sumer, N., and Major, B. (1994). The meaning and impact of partner's accompaniment on women's adjustment to abortion. *Journal of Applied Social Psychology*, *24*(22), 2028–2056.

Crouch, L. (2005). *Disappearing children or data misunderstandings? Drop-out phenomena in South Africa*. Retrieved 10 July 2007 from www.rti.org/pubs

Cunnington, A. J. (2001). What's so bad about teenage pregnancy? *Journal of Family Planning and Reproductive Health Care*, *27*(1), 36–41.

Daguerre, A., and Nativel, C. (2006). Introduction: The construction of teenage pregnancy as a social problem. In A. Daguerre and C. Nativel (eds), *When children become parents: Welfare state responses to teenage pregnancy* (pp. 1–20). Bristol: Policy Press.

Dangal, G. (2006). An update on teenage pregnancy. *Internet Journal of Gynecology and Obstetrics*, *5*(1), 3.

Davis, R. A. (1989). Teenage pregnancy: A theoretical analysis of a social problem. *Adolescence*, *14*, 19–28.

De Boeck, F., and Honwana, A. (2005). Introduction: Children and youth in Africa. In A. Honwana and F. De Boeck (eds), *Makers and breakers: Children and youth in postcolonial Africa* (pp. 1–18). Oxford: James Currey.

De Lange, N., and Geldenhuys, J. L. (2001). A systemic approach to adolescents' experiences of terminating their pregnancies. *Society in Transition*, *32*(2), 246–259.

Delius, P., and Glaser, C. (2002). Sexual socialisation in South Africa: A historical perspective. *African Studies*, *61*(1), 27–54.

DeLuzio, C. (2007). *Female adolescence in American scientific thought 1830–1930*. Balitmore, MD: Johns Hopkins University Press.

Department of Education [South Africa] (2007a). *National curriculum statement Grades 10–12 (General): Learning programme guidelines life orientation*. Pretoria: Department of Education.

Department of Education [South Africa] (2007b). *Measures for the Prevention and Management of Learner Pregnancy*. Pretoria: Department of Education.

Department of Health [South Africa] (2006a). *Saving mothers: Report on confidential enquiries into maternal deaths in South Africa*. Retrieved 5 March 2007 from www.doh.gov.za/docs/reports/2004/savings.pdf

Department of Health [South Africa] (2006b). *Termination of pregnancy data 1997 to 2006*. Pretoria: Department of Health.

Department of Health [United Kingdom] (2007). *Statistical bulletin: Abortion statistics, England and Wales: 2006*. Retrieved 12 November 2009 from www.dh.gov.uk/prod_consum_dh/groups/dh_digitalassets/documents/digitalasset/dh_075705.pdf

Department of Health [South Africa] (2007). *South African Demographic and Health Survey 2003*. Pretoria: Department of Health.

De Villiers, F. P. R., and Kekesi, J. (2004). Social interaction of teenage mothers during and after their pregnancy. *South African Family Practice*, *46*(2), 21–24.

De Villiers, V. P. (1991). Seksonderrig onder tieners in die Paarl. *South African Medical Journal, 80,* 231–232.

De Villiers, V. P., and Clift, H. E. (1979). Tienerswangerskappe: 'n Sosio-ekonomiese probleem met bose kringloop gevolge. *Social Work/Maatskaplike Werk, 15,* 195–199.

De Vries, C. (1986). *Orientation in fundamental education theory.* Stellenbosch: University Publishers and Booksellers.

DiCenso, A., Guyatt, G., Willan, A., and Griffith, L. (2002). Interventions to reduce unintended pregnancies among adolescents: Systematic review of randomised control trials. *British Medical Journal, 324,* 1426. Retrieved 24 February 2009 from http://bmj.com/cgi/content/full/324/7351/1426

Dlamini, L. S. (2002). The problems of teenage mothers in the southern Hho-Hho region of Swaziland. Unpublished masters thesis, University of South Africa.

Donzelot, J. (1993). The promotion of the social. In M. Gane and T. Johnson (eds), *Foucault's new domains* (pp. 106–138). London: : Routledge.

Dovey, K., and Mason, M. (1984). Guidance for submission: Social control and guidance in schools for black pupils in South Africa. *British Journal of Guidance and Counselling, 12*(1), 15–24.

Dubas, J. S., Miller, K., and Petersen, A. C. (2003). The study of adolescence during the 20th century. *History of the Family, 8,* 375–397.

Dudley, W. (2006). *Reproductive rights: Issues on trial.* Farmington Hills, MI: Thomson Gale.

Dunkle, K., Jewkes, R., Brown, H., Gray, G., MacIntyre, J., and Harlow, S. (2004). Gender-based violence, relationship power, and risk of HIV infection in women attending antenatal clinics in South Africa. *The Lancet, 363*(9419), 1415–1421.

Eaton, L., Flisher, A. J., and Aarø, L. E. (2003). Unsafe sexual behaviour in South African youth. *Social Science and Medicine, 56,* 149–165.

Enright, R. D., Levy, V. M., Harris, D., and Lapsley, D. K. (1987). Do economic conditions influence how theorists view adolescents? *Journal of Youth and Adolescence, 16*(6), 541–559.

Ewald, F. (1991). Insurance and risk. In G. Burchell, C. Gordon and P. Miller (eds), *The Foucault effect: Studies in governmentality* (pp. 197–210). Chicago, IL: University of Chicago Press.

Fairclough, N. (1992). *Discourse and social change.* Cambridge: Polity Press.

Fine, M. (1988). Sexuality, schooling, and adolescent females: The missing discourse of desire. *Harvard Educational Review, 58,* 29–53.

Fine, M., and Macpherson, P. (1994). Over dinner: Feminism and adolescent female bodies. In H. L. Radtke and H. J. Stam (eds), *Power/gender: Social relations in theory and practice* (pp. 219–246). London: Sage.

Finer, L. B., Frohwirth, L. F., Dauphinee, L. A., Singh, S., and Moore, A. M. (2005). Reasons U.S. women have abortions: Quantitative and qualitative perspectives. *Perspectives on Sexual and Reproductive Health, 37*(3), 110–118.

Forste, R., and Tienda, M. (1992). Race and ethnic variation in the schooling consequences of female adolescent sexual activity. *Social Science Quarterly, 73,* 12–30.

Frank, S., Esterhuizen, T., Jinabhai, C. C., Sullivan, K., and Taylor, M. (2008). Risky sexual behaviour of high school pupil in an era of HIV and AIDS. *South African Medical Journal, 98,* 394–398.

Franz, W., and Reardon, D. (1992). Differential impact of abortion on adolescents and adults. *Adolescence, 27*, 655–673.

Furstenberg, F. F., Brooks-Gunn, J., and Morgan, S. P. (1987). *Adolescent mothers in later life*. New York: Cambridge University Press.

Garenne, M., Tollman, S., and Kahn, K. (2000). Premarital fertility in rural South Africa: A challenge to existing population policy. *Studies in Family Planning, 31*(1), 47–54.

Geldenhuys, J. L., and de Lange, N. (2001). Swart Oos-Kaapse adolessente se ervaring van swangerskapterminasie. *South African Journal of Education, 21*(2), 92–98.

Geronimus, A. T. (1991). Teenage childbearing and social and reproductive disadvantage: The evolution of complex questions and demise of simple answers. *Family Relations, 40*, 463–471.

Geronimus, A. T. (1996). Black/white differences in the relationship of maternal age to birthweight: A population-based test of the weathering hypothesis. *Social Science and Medicine, 42*(4), 489–597.

Geronimus, A. T. (2003). Damned if you do: Culture, identity, privilege, and teenage childbearing in the United States. *Social Science and Medicine, 57*(5), 881–893.

Geronimus, A. T. (2004). Teenage childbearing as cultural prism. *British Medical Bulletin, 69*, 155–166.

Gilbert, W. M., Jandial, D., Field, N. T., Bigelow, P., and Danielsen, B. (2004). Birth outcomes in teenage pregnancies. *Journal of Maternal-Fetal and Neonatal Medicine, 16*(5), 265–270.

Gillis, L. S. (1990). Teenage pregnancy: Letter to the editor. *South African Medical Journal, 77*, 121.

Glenn, E. N., Chang, G., and Forcey, L. R. (1994). *Mothering: Ideology, experience, and agency*. London: Routledge.

Gold, R. B. (2006). Rekindling efforts to prevent unplanned pregnancies: A matter of 'equity and common sense'. *Guttmacher Policy Review, 9*(3). Retrieved 12 November 2009 from www.guttmacher.org/pubs/gpr/09/3/gpr090302.html

Gómez, L. C., and Zapata, G. R. (2005). Diagnostic categorization of post-abortion syndrome. *Actas Espoaòolas de Psiquiartria, 33*(4), 267–272.

Graham, P. (2004). *The end of adolescence*. Oxford: Oxford University Press.

Greathead, E. (1988). The dilemma of the pregnant teenager. *Nursing RSA, 3*, 20–26.

Greathead, E., Devenish, C., and Funnell, G. (1998). *Responsible teenage sexuality: A manual for teachers, youth leaders and health professionals*. Pretoria: PPASA and J. L. van Schaik.

Greene, M. E., and Merrick, T. (2005). *Poverty reduction: Does reproductive health matter?* Washington, DC: International Bank for Reconstruction and Development/The World Bank.

Grimes, D. A. (1994). The morbidity and mortality of pregnancy: Still risky business. *American Journal of Obstetrics and Gynecology, 170*(5 Pt 2), 1489–1494.

Grimes, D. A., Benson, J., Singh, S., Romero, M., Ganatra, B., Okonofua, F. E., and Shah, I. H. (2006). Unsafe abortion: The preventable pandemic. *The Lancet, 368*(9550), 1908–1919.

Guttmacher Institute (2008). *Facts on induced abortion in the United States*.

Retrieved 3 November 2009 from www.guttmacher.org/pubs/fb_induced_abortion.html

Hall, G. S. (1904). *Adolescence: Its psychology and its relations to physiology, anthropology, sociology, sex, crime, religion and education.* New York: Appleton.

Hann, C. M. (2005). The relationship between certain family variables and the psychological well-being of black adolescents. Unpublished doctoral thesis, University of the Free State.

Harari, S. E., and Vinovskis, M. A. (1993). Adolescent sexuality, pregnancy, and childbearing in the past. In A. Lawson and D. L. Rhode (eds), *The politics of pregnancy: Adolescent sexuality and public policy* (pp. 23–45). New Haven, CT: Yale University Press.

Harding, D. J. (2006). Disadvantaged neighborhoods, cultural heterogeneity, and adolescent outcomes. Paper presented at the American Sociological Association Annual Meeting, Montreal.

Health24 (n.d). *Sex education – why and how?* Retrieved 25 April 2007 from www.health24.com/sex/Sex_and_your_child/1253-2439,11660.asp

Henshaw, S. (1993). Teenage abortion, birth and pregnancy statistics by state, 1988. *Family Planning Perspectives, 25*(3), 122–126.

Henshaw, S., and Feivelson, D. J. (2000). Teenage abortion and pregnancy statistics by state, 1996. *Family Planning Perspectives, 32*(6), 272–280.

Higgs, P. (2003). African philosophy and the transformation of educational discourse. *Journal of Education, 30*, 5–22.

Hofferth, S. L., and Reid, L. (2002). Early childbearing and children's achievement and behaviour over time. *Perspectives on Sexual Reproductive Health, 34*(1), 41–49.

Hollway, W. (1998). Gender difference and the production of subjectivity. In J. Henriques, W. Hollway, C. Urwin, C. Venn and V. Walkerdine (eds), *Changing the subject: Psychology, social regulation and subjectivity* (pp. 227–263). London: Routledge.

Hopkins, N., Reicher, S., and Saleem, J. (1996). Constructing women's psychological health in anti-abortion rhetoric. *Sociological Review, 44*(3), 539–566.

Hosie, A. C. J. (2007). 'I hated everything about school': An examination of the relationship between dislike of school, teenage pregnancy and educational disengagement. *Social Policy and Society, 6*(3), 333–347.

Hotz, V. J., McElroy, S. W., and Sanders, S. G. (1996). The costs and consequences of teenage childbearing for mothers. *Chicago Policy Review, 64*, 55–94.

Hudson, B. (1984). Femininity and adolescence. In A. McRobbie and M. Nava (eds), *Gender and generation* (pp. 31–53). London: Macmillan.

Human Sciences Research Council (2007). *Youth policy initiative – Proceedings of roundtable 4: Learner retention.* Pretoria: Human Sciences Research Council.

Ijumba, P., and Padarath, A. (2006). *South African Health Review 2006.* Pretoria: Health Systems Trust.

Irin news (2007). *Teenage pregnancy figures cause alarm*, 12 March. Retrieved 4 June 2007 from www.hst.org.za/news/20041555

Jacobs, J. L. (1994). Gender, race, class, and the trend toward early motherhood: A feminist analysis of teen mothers in contemporary society. *Journal of Contemporary Ethnography, 22*, 442–462.

Jali, T. I. (2006). Adolescents' experience during pregnancy in a township. Unpublished masters dissertation, University of Johannesburg.

Jaya, J., and Hindin, M. J. (2007). Nonconsensual sexual experiences of adolescents in urban India. *Journal of Adolescent Health*, *40*(6), 573–587.

Jewkes, R., Vundule, C., Maforah, F., and Jordaan, E. (2001). Relationship dynamics and teenage pregnancy in South Africa. *Social Science and Medicine*, *52*(5), 733–744.

Jewkes, R., Brown, H., Dickson-Tetteh, K., Levin, J., and Rees, H. (2002). Prevalence of morbidity associated with abortion before and after legalisation in South Africa. *British Medical Journal*, *324*, 1252–1253.

Jewkes, R., Rees, H., Dickson, K., Brown, H., and Levin, J. (2005). The impact of age on the epidemiology of incomplete abortions in South Africa after legislative change. *BJOG: An International Journal of Obstetrics and Gynaecology*, *112*, 355–359.

Johnston, D. D., and Swanson, D. H. (2003). Undermining mothers: A content analysis of the representation of mothers in magazines. *Mass Communication and Society*, *6*(3), 243–265.

Jones, M. E., Kubelka, S., and Bond, M. L. (2001). Acculturation status, birth outcomes, and family planning compliance among Hispanic teens. *Journal of School Nursing*, *17*(2), 83–89.

Jones, S. (1997). *The archaeology of ethnicity: Constructing identities in the past and present*. London: Routledge.

Kesho Consulting and Business Solutions (2006). *Report on incentive structures of social assistance grants in South Africa*. Pretoria: Department of Social Development.

Kett, J. F. (2003). Reflections on the history of adolescence in America. *History of the Family*, *8*, 355–373.

Klein, A. (1994). Trapped in the traffick: Growing problems of drug consumption in Lagos. *Journal of Modern African Studies*, *32*(4), 657–677.

Koops, W., and Zuckerman, M. (2003). Introduction: A historical developmental approach to adolescence. *History of the Family*, *8*, 345–354.

Lawson, A. (1993) Multiple fractures: The cultural construction of teenage sexuality and pregnancy. In A. Lawson and D. L. Rhode (eds), *The politics of pregnancy: Adolescent sexuality and public policy* (pp. 101–125). New Haven, CT: Yale University Press.

Lesko, N. (2001). Time matters in adolescence. In K. Hultqvist and G. Dahlber (eds), *Governing the child in the new millennium* (pp. 35–67). London: Routledge Falmer.

Letsholo, D. N. M. (2006). The implementation of parent-teacher conferences in the primary school. Unpublished masters dissertation, University of South Africa.

Levine, J. A., Emery, C. R., and Pollack, H. (2007). The well-being of children born to teen mothers. *Journal of Marriage and Family*, *69*, 105–122.

Linders, A., and Bogard, C. (2004). The construction of teenage pregnancy as different kinds of problems in Sweden and the United States. Paper presented at the American Sociological Association Annual Meeting, San Francisco.

Lisack, J. P. (1987). *The changing face of America: Population, education and socioeconomic*. Manpower report 87–6. Office of Manpower Studies, Purdue University, Lafayette. Retrieved 25 May 2009 from http://0-web.ebscohost.com.wam.

seals.ac.za/ehost/detail?vid=17andhid=106andsid=ded5f59a-fc08-4547-b56e-de
331ac5862f%40sessionmgr109andbdata=JnNpdGU9ZWhvc3QtbGl2ZQ%3d%
3d#db=ericandAN=ED304350#db=ericandAN=ED304350#db=ericandAN=
ED304350

Luker, K. (1997). *Dubious conceptions: The politics of teenage pregnancy.*
Cambridge, MA: Harvard University Press.

McHoul, A., and Rapley, M. (2005). Re-presenting culture and the self: (Dis)-
agreeing in theory and practice. *Theory and Psychology, 15*(4), 431–447.

Macintyre, S., and Cunningham-Burley, S. (1993). Teenage pregnancy as a social
problem: A perspective from the United Kingdom. In A. Lawson and D. L.
Rhode (eds), *The politics of pregnancy: Adolescent sexuality and public policy* (pp.
59–73). New Haven, CT: Yale University Press.

McLaughlin, C. C., and Luker, K. (2006). Young single mothers and 'welfare
reform' in the US. In A. Daguerre and C. Nativel (eds) *When children become
parents: Welfare state responses to teenage pregnancy* (pp. 21–44). Bristol: Policy
Press.

Macleod, C. (1999a). Teenage pregnancy and its 'negative' consequences: Review of
South African research – Part 1. *South African Journal of Psychology, 29*(1), 1–7.

Macleod, C. (1999b). The governmentality of teenage pregnancy: Scientific literature
and professional practice in South Africa. Unpublished PhD thesis, University of
Natal.

Macleod, C. (1999c). The 'causes' of teenage pregnancy: Review of South African
research – Part 2. *South African Journal of Psychology, 29*(1), 8–16.

Macleod, C. (2001). Teenage motherhood and the regulation of mothering in the
scientific literature: The South African example. *Feminism and Psychology, 11*(4),
493–511.

Macleod, C. (2002). Deconstructive discourse analysis: Extending the methodological conversation. *South African Journal of Psychology, 32*(1), 17–25.

Macleod, C. (2003). The conjugalisation of reproduction in South African teenage
pregnancy literature. *Psychology in Society, 29*, 23–37.

Macleod, C. (2006a). The management of risk: Adolescent sexual and reproductive
health in South Africa. *International Journal of Critical Psychology, 17*, 77–97.

Macleod, C. (2006b). Radial plural feminisms and emancipatory practice in post-
Apartheid South Africa. *Theory and Psychology, 16*, 367–389.

Macleod, C. (2008). Developing principles for research about young women and
abortion: a feminist analysis of difficulties in current South African studies.
Feminist Africa, 11, 55–72.

Macleod, C., and Bhatia, S. (2008). Postcolonialism and psychology. In C. Willig
and W. Stainton Rogers (eds), *The SAGE Handbook of Qualitative Research in
Psychology* (pp. 576–589). London: Sage.

Macleod, C., and Durrheim, K. (2002). Racializing teenage pregnancy: 'Culture'
and 'tradition' in the South African scientific literature. *Ethnic and Racial Studies,
25*(5), 778–801.

Macleod, C., and Luwaca, P. (in press). Working on the horns of a dilemma:
Abortion health service providers. *Curationis.*

Major, B. (2003). Psychological implications of abortion: Highly charged and rife
with misleading research. *Canadian Medical Association Journal, 168*(10),
1257–1258.

Major, B., Appelbaum, M., Beckman, L., Dutton, M. A., Russo, N. F., and West, C. (2008). *Report of the APA task force on mental health and abortion.* Retrieved 11 June 2009 from www.apa.org/pi/wpo/mental-health-abortion-report.pdf

Makiwane, M., and Udjo, E. (2006). *Is the child support grant associated with an increase in teenage fertility in South Africa? Evidence from national surveys and administrative data.* Pretoria: Human Sciences Research Council.

Maleck-Lewy, E., and Ferree, M. (2000). Talking about women and wombs: The discourse of abortion and reproductive rights in the G.D.R. before and after the *Wende.* In S. Gal and B. Kligman (eds), *Reproducing gender: Politics, publics, and everyday life after socialism* (pp. 92–117). Princeton, NJ: Princeton University Press.

Manlove, J. (1998). The influence of high school dropout and school disengagement on the risk of school-age pregnancy. *Journal of Research on Adolescence, 8*(2), 187–220.

Manzini, N. (2001). Sexual initiation and childbearing among adolescent girls in KwaZulu Natal, South Africa. *Reproductive Health Matters, 9*(17), 44–52.

Mattes, B. (2001). Post abortion in men. Paper presented at the National Alliance for Life conference. Retrieved 2 March 2007 from http://216.239.59.104/search?q=cache:Jv5sONBUE3oJ:www.nal.org.za/Files/Mattes%2520Brad%2520Mr%2520-%2520Post%2520Abortion%2520in%2520Men.doc+postabortion+syndrome andhl=enandct=clnkandcd=3andgl=za

Miller, B. C. (1993). Families, science, and values: Alternative views of parenting effects and adolescent pregnancy. *Journal of Marriage and the Family, 55,* 7–21.

Miles, R. (1989). *Racism.* London: Routledge.

Mitchell, E. M. H., Halpern, C. T., Kamathi, E. M., and Owino, S. (2006). Social scripts and stark realities: Kenyan adolescents' abortion discourse. *Culture, Health and Sexuality, 8*(6), 515–528.

Mkhize, Z. M. (1995). Social needs of teenage mothers in the rural communities of Ongoye and Enseleni districts. Unpublished masters thesis, University of Zululand.

Mkhwanazi, N. (2004). Teenage pregnancy and gender identities in the making in a post-Apartheid South African township. Unpublished doctoral thesis, University of Cambridge.

Mohanty, C.T. (1995). Feminist encounters: Locating the politics of experience. In L. Nicholson and S. Seidman (eds), *Social postmodernism: Beyond identity politics* (pp. 68–86). Cambridge: Cambridge University Press.

Mokgalabone, M. B. (1999). Socio-cultural condition, teenage pregnancy and schooling disruption: Themes from teachers and teenage mothers in 'poor rural' schools. *South African Journal of Education, 19*(1), 55–66.

Moore, A. M., Awusabo-Asare, K., Madise, N., Jon-Langba, J., and Kumi-Kyereme, A. (2007). Coerced first sex among adolescent girls in sub-Saharan Africa: Prevalence and context. *African Journal of Reproductive Health, 11*(3), 62–82.

Moran, J. P. (2000). *Teaching sex: The shaping of adolescence in the 20th century.* Cambridge, MA: Harvard University Press.

Moreira, T. (2007). How to investigate the temporalities of health. *Qualitative Social Research, 8*(1), 1–17.

Moses-Europa, S. (2005). Postnatal depression: Exploring adolescent women's experiences and perceptions of being depressed. Unpublished masters' dissertation, University of the Western Cape.

Nardinelli, C. (1980). Child labour and the factory acts. *Journal of Economic History*, 40(4), 739–755.

Ncayiyana, D. J., and Ter Haar, G. (1989). Pregnant adolescents in rural Transkei. *South African Medical Journal*, 75, 231–232.

Neobirth Pregnancy Care Centre (n.d.). *Abortion*. Retrieved 12 July 2007 from www.neobirth.org.za/abortion.html

Nicholas, L. J., Daniels, P. S., and Jurwitz, M. B. (1997). South Africa. In R. T. Franceour (ed.), *International Encyclopedia of Sexuality*. Retrieved 25 April 2007 from www2.rz.hu-berlin.de/sexology/GESUND/ARCHIV/IES/BEGIN.HTM# CONTENTS

No minor matter (1998). *Eastern Cape Herald*, 17 June, 4.

Ntombela, B. B. (1992). The perception of pregnancy of the black primigravida in the Umlazi area of KwaZulu. Unpublished masters thesis, University of South Africa.

Offer, D., Ostrov, E., Howard, K. I., and Atkinson, R. (1988). *The teenage world: The adolescent's self-image in ten countries*. New York: Plenum Medical.

Olivier, M. A. J., and Bloem, S. (2004). Teachers speak their minds about abortion during adolescence. *South African Journal of Education*, 24(3), 177–182.

Olivier, M. A. J., Myburgh, C. P. H., and Poggenpoel, M. (2000). Adolescents' views on termination of pregnancy. *South African Journal of Education*, 20(3), 213–221.

Osofsky, J. D., Eberhart-Wright, A., Ware, L. M., and Hann, D. M. (1992). Children of adolescent mothers: A group at risk for psychopathology. *Infant Mental Health Journal*, 13, 119–131.

Parker, I. (1990). Discourse: Definitions and contradictions. *Philosophical Psychology*, 3, 189–204.

Parker, I., and Shotter, J. (1990). *Deconstructing social psychology*. London: Routledge.

Pomfret, D. (2001). Representations of adolescence in the modern city: Voluntary provision and work in Nottingham and Saint-Etienne. *Journal of Family History*, 26(4), 455–479.

Posel, D. (2001). What's in a name? Racial categorisations under apartheid and their afterlife. *Transformation*, 47, 50–74.

Preston-Whyte, E. (1991). Teenage pregnancy in selected coloured and black communities. Unpublished report, Human Sciences Research Council, Pretoria.

Preston-Whyte, E., and Zondi, M. (1991). Adolescent sexuality and its implications for teenage pregnancy and AIDS. *South African Journal of Continuing Medical Education*, 9, 1389–1394.

Preston-Whyte, E., and Zondi, M. (1992). African teenage pregnancy: Whose problem? In S. Burman and E. Preston-Whyte (eds), *Questionable issue: Illegitimacy in South Africa* (pp. 226–246). Oxford: Oxford University Press.

Prinsloo, F. R. (1984). Trends in adolescent pregnancies at Tygerberg Hospital, 1976–1980. *South African Medical Journal*, 65, 695–699.

Puri, M., Ingham, R., and Matthews, Z. (2007). Factors affecting abortion decisions among young couples in Nepal. *Journal of Adolescent Health*, 40(6), 535–542.

Quinton, W. J., Major, B., and Richards, C. (2001). Adolescents and adjustment to abortion: Are minors at risk? *Psychology, Public Policy, and Law, 7*(3), 491–514.

Ramirez, F., and Boli, J. (1987). The political construction of mass schooling: European origins and world-wide institutionalization. *Sociology of Education, 60*(1), 2–17.

Rattansi, A. (1994). Changing the subject? Racism, culture and education. In J. Donald and A. Rattansi (eds), *'Race', culture and difference* (pp. 11–48). London: Sage.

Reardon, D., and Cougle, J. R. (2002). Depression and unintended pregnancy in the National Longitudinal Survey of youth: A cohort study. *British Medical Journal, 324,* 151–152.

Reardon, D. C., Cougle, J. R., Rue, V. M., Shuping, M. W., Coleman, P. K., and Ney, P. G. (2003), Psychiatric admissions of low-income women following abortion and childbirth. *Canadian Medical Association Journal, 168*(10), 1253–1256.

Rees, H., Katzenellenbogen, J., Shabodien, R., Jewkes, R., Fawcus, S., McIntyre, R., Lombard, C., and Truter, H. (1997). The epidemiology of incomplete abortion in South Africa: National Incomplete Abortion Reference Group. *South African Medical Journal, 84*(7), 417–418.

Remennick, L. I., and Segal, R. (2001). Socio-cultural context and women's experience of abortion: Israeli women and Russian immigrants compared. *Culture, Health and Sexuality, 3*(1), 49–66.

Renzo, R., Novarin, S., Forza, G., and Cosentino, M. (1991). Personality and psychological distress in legal abortion, threatened miscarriage and normal pregnancy. *Psychotherapy and Psychosomatics, 56*(4), 227–234.

Rhode, D. L. (1993). Adolescent pregnancy and public policy. In A. Lawson and D. L. Rhode (eds), *The politics of pregnancy: Adolescent sexuality and public policy* (pp. 301–335). New Haven, CT: Yale University Press.

Rodman, H. (1991). Should parental involvement be required for minors' abortion? *Family Relations, 40*(2), 155–160.

Rogow, D., and Haberland, N. (2005). Sexuality and relationships education: Towards a social studies approach. *Sex Education, 5*(4), 333–344.

Rose, N. (1996). Identity, genealogy, history. In S. Hall and P. du Gay (eds), *Questions of cultural identity* (pp. 128–150). London: Sage.

Ross, R. (2000). A comparison of mother-child interaction between *adolescent* and *adult mothers* of preschoolers. *Dissertation Abstracts International. Section B: The Sciences and Engineeering, 61*(2-B), 783.

Rubin, L., and Russo, N. F. (2004). Abortion and mental health: What therapists need to know. In J. C. Chrisler (ed.), *From menarche to menopause: The female body in feminist therapy* (pp. 69–90). New York: Haworth Press.

Rudmin, F. W., and Ahmadzadeh, V. (2001). Psychometric critique of acculturation psychology: The case of Iranian migrants in Norway. *Scandinavian Journal of Psychology, 42,* 41–56.

Russell, S. T., Lee, F. C., and The Latina/o Teenage Pregnancy Prevention Group (2004). Practitioner's perspectives on effective practices for Hispanic teenage pregnancy prevention. *Perspectives on Sexual and Reproductive Health, 36*(4), 142–149.

Sanchez, L., and Thomson, E. (1997). Becoming mothers and fathers: Parenthood, gender, and the division of labor. *Gender and Society*, *11*(6), 747–772.

Sanger, C. (2004). Regulating teenage abortion in the United States: Politics and policy. *International Journal of Law, Policy and the Family*, *18*(3), 305–318.

Santelli, J., Rochat, R., Hatfield-Timajchy, K., Gilbert, B. C., Curtis, K., Cabral, R., Hirsch, J. S., Schieve, L., and Unintended Pregnancy Working Group (2003). The measurement and meaning of unintended pregnancy. *Perspectives on Sexual and Reproductive Health*, *35*(2), 94–101.

Santrock, J. W. (2002). *Life-span development*, 8th edn. Boston, MA: McGraw-Hill.

Santrock, J. W. (2008). *Life-span development*, 9th edn. Boston, MA: McGraw-Hill.

Schettini, A. M. (2002). Parents, peers and health risk behaviour in adolescence. Project proposal for the National Institute of Mental Health.

Schmiege, S., and Russo, N. F. (2005). Depression and unwanted first pregnancy: Longitudinal cohort study. *British Medical Journal*, *331*, 1303–1308.

Sexology SA (n.d.). Postgraduate diploma in educational sexology. Retrieved 25 April 2007 from http://sexology.co.za/AcademyCourseTeacher.html

Sharp, J. (1988). Two worlds in one country: 'First world' and 'third world' in South Africa. In E. Boonzaier and J. Sharp (eds), *South African keywords: The uses and abuses of political concepts* (pp. 111–121). Cape Town: David Philip.

Shaw, M., Lawlor, D. A., and Najman, J. M. (2005). Teenage children of teenage mothers: Psychological, behavioural and health outcomes from an Australian prospective longitudinal study. *Social Science and Medicine*, *62*(10), 2526–2539.

Shields, W. C. (2006). Mandating parental involvement in adolescents' abortion: Implications of a short-sighted policy. *Contraception*, *73*, 211–213.

Shoveller, J. A., and Johnson, J. L. (2006). Risky groups, risky persons: Dominating discourses on youth sexual health. *Critical Public Health*, *16*(1), 47–60.

Shweder, R. A. (1991). *Thinking through cultures: Expeditions in cultural psychology*. Cambridge, MA: Harvard University Press.

Silverman, J. G., Raj, A., and Clements, K. (2004). Dating violence and associated sexual risk and pregnancy among adolescent girls in the United States. *Pediatrics*, *114*(2), e220–e225.

Smit, J., Beksinska, M., Ramkissoon, A., Kunene, B., and Penn-Kekana, L. (2004). Reproductive health. In Health Systems Trust, *South African Health Review*. Pretoria: Health Systems Trust.

SmithBattle, L. (2005). Teenage mothers at age 30. *Western Journal of Nursing Research*, *27*, 831–850.

Smyth, L. (2002). Feminism and abortion politics: Choice, rights, and reproductive freedom. *Women's Studies International Forum*, *25*(3), 335–345.

Special Assignment (2006). *Silent cries*. Retrieved 27 February 2007 from www.sabcnews.com/specialassignment/20061114.html

Speckhard, A. C., and Rue, V. M. (1992). Postabortion syndrome: An emerging public health concern. *Journal of Social Issues*, *48*(3), 95–120.

Stadler, A. (1987). *The political economy of modern South Africa*. Cape Town: David Philip.

Steiner, A. (1997). Letter: Argument on abortion 'at whim' flawed. *The Star*, 25 April 13.

Stotland, N. L. (2001). Psychiatric aspects of induced abortion. *Archives of Women's Mental Health*, *4*, 27–31.

Taffa, N. (2003). A comparison of pregnancy and child health outcomes between teenage and adult mothers in the slums of Nairobi, Kenya. *International Journal of Adolescent Medicine and Health*, *15*(4), 321–329.

Tanga, T. T. (1991). The health support systems for the unmarried pregnancy adolescents with particular reference to parents. Unpublished masters thesis, University of Natal, Durban.

Temba. V. N. (2007). A phenomenological study of the experiences of pregnant, black adolescent girls living with HIV/AIDS. Unpublished masters thesis, University of Pretoria.

The Asylum Forum ElectroChat Therapy (2006). *Special Assignment*. Retrieved 27 February 2007 from http://asylum.za.org/viewtopic.php?t=685

Thorogood, N. (2000). Sex education as disciplinary technique: Policy and practice in England and Wales. *Sexualities*, *3*(4), 425–438.

Thorp, J. M. (2003). Long-term physical and psychological health consequences of induced abortion: Review of the evidence. *Obstetrical and Gynecological Survey*, *58*(1), 67–79.

Time (2006). *Killing of potential*. Retrieved 27 February 2007 from http://blogs.24.com/ViewComments.aspx?blogid=e092f4b1-f0e8-4128-9105-2cb9fc40 f200&mid=0e7e5764-9225-42fc-97c5-375432ef81ce.

Timesonline (2009). *Children having children: England and Wales can tackle teenage pregnancy – with a minor social revolution*, 27 February. Retrieved 12 March 2009 from www.timesonline.co.uk/tol/comment/leading_article/article58 11643.ece

Trad, V. (1993). Abortion and pregnant adolescents. *Family in Society: The Journal of Contemporary Human Services*, September, 397–409.

Van Rooyen, L., and Ngwenya, M. (2003). *Sexuality education: From babyhood to adolescence*. Pretoria: Kagiso.

Van Rooyen, M., and Smith, S. (2004). The prevalence of post-abortion syndrome in patients presenting at Kalafong hospital's family medicine clinic after having a termination of pregnancy. *South African Family Practice*, *46*(5), 21–24.

Varga, C. A. (2002). Pregnancy termination among South African adolescents. *Studies in Family Planning*, *33*(4), 283–298.

Vinovskis, M. A. (1988). *An 'epidemic' of adolescent pregnancy: Some historical and policy considerations*. New York: Oxford University Press.

Vinovskis, M. A. (1992). Historical perspectives on adolescent pregnancy. In M. K. Rosenheim and M. F. Testa (eds), *Early parenthood and coming of age in the 1990s* (pp. 136–149). New Brunswick, NJ: Rutgers University Press.

Walkerdine, V. (1989). *Counting girls out*. London: Virago.

Welfare and Population Development Portfolio Committee (2000). *Minutes of meeting 27 September 2000 on Developmental Welfare Governance Bill, Social Assistance Act Amendments*. Retrieved 23 February 2007 from www.pmg.org.za/docs/2001/minutes/000927pcwelfare.htm

Wetherell, M., and Potter, J. (1992). *Mapping the language of racism: Discourse and the legitimation of exploitation*. New York: Harvester Wheatsheaf.

White, B. W. (1996). Talk about school: Education and the colonial project in French and British Africa (1860–1960). *Comparative Education*, *32*(1), 9–25.

Whittaker, A. (2002). 'The truth of our day by day lives': Abortion decision making in rural Thailand. *Culture, Health and Sexuality*, *4*(1), 1–20.

Wiemann, C. M., Agurcia, C. A., Rickert, V. I., Berenson, A. B., and Volk, R. J.

(2006). Absent fathers as providers: Race/ethnic differences in support for adolescent mothers. *Child and Adolescent Social Work Journal*, *23*(5–6), 617–634.

Wight, D., Raab, G. M., Henderson, M., Abraham, C., Buston, K., Hart, G., and Scott, S. (2002). Limits of teacher delivered sex education: Interim behavioural outcomes from randomised trial. *British Medical Journal*, *324*, 1430. Retrieved 11 March 2009 from www.bmj.com/cgi/reprint/324/7351/1430

Wood, K., and Jewkes, R. (1997). Violence, rape, and sexual coercion: Everyday love in a South African township. *Gender and Development*, *5*(2), 41–46.

Wood, K., Maforah, F., and Jewkes, R. (1998). 'He forced me to love him': Putting violence on adolescent sexual health agendas. *Social Science and Medicine*, *47*(2), 233–242.

World Health Organization (2009). Teenage pregnancies cause many health, social problems. Retrieved 3 November 2009 from www.who.int/mediacentre/multimedia/podcasts/2009/teenage-pregnancy-20090213/en/index.html

Young, A. (1987). How medicine tamed life. *Culture, Medicine and Psychiatry*, *11*, 107–121.

Zabin, L., Hirsch, M. B., and Emerson, M. R. (1989). When urban adolescents choose abortion: Effects on education, psychological status and subsequent pregnancy. *Family Planning Perspectives*, *21*(6), 248–255.

INDEX